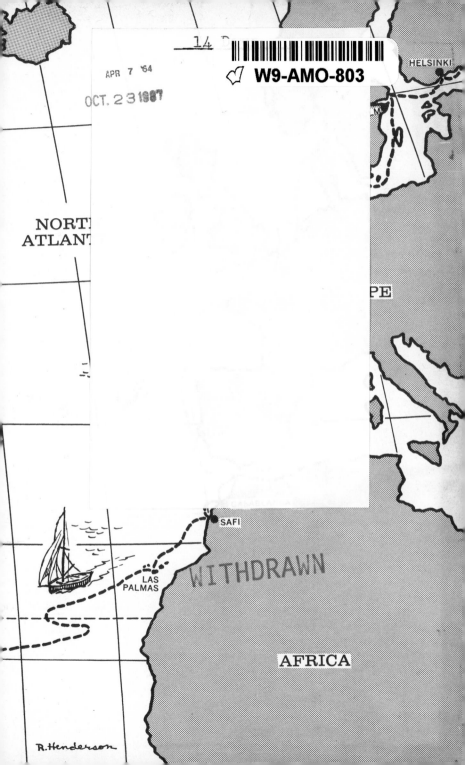

14

W9-AMO-803

HELSINKI

NORT
ATLANT

PE

SAFI

WITHDRAWN

LAS
PALMAS

AFRICA

R. Henderson

"If ever a book deserved to be called a twentieth century Mayflower story it is this one about the escape to freedom of Teppo Turen and his companions . . .

"Today Turen is a Chicago insurance executive, employed by the man who (finally) made it possible for him to become an American, W. Clement Stone. But his fellow pilgrims and the adventure they experienced together obviously are vivid in Turen's memory . . .

"The story of their flight is a stirring affirmation that there are still men and women worthy to stand beside the pilgrims."— Richard Philbrick in the *Chicago Tribune*

" . . .This is the story of a Finnish couple and some countrymen who, having endured the hardships of World War II, decide to strike out for America. They do so — nine of them — in a cranky, leaky old boat called the Tuntsa, only 30 feet or so long. Inexperienced, part-hampered, part-blessed by an erratic, colorful, drunken navigator, they make their way down to Africa, then across the Atlantic through storms, police arrests, language hurdles, and every conceivable kind of barrier, including sharks. Their journey, which eventually brought them piling up on White Horse Reef, is more than a story of adventure at sea, more than a study of the people involved. It is in its way an apotheosis of the man who wants to come to America and who will let nothing stand in his way. Very readable."— Virginia Kirkus

the TUNTSA

by TEPPO TUREN
with ELIZABETH MADDOX McCABE

HENRY REGNERY COMPANY
CHICAGO 1961

My warmest thanks are due to Miss Joan Furfey for her generous help and encouragement, and particularly for her labor in helping to shape the first few chapters of this book.

First printing, July, 1961
Second printing, March, 1962

to **Rita** *and* **Eero**

CONTENTS

ILLUSTRATIONS

INTRODUCTION

1961 was the year May and I finally became American citizens. On the day we swore allegiance, we tried to sit down that evening with our children and explain to them what this meant. Our words seemed hopelessly inadequate. We found ourselves simply telling all over again about the shipwreck and then harking back to the voyage of the *Tuntsa*, to which our children listened willingly enough, for adventure and hairbreadth escapes seem to have particular appeal to this generation—though not to ours, which had too many of them.

Long ago I had begun to put the incredible story into writing. The voyage of the *Tuntsa* was where the meaning lay, I was sure of it. I had pages in Finnish, and more pages in English, stuffed into drawers all over the house. The *Tuntsa* reached America only in spirit, for our last disaster occurred miles off the coast and somehow I wanted to do her the justice of an explanation. It was she, the *Tuntsa*, who got us here, although my own first view of the United States was from a plane. With unbelievable ease it carried us over the final portion of our journey—the ending made possible by the goodness of that fantastically generous American of whom May had said, "Teppo, there really are such people."

It was this American, Mr. W. Clement Stone, who sent to the airport the first American we met on American soil, Lennard McCabe, who would later convince us that we should try after all to put into words the unforgettable story locked in our hearts. Patiently, almost sentence by sentence, he and his wife drew it forth, and Mrs. McCabe wrote it down.

"On the reef," she would say, "was the coral sharp?"

"Oh, very sharp," I would tell her. How could my inadequate English picture what it was—that reef. I could not even do it in Finnish. The horror of the roaring water —the utter desolation of our little band clinging to the ship, as if in all the pitiless world there were no other living creatures but ourselves.

"The coral stood up in horns," said May. "And farther below, in big peaks, like mountains under the ocean."

Mrs. McCabe wrote.

"Tell me," she said. "Did you think you would ever get here?" Her head a little to one side—her eyes interested, friendly—she waited.

The children were in the next room doing their homework. I could hear the rustle of turning pages. A phrase flashed through my mind, "My cup runneth over." To how many is it given to live what we lived and see such a dream come true? Did we think we would get here— "here" was this warmth, our home.

As if a key had turned to unlock everything we had vainly tried so long to say, May and I suddenly both began to talk at once.

Betty McCabe's pencil hurried down the page. She struggled to keep up. "This is it," she said at last. "Now you're telling how it really was and what it meant."

But it proved to be a long process, and before it was over we marvelled at the patience of the McCabes. May and I could not be content with a mere catalogue of events, because so much of our story was in what was thought and said and felt by all of us on the *Tuntsa*. This had been far more than just an adventure—events and words were inscribed on our hearts and in our minds. When at last we finished and sent the result of our labors to our fellow voyagers, they wrote back that the essence of the *Tuntsa* had indeed been set down.

Betty had rewritten some scenes for us as often as ten times before we were satisfied that they reproduced the actuality of the strange journey which had been the pivot of our lives. In the front of the book we wanted to express somehow our gratitude to her, but she and Lennard would not have it.

"Dedicate it to the children," she said.

That is what we did.

TEPPO TUREN
Chicago, Illinois

an **END —**
and its **BEGINNING**

A savage, crashing, spine-snapping force threw me from my bunk. Still half asleep I got up clutching a bulkhead. The cabin was tilting at a crazy angle. I heard the horrifying gurgle of water.

In the darkness I struggled toward the ladder to the forward hatch and started to climb. Because of the boat's unnatural list, I found I was almost crawling on my back.

Halfway up I lost my hold as the boat lifted and rose so suddenly and so high it seemed like miles—then dropped. It slammed onto something unseen. I fell on my left side. As I groped back to the ladder, my shoulder ached agonizingly, and I wondered hazily if it had been fractured. Then I heard another explosive crash of timbers. The boat lurched into stillness. She seemed to hang a moment in space, before she began careening from side to side in a thunderous rush of waters.

3

As I forced open the hatch, an avalanche of spray struck me in the face. Mountainous waves were crashing across the deck.

Clutching the edge of the cabin roof, I fought to reach the lifeline along the rail. In the dark I could dimly see three figures clinging to it near the bow. To reach them I had to cross the deck, whipped by spray which stung my eyes like hypodermic needles, blinding me and bringing sharp pain. I stopped to cling to the corner of the cabin, and instinct made me glance over my shoulder. A black wall of water, crazily streaked by gleams of green from our starboard lantern, towered, moved, roared, fell. Breath-cutting weight crushed me to the deck. The planking rose under me and my hands lost hold. I struggled for another grip, but my body became so numb I wondered if I had been swept overboard. I choked, twisted, gripped, tried to move—gripped again and fought for breath.

Once more the ship lifted dizzyingly. In a deafening roar of water receding, I felt another forward surge and heard the renewed grinding of timbers. The swaying eased. Whatever we had struck, that mountainous wave had taken us partly over it. I scrabbled along the rail, clutching to each stanchion with raw hands. The boat tilted anew with every wave, but now swaying from side to side, not in vicious fore-and-aft lurches. Nearing the figures at the bow, I could see their white faces.

We were accustomed to thinking of the *Tuntsa* as a miracle ship. After all these months, now that we were almost at our goal, would she snuff us out on an unknown reef? I would not believe it!

PLANS

escape

red-headed Masa

our group forms

It was three years before this moment, now lived so
uncertainly on the *Tuntsa*'s dark deck, that my dream
had become a fixation. The dream had been set for me
in my childhood, in the days after the First World War,
in my native Finland, during the time of her new-won
independence from Imperial Russia.

I was barely old enough to start school, when my
father began to say to me, "Teppo, for you I want independence to be a certainty. That isn't true here—I don't
think it ever will be. You will have to go away. Prepare
yourself, and be sure that you will go—that you will do
it before it is too late."

And in my teens, as our country was pressed on one
side by Nazi Germany and on the other by Soviet Russia,

my father would repeat, "Teppo, as soon as you grow up, you must go to America. It's a land of freedom, and some-day it may be the only one. I should have gone myself, Teppo."

Dreams do not fulfill themselves when the time is eas-iest. Circumstances have a way of intruding and present-ing themselves as real and pressing, while a dream can be postponed. First there was my schooling to finish— after that I fell in love and began saving to get married —then came the war, which interrupted all hopeful thinking and normal living. But after the war, when my country's bitter five year conflict with the Russian invad-ers ended, and Russia under the Soviets began to flow back over Finnish soil, annexing my very birth-city of Viipuri, my dream returned and became the whole goal of my existence.

The annexation of Viipuri was not the first time our family had been made homeless. In 1918, when the Bol-sheviks attempted to establish their rule over Finland, our house was burned. We rebuilt it after Finland won her independence. Twenty-one years later, in 1939 when Russia invaded us, it was again destroyed, this time by a Soviet air raid. After the war ended, my father died. It seemed to me more accurate to call his last illness a broken heart rather than the heart attack the doctor named it. I came away from his bedside determined that in our generation the quest for freedom would be ful-filled. There would be no more postponement. In the shortest possible time, my wife, our son, and I would get out of Finland. And somehow we would reach America.

It was a difficult project. No able-bodied man was allowed by the Finnish government to leave the country. In the years after the First World War so many had fled to escape the aftermath of economic chaos, that all possible measures were taken after World War II to halt a similar exodus. Every man was needed to help pay the staggering reparations Russia exacted after our defeat. Harbors, railroad stations, airports, and all borders were watched. Penalties were heavy. Few dared try escape, and even fewer could get the papers needed to emigrate legally. That my country had become like so many others in Europe a virtual prison, seemed to me a dread symptom. The very fact that those in power were finding it necessary to make leaving impossible stiffened my determination. The lengthening shadows stifling Eastern Europe would not fall over us. That would not be the future of our son. I swore it.

I was then a first lieutenant in the Finnish army. Work was hard to find, and I had a wife and small child to support while I cast about for a way of escape. Our family means, though once comfortable, had been wiped out by the war. I stayed in the army, saved my pay, kept my own counsel and searched for contacts which might help us leave the country.

During all of 1944 and 1945 my efforts were futile. My wife pointed out the reason.

"The army is the worst possible place to meet people who are going to try anything like that," she said. "It's not the army temperament, Teppo. People who think the way we are thinking simply don't stay in armies."

I glanced at May's face, whose youthful roundness contrasted with her straight brows and firm chin, and I decided that she was right. However, I pointed out that I might not be able to make as comfortable a living in any other way at present. Unemployment was diminishing, but real opportunity was slight. Most of the work to be done in postwar Finland consisted of swinging a a pick and a shovel.

"Why don't we wait then, Teppo?" she asked. "If we do get out, it will be in some terribly hard way—hiding in the bottom of a wagon or walking across Germany. We haven't any money, not any money at all. Eero is a baby. How could we manage?"

"We have to," I said.

May simply shook her head.

At last she said in a low voice. "I agree with you, really."

"I know."

"Eero can stay with your mother. We can send for him after we get out. It is only men they won't let leave."

"You could stay with Mother too," I pointed out.

May's pretty mouth folded into a line. Her square chin lifted. "If and when you go, I go too. Unless," she added in a different tone, "you don't want me."

I got up and put my arms around her. "May, you know better than that."

She did. And so did I.

A few weeks later I resigned my commission. I had been successful in finding a civilian job—not a very good one or well paid, but one which would let me move around and meet a maximum number of people. I became an insurance salesman.

Oddly enough, it turned out that I liked the insurance

business, not only as a possible means of reaching our goal and finding others who wanted to escape, but simply for itself. There was freedom and a chance to work as an individual, and still be my own man while acting as a member of a team. Besides, I quite simply enjoyed meeting people and discussing their problems. Two months passed, however, before I felt any closer to our real goal. Then without warning, I happened upon what for the first time seemed a possible solution.

I had just sold a client a policy during an appointment at his home. His name was Masa Korpi, and he was a skilled radio repairman and automobile mechanic.

"How about a cup of coffee?" he asked as I put the papers into my briefcase.

I accepted, and noticed how pleased he seemed at being released from the strain of sitting still. He was a stocky, powerfully built man who moved quickly, enthusiastically, in start-and-stop spurts. His red hair became unruly as he darted about fetching cups and coffee pot. The muscles of his arms rippled under the sports shirt he was wearing. Somehow during our talk I must have won his trust, for he suddenly told me that his consuming passion was to get out of Finland.

I spilled part of my coffee.

"Does that shock you?" he asked anxiously.

I could imagine his feelings. There was always the danger of being reported to the authorities.

I replied quickly. "I am not shocked at all."

Soon our coffee was getting cold as we talked.

He was twenty-six years old and he felt that to stay in Finland would waste his life. Leaning across the table, he said earnestly, "I want to get as far from here as possible. Finland is strangling to death. There's a tide coming over us. . . ." He did not finish, but ran his hand through his hair again and watched my face. Then he suddenly suggested we go to America together—by sailboat.

I must have looked as incredulous as I felt, for he hurried to go on.

"Look, I'm not crazy—really! A sailboat is the best way. There are always boats going in and out of Helsinki harbor. Who can keep track of them? And the trip isn't impossible. Truly, it is not!" He went on to tell of an acquaintance of his, Walvi Erickson, who had actually once navigated a small sloop all the way to the Canary Islands.

"It's dangerous, sure, but with an experienced navigator, the danger is cut in half. Walvi would be glad to tell us everything he can. In fact. . . ." Masa's voice stopped as we arrived simultaneously at the same thought.

"Would your friend be our navigator, do you think?" I asked.

Masa sprang to his feet. "Of course!" He stood tensely, as if he expected to sail that very night.

The following evening, Masa, Walvi Erickson, and I huddled over Masa's kitchen table. Erickson's nature seemed somewhat surly. He chewed a black cigar and looked me over. He was a heavy-set man with bushy eyebrows and graying hair. He had been born, probably, some forty years earlier. He moved slowly, deliberately, heavily. But he had indeed once navigated a sailboat to the Canaries, and when I asked him how well such a boat stood up on a long ocean journey, he seemed to take pleasure in displaying his superior knowledge and began to tell us in detail about his trip.

"Sailing isn't as haphazard as it looks. It's a definite science, something you can learn. There's a school right here in Helsinki that is pretty good. You ought to take their course in navigation."

"I will," I said. "But a course is no substitute for experience. I am sure we would need a navigator anyhow."

"I'll be your navigator," he said. He stretched. "And there isn't a better one in the business, if I do say so myself."

I was overjoyed. Masa sprang up and shook Walvi's hand. Walvi grinned. He was clearly delighted to have done something which won so much approval. I thought that perhaps like many heavy-natured men, he secretly craved warmth and companionship and found in them his greatest pleasure.

Our plans now began to move swiftly. In early January of 1947, I changed companies. I hoped to meet more people who wanted to escape, and I felt that I had exhausted the possibilities where I worked.

At the new agency I met Karl Virta. Through office conversation I heard that he had gone to the Dominican Republic before the war to try rice farming, but malaria and a liver abscess had forced his return. Perhaps now he might like to go back to the Republic, or even on to the United States?

I observed him closely for a few days.

In conversation, Karl Virta's answers were always precise, polite, and scrupulously accurate. His appearance carried out this impression of meticulous exactness. His thinning brown hair was faultlessly groomed above his high forehead. His frame was nondescript; his height a slender five feet, ten. His suits were perfectly tailored. Even his shoes were scuffless and spotless, undoubtedly shined each evening and touched-up in the men's room at noon. He always said the right thing, smiled only when a smile was expected, and never showed overt emotion. Yet one could not help liking him. He had a host of friends, all of whom seemed to joke unmercifully about his perfect manners, but he never showed anger or irritation. And there was the most sincere respect for his ability and integrity.

So, late one afternoon I stopped at his desk. After asking a question about the policy I was holding and receiving a stiff and proper answer, I remarked casually, "Did you ever think you might like to try rice farming again?"

His eyes were immediately alert, although his expression was unchanged. He looked around casually. No one was near us. He nodded to the chair beside his desk. I sat down.

"With a wife and two small children, it wouldn't be easy. You're a married man too, aren't you?"

"Yes," I said. "But my wife and I are thinking of taking a trip."

Again he looked indifferently around the office. "Where?"

"America."

At that moment I heard footsteps behind us. Karl quickly pointed to the policy I was holding. "If there's anything there you don't understand, just let me know."

I nodded, then bowed to the other man approaching

us. I walked back to my desk, but I could not concentrate. Was my trust in this correct, outwardly aloof man safe? Would he help us? Did he, as I thought, perhaps have the same hope for himself? Or would he turn informer? I could only wait.

It was then four o'clock. The intervening hour before the office closed seemed to drag like half a day. Finally I saw Karl get up to leave. He stopped, nodded politely, dropped his card on my desk, and said simply, "Stop by my house tonight. After nine."

It was a little after half-past-nine when May and I rang his bell.

He helped me off with my coat and introduced us to his wife, Kati, who had come out to the entrance hall. Something about her at once startled me, and I realized that it was her eyes. One was blue, the other brown. She wore thick glasses, whose heaviness contrasted oddly with her delicate features. But she had silken, wavy blonde hair, a well-shaped nose, and a sweet, lovely mouth. And later, when she took her glasses off, I saw that she actually was beautiful. She was slightly built, scarcely more than five feet tall. I guessed her age to be twenty-eight or nine.

As Karl led us into the living room, I noticed a man leaning expectantly forward in a deep-cushioned chair.

"May I introduce my brother-in-law, Arvi Teras?"

Teras rose quickly, shook my hand decisively. Here, I thought, was a man who got things done, quietly but efficiently. He was over six feet tall, lanky, with well-tanned features and straight brown hair. He was probably in his late thirties.

Karl spoke to me. "I am interested in what you said earlier. But I doubt if I can think of such a trip myself for reasons already explained. Arvi, however, wants very much to get out of Finland." His brother-in-law nodded, resolutely but without comment.

I glanced at Arvi's face. Like Karl's wife, he wore thick lenses which masked the expression in his eyes. "Do you wear glasses all the time?" I asked, wondering if this bespectacled man would be equal to active life on a sea-going boat.

"Only when my eyes are tired," he replied, taking his glasses off and putting them in his pocket.

Then, matter-of-factly, he explained that he had been a pilot during the war. On one flight, the cowling over his cockpit had ripped loose and the rush of icy wind had injured his eyes. "That finished my service days," he explained calmly.

When he returned to civilian life, he bought an interest in a furniture business, but taxes were so high that he wanted to sell out. "Nothing has gone well, and Finland is in such a mess that frankly I decided that if my wife and I could get out—preferably to America—we would do it."

He asked how I planned to go. I told him about Masa and Walvi and our decision to sail. He showed the same surprise I had felt when Masa first suggested the idea, so I hastily explained Walvi's navigating experience in sailing to the Canaries.

All this time, I had been stared at by two bright eyes from the darkness behind a rocker at the far end of the room. Now the eyes moved toward me—quite close to the floor. As the pin-points of light emerged from the shadows, I saw they belonged to a hairy bundle of a dog, an inquisitive-looking little fox terrier. Shaggy-faced curiosity confronted us for a moment. Then he gravely sniffed May's ankles and wagged his stump of a tail. May leaned over to pat him gently.

"He is nice," she volunteered to Karl's wife.

"He's a good little dog," Kati said. "But he isn't ours. He belongs to Arvi. He follows him everywhere." She smiled at May, and I could see that May liked her.

The dog moved on and sniffed my shoes. Arvi laughed. "Well! You've passed inspection! His name is Tuntsa.* Karl brought him to me from Lapland after the war."

I mentioned what a cheerful companion he would be on an ocean voyage, and Arvi remarked laconically that as a dog who had survived the war, he would make us a good mascot.

Four nights later, Walvi, Masa, Arvi and his wife Anna, May and I met at Karl's. Masa's wife remained at home. She would leave all decisions to him, for she would have to remain in Helsinki until Masa was settled because they had no one with whom they could leave their baby daughter.

Kati and Karl sat closely side by side as Walvi recounted his experiences in sailing to the Canaries. The big, sullen man was a vivid story-teller, and he obviously enjoyed being the center of a new and larger audience.

* "Tuntsa" is an alternate term for "tundra," the moss and lichen covered plains of Lapland, whose stubborn vegetation persists despite the frozen subsoil. Little Tuntsa's shaggy coat and hardy nature were responsible for his name.

Before a half hour passed, I saw that Karl's face was showing excitement. With a shake of his well-groomed head, he finally murmured, "I give up. We'll go with you."

Behind her glasses, Kati's eyes were first startled, then worried, then resigned. I had the impression that Karl's decision, sudden though it seemed, was not wholly unexpected. She glanced at May, and said that like May she would go too, if her mother would keep her two little girls. May had already told her that our son, then about one-and-a-half, was to stay with my mother until he could be sent for. Karl and Kati's children were one and two years old, and it would be impossible to take them.

A rapid, animated discussion followed. I was soon aware that we were distinct and very different personalities. Karl had on the same flawlessly-cut suit he had worn to work, only now it was freshly pressed. He presented a picture of absolute calm—except for the momentary betrayal of his real feelings in his one excited outburst. Kati had taken off her glasses and was sitting stiffly forward in her chair, looking worried most of the time, but extraordinarily fragile and pretty. Energetic, red-headed Masa, in a loose-fitting bright green jacket and checked slacks, twiddled his thumbs, sprawled, changed chairs, twirled cigarettes, crossed and re-crossed his knees in an endless flow of restless energy.

In contrast to his restlessness, was Karl's brother-in-law, Arvi, sitting quietly on his straight-backed chair with an outward self-control belied only by his taut mouth and shining eyes. Arvi's wife Anna, however, was as self-consciously nervous as her husband was disciplined, as talkative as he was taciturn. Anna was Karl's sister but seemed quite unlike him in temperament. A sculpturesque brunette in her late twenties, she soon made it clear that she was aware of the drama of the discussion and inclined to make the most of it. She kept breaking in with questions, stories of her experiences, or statements about her likes and dislikes. She liked canned foods. Some were good, however, and some were not. We must be sure to buy the proper brands—which she knew.

I looked around and tried to predict how we might all get along together as a group. May and Kati would be friends. Anna might be difficult, but she seemed capable. There was a likeable quality about her energy, and her questions showed drive and enthusiasm. Who knew where we could get a boat? How much would it cost? Could Walvi estimate how much food we needed? How would it be cooked? How often could we stop for supplies? How many clothes could we take?

Walvi answered between irritable puffs on his cigar. A sailboat? "A good one probably won't be for sale at all. A boat of any kind will be hard to find, and sure to be expensive." How much would it cost? "Well, it shouldn't cost more than 340,000 marks."* How much food would we need? "To cross the Atlantic? Six weeks supply with good weather. You women should figure that out." What ports would we visit? "We have to stop for oil, gas, water, and food when we need it. Every third or fourth day, maybe, if we can." How many clothes? Walvi's normally monotonous, low voice went up a full octave. "Good heavens, woman! With salt water drenching you

* Approximately $1,500.

and only the dirty waterfront stores and cafes in port, what difference does it make? You'll wear slacks and low-heeled shoes, if you're smart."

Anna, who had been an editor of a women's fashion magazine before she married, looked suddenly moody. May and Kati glanced soberly at one another. Then Walvi directed his talk pointedly to the men. Women's questions annoyed Walvi because they took away his audience. He preferred to expound to the male members of the crew.

He said that we should visit the waterfront as often as we could, singly or in pairs, and ask where we could get a small sailboat, "strictly for weekend sailing." We would not dare buy a big boat even if we had the money. "Thirty feet or less," instructed Walvi. "It's the only way to avoid suspicion."

None of us had much ready cash, but Karl, Masa, Arvi, and I thought that together we could raise the down payment on a boat that size. Then we would sell our personal belongings to complete the payments and buy supplies. It was agreed that Walvi's services as navigator relieved him of financial obligation.

Now that we had reached the point of actually planning to buy a boat, conversation became solemn. Each of us thought of family and friends, and all we must leave behind. The United States was merely a dream. We knew no one there, we had no entrance papers, and we could not conceive how we could live once we arrived. Except Walvi, none of us had ever sailed the ocean; and the thought of rough waters and storms was sobering. During the war we had learned to face with outer calm and inner stoicism the possibility of death. But then we knew that if we survived we would have family, friends, and familiar landmarks to return to, battered and changed only in part. Now, however, except for our own selves, all would be new and unfamiliar. I asked myself over and over: is the dream a good one? In my own mind the answer was always, yes. And the others must have felt the same, for without more discussion we set our plans into motion.

the **BOAT**

an ancient mariner

the old potato lugger

you can't sail a piano

Tuntsa

Peering out from the hoods of their fur-lined parkas, captains, sailors, and wharf hangers-on stared at us in disbelief. Buy a sailboat in the dead of winter when ice covered all rivers and lakes and most of the Baltic? Impossible. Wait until spring. Then owners of boats for sale would advertise or spread the news in waterfront gossip.

But we felt we must not wait. Walvi said we could leave no later than the following August so we would reach the Virgin Islands before the hurricane season began. Less than six months remained until his deadline for our departure, and even that might be too little time to make a used boat seaworthy.

Finally, early in March, after an entire month of

search, Masa and Walvi returned from the Helsinki docks, where Walvi had spent an hour with a friendly sailor exchanging anecdotes about the sea. When Walvi at last mentioned that he would like to have his own boat for weekend excursions, the sailor commented that he had heard of one for sale in Kotka, about a hundred miles east, on the Gulf of Finland.

"She's around ten years old. Been used to carry potatoes across the Bay to Estonia. Kotka's a friendly city. Someone there will tell you how to find the owner."

So Masa, Arvi, Karl, and I decided to take the afternoon train that Saturday. Walvi, after relaying the information, said he would not go. "It's your money. You decide what to spend it on."

It seemed odd to me that Walvi showed so little interest in the boat he was to navigate. However, I merely attributed it to his somewhat phlegmatic nature. Walvi disliked moving about, as much as he enjoyed talking and attentive listeners.

Karl and Arvi, Masa and I arrived in Kotka at dusk. It was twenty degrees below zero, and we were nearly frozen after the quarter mile walk to the boat owner's salt-streaked, weathered shack. A broad ray of light from a single window cast a welcome, warming glow about our feet. Masa knocked.

The door opened a scant inch. We must have looked miserable, for the crack widened and an old man with a deeply wrinkled face sullenly looked out.

"What do you want?" he asked suspiciously. The seafarers in this part of the country were not noted for hospitality.

"We would like to see the boat you have for sale, sir," said Karl.

Curiosity seemed to melt some of his hostility. "You're sailors?"

"No sir, we want to learn." Karl hesitated, and then took up our agreed-on story. "We want to use the winter to refit a boat and then take out people on pleasure trips in the summer. It pays well."

The old man blinked. "You're crazy!"

He gave us another prolonged stare, and shook his head. "You'll be shark bait—the lot of you." Then, unexpectedly, he opened the door wide. "Come in."

Inside, the ancient mariner began to pace the small room, his back bent slightly forward and his hands clasped tightly behind. He stopped to look out the window at the frozen Bay. "Let me tell you something," he said, "the sea is evil. It attracts people like you, gets them to sail on it, then it starts to plot. It rocks you—oh, so comfortably—until you relax." He turned. "Then it hits!"

We faced him silently. He jerked his head toward the gray waters. "That's not a playground out there. You're not sailors, never will be. I can see it from the look of you. You'll be drowned—the whole lot."

A long pause followed. Finally I said, "May we see the boat, sir?"

Abruptly he put on his coat and got a flashlight.

The boat looked even worse than we had expected. It listed in the ice like a bloated pig, its one mast inclined shoreward. Its bow was almost covered by hard-packed snow so we could not see the condition of the wood.

Masa tried to sink a knife into the hull but the ice was deeper than the length of his blade.

We squirmed onto the deck. The rigging seemed in bad condition. Then Arvi took the flashlight and led the way below through the one small hatch. The space was so small two men could not have shaken hands, so we entered one by one. Heaven only knows how a crew had ever slept, eaten and washed in that black hole.

I noted with misgiving that thick tar had been smeared over the ribbing of the inner hull to keep it from leaking. Dirt was caked over bulkheads—ribs—everything.

There was no pump. No water tanks. The crew must have used portable ones. There was a small one-cylinder auxiliary motor, but unmistakably worn-out. I could hear Masa curse softly as he looked at it. Finally we huddled by the mast, and numb with cold and disappointment, looked questionably at one another.

"Wait until the ice melts off her—then there will really be trouble!" Masa predicted. "I bet she leaks and needs reinforcing all along the keel."

Karl regarded us solemnly. "She's the *only* sailboat we have heard about. If we want to go in August, how can we wait until spring to find something better?"

"Well, let's see how much he wants for her," I said.

We hurried toward the house. Our eyes and noses were running from the cold. Inside, we clustered around the wood stove in the center of the room.

"How much do you want?" I asked.

The old seaman's shrewd eyes narrowed. He had already decided we must be demented. No use to try to dissuade us further. And it was now a matter of money, which came hard on that bitter coast. We could see him weighing the intensity of our insane desire for a boat, the rarity of available craft, and mentally raising his price.

"450,000 marks,"* he said at last.

I felt my face, warming from the heated stove, go stiff. "What?"

"That's my price."

"Look here, my good man. . . ." began Karl, uncrossing his legs and leaning forward in the seat he had just taken.

"Don't 'my good man' me," the old sailor said sharply.

"But listen!" said Arvi. "She'll cost almost that in repairs alone!"

Masa angrily ran a hand through his red hair. "You're sure of yourself, aren't you?" he asked angrily.

The seaman's shrewd smile spread like ripples from an oar. "There ain't another boat you'll find for sale in a thousand miles."

Karl, still in his pose of casualness, said, "What if we don't buy?"

The seaman shrugged, got up from his rocker, and moved toward the adjoining room. "Talk it over," he said. The door closed, and we heard the creak of springs as the heavy figure sank onto the bed. In that cold, going to bed was the only thing to do in a room without a fire.

The price was 110,000 marks more than Walvi had told us our top payment should be. And we could not guess how much work or money would be required to make the old boat seaworthy. Nevertheless, we were

* Approximately $2,000.

convinced that nothing else would appear on the market until the ice thawed, and we would not then have enough time to complete repairs and buy supplies. And if we waited until next year, we could not know how many more security measures against such plans as ours would go into effect. If we did not go now, we might never go at all.

"Well, now that we have found it, how do we pay for it?" Karl asked.

We gave him a startled stare, then smiled rather sheepishly at one another. We had each privately decided that regardless of price we had to buy the boat.

Arvi had 56,000 marks with him. Karl and I each had close to the same amount. Masa had several thousand less. Together we could count scarcely half the sum.

We estimated funds we would get from selling furniture and belongings. Finally it seemed enough. Arvi suggested, "Since we're short of the price for now, why don't we offer to deposit 60,000 marks and pay the rest in sixty days."

We called the boatman. He balked, however, when we broached the installment idea. He wanted his money at once.

"We can't do it any other way," Karl said coldly.

The old man rocked meditatively back and forth in his chair. Finally he shrugged and agreed. Once he had his down payment, he became cordial, shaking hands all around, and wishing us "good luck." But it was obvious that he considered us doomed.

Going back on the train, we discussed our future needs

as boat owners. The car was vacant except for a bearded snorer and his sleeping granddaughter at the far end, so we felt free to talk.

"We have to get new sails and rigging," Karl said.

"And a permanent bilge pump, plus possibly a portable one for emergencies," added Masa. Arvi nodded. He and Masa had already found common ground in a knack for things mechanical.

"We will be ripping out a large section of deck for a cabin. And we have to put in water tanks," I said. "It will be a big job." It was obvious that even if we did most of the construction ourselves we would still need expensive supplies. We would soon be in dire need of more money.

"I'll sell my workbenches and larger tools," Masa said thoughtfully. "There's a lot I couldn't use for work on the boat anyhow."

May and I had already realized that we would have to sell all our furniture, and most of our clothes. May's beloved piano should quickly find a purchaser, even in these times. I told Karl about the piano. "It's a shame," he said, "but it will bring a good price. Pianos are almost as scare as boats."

"With less foolishness needed to buy one," I commented. "You don't have to *sail* a piano!"

At the end of the cold, five-hour trip from Kotka to Helsinki, we planned to meet the following night at Karl's apartment, if Walvi was free.

Walvi was horrified by the price, but he was as well acquainted as we with the demands made possible by

postwar scarcities. If one was so unfortunate as to need
some specific object, the owner could extort almost any
sum he cared to name. Walvi finally gave one of his
heavy sighs and drew his bushy brows together into a
scowl of resignation. "I suppose you were lucky to find
a boat at all," he said. "But I'm glad it's your money, not
mine."

Taking up a nautical almanac, he began to leaf
through it, commenting when he came to a bit of information which recalled a personal experience. Again and
again he asked for a description of the boat, frowning
whenever we mentioned that it was a sloop. "For a trip
like this, you need a two master. If you're going to invest
in new sails and rigging and a built-in cabin, you'll be
in for a major overhaul anyhow. You may as well get a
second mast and make her into a ketch."

Our meetings became more frequent, our discussions
longer. Walvi enjoyed instructing us, and we went over
every detail of our plans until refitting the boat began
to seem possible, even easy. The trip no longer appeared
perilous but took on the glamor of a great adventure. To
Tuntsa, the little fox terrier, the group became so familiar
that he was at home with all of us. He would greet us
spunkily, his tail wagging, ears alert. As we came or left,
he was the personification of energy and enthusiasm. As
far as *Tuntsa* was concerned, the adventure had already
begun.

During the next few days, May again and again
rubbed her hands lovingly over her piano's polished mahogany surface and then sat down to play her favorite
melodies. It turned out that her piano was the first large

item sold. Then followed books, chairs, china, silver, linens, and furniture. Stoically May watched them go and even pretended to be pleased.

"They were a lot of trouble, Teppo," she would say, but sometimes her lips were trembling.

Masa got excellent prices for his heavier shop equipment. Karl and Kati, Arvi and Anna sold clothing, rugs, and furniture. Karl advertised in the newspaper "buyers wanted" columns. We never knew when a member of the secret police might hear about some specific sale and investigate, so in each household the planned reply to any question was that the family was moving to another city.

Within five weeks after making the down payment on the boat, we had accumulated enough money to fill out its total price and start buying materials for remodelling. Kati acted as treasurer and early in April told us we could go ahead. Arvi and Masa, as the most skilled in construction, would return to Kotka as soon as the waterways were open. They would send back specifications for supplies which they found unavailable or too expensive. Karl and I would stay behind in Helsinki to get them.

Except for Walvi, who was to take no part in the actual labor of refitting, all of us left our jobs by the end of April. On the first of May, Arvi and Masa arrived in Kotka. That Saturday, Karl and I in Helsinki received sketches of the proposed cabin area, a long list of materials needed, and the following note at the end: "She's 30 feet, 6 inches long, 12 feet wide, with a 33 foot mast and 17 ton displacement. It's a floating hotel! Masa."

Arvi had scrawled below: "Seriously, it looks much better than we hoped. Rush supplies. We're on our way for sure."

Rushing supplies was more easily said than done. Most items, even nails, were scarce; and the war tax was high. Together May and Kati cast up a reckoning based on an estimate of costs. The forecast was soon seen to be pathetically optimistic and the estimates far too low. In spite of all difficulties, however, Arvi and Masa overhauled the motor, re-installed it, and finished most of the cabin. After sawing out the greater portion of the center deck and leaving only a narrow catwalk on either side, they erected as roomy a cabin as possible and built in rough bunks. Part of the mid-cabin was left open for storage.* Then, unable to do any more because Karl and I had been unsuccessful in obtaining some of the essentials, they came back to Helsinki after three weeks of back-breaking labor.

Meanwhile, I had started the navigation course Walvi recommended. "I'm a real sailor now," I told Karl proudly. I would find out later, however, that it took more than books to make a seaman.

We had major items yet to buy: the second mast, new rigging, bilge pump and reserve portable pump, dinghy, life preservers, stove, marine toilet, water tanks, possibly a new rudder, and lumber for lockers, storage cabinets, and decking. Walvi also said we must have an iron keel to balance the weight of the new masts. The greatest problem of all, however, was sails. Canvas was almost unobtainable.

* See illustration.

Arvi asked, "How much will we need?"

Walvi jotted down dimensions, made sketches, multiplied, added, then replied, "About sixty-seven square yards."

I started. I had never dreamed it would take so much. Where would we ever find any such quantity as that?

Karl, however, with his special brand of good manners was to be of unexpected help.

We went to a sail-loft in Sorkka, a part of Helsinki which was the haunt of waterfront toughs and the center of the post-war black market. The natives of the area had their own dialect, a combination of Finnish and Swedish hard to understand. They regarded all outsiders with suspicion.

As we made our way to the sailmaker's shop down narrow, filthy, uneven streets lined with run-down frame buildings, the inhabitants glared at us and lounged on corners, hands in pockets. It was a relief when we reached our destination.

The door opened hard, squeaking as we pushed. A single bulb gleamed dustily above a cluttered desk in one corner. An unbelievably dirty assortment of precariously-balanced boxes filled most of the space.

A tall young girl rose from the desk and came grudgingly toward us. Her unkempt hair drooped over her face and sagged over her shoulders. Her badly fitting, soiled dress was torn at the waist.

"What do you want?" she asked in a hostile voice whose sharp edge matched her bitterly pinched features.

"We would like to see the sailmaker," said Karl politely.

"He's not here."

Discourtesy invariably made Karl more courteous. He spoke with quiet precision. "We would like to order some sails. We need approximately sixty-seven square yards of canvas."

He had her attention now. She stared in sheer disbelief. "Well, how are you going to get it?" she asked. "Steal it off some boat?"

Karl gazed thoughtfully down at her. "To whom am I speaking?" he asked gently at last. To Karl, any woman, in any place, deserved the utmost consideration. The rougher the surroundings, the more automatically he compensated with good manners.

The girl hesitated. She had obviously been about to make a sharp retort but now she seemed to change her mind. "My name is Erika," she brought out hesitantly.

"A lovely name," replied Karl, and bowed. The girl gazed at him in wonder.

"My uncle isn't at home," she said awkwardly. She suddenly put her hands with their bitten nails behind her back.

"Your uncle is the proprietor?" Karl asked.

She nodded, looking at him with increasing awe.

"I have a problem," said Karl. Quite oblivious to Erika's reactions, he was simply looking as worried as he felt.

Her expression immediately copied his. She grew worried too. She frowned.

"A very serious problem," Karl went on in his precise and courteous way. "My friends and I have to make a trip to Kotka. But our boat is in such condition that we do not dare risk her on the Baltic in her present condition. The sails have rotted beyond repair. To go out with them as they are would be extremely dangerous."

"You must not do that," Erika said earnestly. "You might be killed."

Karl smiled slightly. Suddenly Erika turned. "Wait!" she exclaimed over her shoulder. "I'll get my uncle!" Quite forgetting that she had told us her uncle was not in, she hurried into the rear of the shop.

Mystified, Karl looked after her.

There was a sudden din from the adjoining room. "I thought I told you! . . ." A rough voice roared and then sank. There was the sound of Erika's urgent pleading, and then the door was jerked suddenly open. A fat old man with a sailor's cap cocked over one ear came striding toward us. He launched into a tirade against the times, the black market, shortages. . . . Impossible, he said, for an honest man to make a living. "Everyone wants me to get something for them!" He spread his hands eloquently. "How can I? The war tax is so high! No one can pay! It takes all my profit."

"We need sailcloth desperately," Karl said.

Erika stood clasping and unclasping her hands. Karl took out his packet of cigarettes and offered them to the old man, who accepted one, lighted it, and inhaled, glancing at Karl sourly.

"We need sixty-seven square yards of canvas," said Karl. The sailmaker gave a whistle of incredulity. Erika nudged him into silence.

"Of course," Karl went on, "I wouldn't expect you to get all that from one place. Nor would I expect the sails to be cheap."

The old man took a long puff on his cigarette and let the smoke out, while Erika gazed at him pleadingly. "Well," he said at last, "my niece has got it into her head that for some reason you have to have these sails. She's got a feeling about it, she says. And if you're willing to pay. . . ."

"Your niece is a very perceptive young woman," replied Karl, smiling at Erika and making another bow in her general direction.

"I don't know what she is," said the sailmaker irritably, "but when she gets a 'feeling' I generally try to do something, because if I don't, my dinners won't be fit to eat for a month. I'll see what I can do for you."

"We are most grateful," said Karl, "both to you and to your niece." He handed the sailmaker the diagrams Walvi had made of our mainsail, mizzen, foresail, and jib—both working and storm sails.

"Come back in two weeks," said the old man, eyeing the diagrams dubiously. "Mind now, I'm not making any promises."

As we went out, I heard Erika's voice raised in what was clearly to be a long monologue.

"You'll get the sails," I said to Karl in the street.

"How do you know?"

"I couldn't possibly explain," I told him, "but you'll get them. I'm positive."

Two weeks later when we went back, the sailmaker presented us with our completed working and storm sails plus a bill not much higher than we expected. Erika gazed at Karl with dewy eyes. She was a heroine who from her lowly place in the world was saving a hero.

Karl looked back with some bewilderment, but certainly with sincere gratitude. Our biggest problem was solved.

Shortly thereafter, we bought line and wire for the rigging and ordered our iron keel and water tanks. We secured two second-hand water pumps and an old portable bilge pump from a junk yard, all to be repaired by Arvi and Masa. We also found a two-man dinghy at a ship chandler's. Then we returned to Kotka to get the boat and sail it back to Helsinki. It was early June, but it was a harsh and late spring. The temperature was still below freezing.

But when we actually stood on the icy beach, we forgot the inclement weather and all our difficulties. We gazed out at our boat and felt the pure delight of ownership. Little Tuntsa pranced at the end of his leash and barked eagerly, as if urging that whatever we had in mind should start at once. Our ship seemed to roll as if she too was straining to get on with the adventure.

"It's time for a formal christening," said Karl. "What shall we call her?"

We looked proudly at the impatient little craft, bobbing on the waves and sending up sprays of icy water on each side of her bow. She seemed as impatient at being still tied to her mooring as Tuntsa was at being held by the leash in Arvi's hand.

"Let's call her the *Tuntsa*," Masa said.

"Perfect!" I exclaimed.

Indeed it was the terrier spirit that our boat suggested. She seemed ready to take to the high seas with exactly the same defiant confidence with which little Tuntsa faced the world.

Masa searched the refuse by the water's edge. Finding no bottles, he picked up a chunk of ice. Arvi and I hauled in the boat and Masa stepped forward. His entire crown of red hair seemed to stand high in a single mountainous cowlick. "I christen you TUNTSA!" he exclaimed and shattered the ice across the bow.

We cheered.

an OLD BOAT GROWS NEW

landlubbers on deck

the clipper-ship captain

fools are not suspect

no palace, but it floats

our first test

We went aboard the *Tuntsa* and looked in her locker for her old sails, with which we thought we could get her back to Helsinki. But when we saw them, we groaned. The mainsail and jib were rotten. They fell apart in four or five places as we held them up. Masa cursed eloquently.

Finally, Arvi had to go back to town for sailmaker's palms, curved needles, waxed thread, and canvas. We spent the whole of the precious day patching the crumbling canvas.

Then we hired the ex-owner's grandson to handle the boat for us on the trip to Helsinki. He was a gangly, pimply-faced veteran of sixteen, who like his grandsire, regarded us as utterly insane. The mainsail ripped apart half-way across the Bay and he went below to start the motor. When he returned to see our clumsy attempts to lower the torn sail, he burst into mocking laughter. We could only watch humbly the professional ease with which he stowed the ripped canvas and brought us back on course, but inwardly we were seething. We studied his every movement for our own future use. We might be landlubbers at present, but we had no intention of remaining so.

I noticed with relief that the *Tuntsa* seemed to handle well. In spite of the handicap of having only half a mainsail, her remaining canvas and one-cylinder motor carried us into Helsinki's harbor.

We went directly to the shipyard to see if they were ready to put on the iron keel. When we left, they had promised immediate installation as soon as we returned, but now they said they had received a Russian order to build fishing boats, and the Russians, of course, went to the head of the line—in this as in everything else. We would have to wait till the crane was free again.

It was almost three weeks before the shipyard notified us that the crane was at last available. While the shipyard men worked, we prepared the newly delivered water tanks. Our first concern was that they would keep our water fresh, particularly during our long Atlantic crossing. While we conjectured, an old sailor approached us. He had evidently overheard our inept conversation.

He seated himself on a packing case near us. "I have just what you need."

"What's that?" I asked bluntly.

He puffed at a malodorous pipe, then replied, "A recipe for them tanks."

"You mean something to keep water fresh?"

"Yep."

We waited. After some moments, he asked pleasantly, "Do you want it?"

Arvi pressed a few coins into his hand and answered, "Yes, of course. Take this for some tobacco."

The weathered face wrinkled with surprise. "I'm not selling anything. I just wanted to be sure you wanted my private recipe."

He then gave us a list of what seemed to us highly unlikely ingredients. They made a strange concoction, but we used it—cement mixed with skimmed milk and salt, and applied in thin layers until nearly a half-inch thick. We had considerable misgivings at the time, but we later had very good luck with our water, which so often fouls in storage, and we often thought gratefully of our sailor friend and his "private recipe."

While Karl and I lined the tanks, Masa and Arvi painted the outer hull white before the crane lowered it back into the water. Arvi nailed the letters "TUNTSA" in brilliant brass on both sides near the bow. Then into the waiting white and gold *Tuntsa*, now proudly waterborne in all her new glory, Karl and I lowered the tanks midship, one on each side between hull and cabin bulkhead. Each tank had a single opening through the deck to which a small hand pump was attached for use when drinking or cooking water was needed. Cross baffles prevented sloshing in heavy weather from damaging the lining.

Arvi and Masa installed our permanent bilge pump after a complete overhauling, and cleaned up a portable pump to be held in reserve. Then they finished partitioning the midships area and built in the rough bunks, while Karl and I continued our hunt for supplies. It required the utmost ingenuity, and it was an exhausting pursuit both physically and nervously, for we never knew when our activities might stir up the security police and expose the whole plan.

Finally by the end of June we were ready to sail to Valkom, a small seaport about fifty miles east of Helsinki, where two new masts would be set. We sewed together the torn sail for what we hoped would be the last time, and five of us—Arvi and Anna, Masa, Karl, and I (no, six of us, I almost omitted Tuntsa, who of course came with Arvi) cast off from the Helsinki pier and headed for Valkom.

That short voyage was exhilarating. Together we learned basic fundamentals of navigation and sailing. I had brought my textbooks for safety in reference, and one at a time we worked the sails or took the helm while the others critically looked on. The *Tuntsa* seemed to us a craft of utterly perfect beauty, and I began to understand why sailors call their boats "she" and become attached to them with affection and pride. Our *Tuntsa* was a sensitive little boat, quick to answer her helm, and rising sturdily to meet the choppy sea. Her agility and something about the shape of her bow gave her that air of impudence we had noted on the day we named her after Arvi's indomitable terrier, now running about briskly on deck, obviously trying to show us that in all the world there could be no better sailor than he. The resemblance between his personality and that of our boat, with her daring and perhaps impossible assignment, made us laugh with pride and pleasure.

We moored at Valkom that evening. Two days later, the installation of the two masts was complete—and we were out of money. The costs had been appalling.

"Well, we've sold everything we own," I said. "Even if we wanted to change our minds, it's too late."

There was a silence.

"Maybe we could do the rigging ourselves," suggested Arvi.

"My God, no!" Masa protested. "I don't know a backstay from a hole in the deck!"

"We'll have to learn," Karl said quietly.

"Maybe someone would show us." Masa's red forelock hung down over his forehead. Even little Tuntsa, panting at our feet, looked dejected. Finally Arvi went out to buy a book on rigging. It illustrated with endless complexity how and where every piece of line went, but, after careful checking, the directions seemed to fit any kind of boat but our own.

"The *Tuntsa's* a bastard," said Masa angrily. "Walvi had us make a boat there's never been anything like before."

Karl's face showed strain. "We've got to rig her right. If we don't, our first storm will be our last."

The shadow of someone looking on fell across the deck. This was nothing new. From the beginning, dockside loafers and stray seamen had been attracted to jeer at our group of landlubbers and their incomprehensible boat. At this point one more sneer would have made us take to our fists. We were careful to look up casually, hoping to discourage comment.

A husky, aging man with a smiling sun-burned face topped by sun-yellowed white hair was standing over us. He wore his navy blue visored cap with the air of confident status that could only belong to a former skipper.

"You look as though you need help."

In bitter silence, Arvi straightened his bent back and wiped the perspiration from his forehead.

"We haven't any money to pay you," I answered curtly.

"I don't want money. I used to sail the old clippers. That boat of yours now—I've never seen anything like it. It'd be a pleasure to rig her. You don't know much about rigging, do you?" His voice was disarming. If he had any tendency to be amused, it was lost in the intensity of his interest.

"No, sir," replied Karl.

The white haired skipper beamed.

How long had it been, I wondered, since the old man had felt himself in a position of command? Too long, apparently; for, asking us our names, he stepped on deck and at once started barking orders. Beaming with pleasure and striding about, he had us set the stays, hang the booms, rig hundreds of feet of line. While we worked, he gave us what was in effect a practical lecture. The terms—stays, sheets, shrouds, backstays—rolled off so swiftly that we could only stare. But he would note our stricken expressions, laugh, and then patiently explain.

As we worked, sweated, and listened, we had more unsolicited company. The harbor people were naturally delighted with the discomfort of the amateurs, but we were so pleased with our preceptor and his invaluable instruction that we now merely grinned, with what must have seemed to the onlookers a new good temper as mystifying as the rest of our activities.

As we worked, Anna made herself invaluable. She cooked imaginative meals for us, got Tuntsa out from underfoot by taking him walking, shopped for food and supplies, and cleaned up after us. She would rail about our poor housekeeping, but moments later would be smiling and singing as she painstakingly folded the two gray blankets we had over each bunk, or tackled some other cabin duty. We soon learned that her quick tongue merely covered an intense desire to do everything as perfectly as possible. She would have been indignant if we had been good housekeepers—that was her own cherished realm.

On deck, she helped by handing us line or nails or tools. Her impulsiveness and high spirits found the heckling of the spectators stimulating rather than offensive. Hands on hips, her junoesque figure impressive in her tight jersey, she would give back spicier language than she received and then laugh explosively. The insinuations of the dockside characters only made her smile. A speck of dirt on one of our precious blankets would have upset her far more.

When the rigging was finished, our impromptu instructor wandered off as casually as he had wandered in. The throng of derisive bystanders, however, increased. To drown out distracting comments, we finally took to singing at the top of our lungs and pounding with unnecessary vigor. We tried to turn the dockside atmosphere to advantage by seeming even more absurd and inept than we were. It had been hopeless from the beginning to try not to attract attention, but if everyone for miles around got it firmly fixed in mind that we were a group of comic fools, it would be unlikely to occur to anybody to suspect us of being capable of anything as serious as a plot to flee the country.

"I feel safer," said Karl, "when I see them so busy laughing."

Two weeks from the time we moored in Valkom, we had completed all but the cabin roof. While we did this, Anna cleaned and painted the inner hull. Then, three coats of white paint above deck, and we were ready to get out of the limelight and sail back to Helsinki to search for an inconspicuous mooring.

In order to make the trip a real trial run, we decided not to hug the shore but to head for open water, and to send for Walvi and Kati and May so we would be voyaging with our full crew. Our trip over had been so delightful that we thought it would be even more pleasurable on the way back, and we wanted our wives to enjoy it. We anticipated no trouble. In this, we were sadly mistaken, for on the deceptively beautiful Baltic, in the very sight of our own shores, we were to come almost as close to death as we ever came later.

＊

Walvi, May, and Kati arrived at Valkom by bus. Kati and May were enthusiastic. "The *Tuntsa* is lovely!" exclaimed Kati taking off her sunglasses and gazing happily about. May was delighted to see the gleaming white cabin. But Walvi seemed oddly uninterested and preoccupied. Looking at the rigging, he muttered, "My God!" May murmured to me, "Something is bothering him—I don't know what. All the way on the bus he sat like a bump."

There were delighted "oohs" as the girls stepped aboard the sparkling gold and white boat. Trying to draw the silent Walvi into comment, they exclaimed with delight at the skylights atop the cabin. Then they saw the two hatchways, one just forward of the wheel, the other near the bow. "Let's try the front one," Kati suggested, "and come out the one near the back—oh, I mean the stern." Tuntsa, barking proudly, led the way.

I heard the girls laugh as they began the steep descent down the hatch ladder. "It would be easier to jump— like Tuntsa!" said May. Karl, Masa, and I followed. We stepped from the ladder into sudden silence. Laughter and chatter had stilled when our wives saw the "beautiful galley, fully equipped" which we had promised.

On a rickety table sat one blowtorch, one skillet, one pot, and one salt shaker, with paper plates and kitchen knives and forks. There was no stove and no refrigerator. "Of course, it still needs a few things," Karl explained lamely.

"We'll buy a stove in Helsinki," I hastily told May, who looked at me miserably.

"Anna will tell you the blowtorch cooks very well," Karl said, and I moved quickly to distract them by showing the rest of the "galley."

Butted against the table to starboard was a single

bunk; facing it to port, another single. By day these
would be seats for eating; at night, beds for Arvi and
Anna. The hatch ladder invaded the center area, allow-
ing narrow passage around it.

"We don't dare gain weight do we?" asked May with
an attempt at humor. In single file, we passed the cur-
tained toilet area on one side and our storage cabinets
opposite. The quarters were so tight that we all scraped
elbows against curtain or doors.

"I hope no one has claustrophobia," Kati said.

In the center section of the cabin were two double
bunks.

"There certainly isn't much room," observed May,
gazing up at the close ceiling overhead. "Who . . ." Then
realizing the answer, she looked at us indignantly,
"Maybe I'll just sleep on deck with Tuntsa!"

Kati, realizing that she and Karl would occupy the
other double bunk, was speechless. Karl put his arm
around her. She looked ready to cry.

We heard voices and looked around to see Arvi and
Anna standing in the doorway. They had returned from
buying food for our run back to Helsinki. "It isn't so
bad," said Anna, looking at May and Kati. "I've been
living in it. Honestly, it's all right—as soon as you get
used to it."

There was little more we could say. We had made the
best of our supplies and the available space, as the girls
could see for themselves. We went back on deck to let
them get settled. Tuntsa went importantly with us. He
was establishing himself as one of the male crew.

We found Walvi gloomily roving about. "Hey, Masa,"

he shouted when he saw us, "give me a hand. Teppo, get up the mizzen. Karl, take the foresail. Arvi, get ready to raise anchor." His voice was peremptory, demanding, loud. The ease and enjoyment he seemed to have experienced during our meetings was totally gone.

Adding to the unpleasantness was noise from the pier. The entire waterfront population, it seemed, had come to see us leave, and now that we were actually about to go out upon the water, it suddenly came home to us how seriously the criticism underlying their jibes might be justified.

"My God, look at her roll," someone cried.

"She's top-heavy," a quieter voice replied.

"There's not one of them can sail," an old man said soberly. "Look at them."

Laughter was somewhat stilled. We had the benefit of a few moments silence.

"If you go out in that thing, you'll kill yourselves," a sailor called earnestly at last.

There was a rumble of agreement.

We glanced at one another. We were used to jests at our expense, but this solemn foreboding had quite another quality. We lumbered about on deck, feeling our own clumsiness more deeply every moment. As we cast off, the little crowd on the pier stopped talking. In ominous silence they stared after us.

Walvi did not ease our concern. He seemed to have become a stranger. He cursed our inept straining at the lines. "You'd be smart to go home and stay there," he said at last. "Where did you ever get the idea you could do this?"

"Partly from you," said Karl. Walvi did not answer.

Tuntsa cringed and slunk off to the foredeck. There he lay with his head between his paws.

Even the ship seemed unlike herself. She plopped down each wave half sideways and seemed as sullen as Walvi.

Thus we began our test run across the Baltic.

a **STORM**

while you sleep is when the wind changes

breakers ahead!

Baron Otto Alexander von Haart

the Russian zone

a night of triumph

Out on open water, we discovered only too soon that the men in the harbor had been right. Our inexperience was deadly. Furthermore, all steadiness seemed to have gone out of the *Tuntsa*. She rolled wickedly. In our naivete we had neglected to fill the water tanks, an oversight which subtracted nearly four-thousand pounds from our ballast. We needed it desperately to balance our proud new masts.

As night closed about us, Walvi suggested curtly that we cut the trial run, and head for a lee shore. "We can see our weaknesses," he said ironically. "We don't have to kill ourselves proving them. Let's just try to make it to land."

We dropped anchor in the shelter of an island, furled our sails, and stumbled to our bunks.

A few hours later, we woke abruptly. The boat didn't feel right. Tuntsa was barking.

We tumbled out and hurried on deck. Tuntsa was racing wildly about. The anchor was dragging. The wind had changed and was driving us upon the shore. The island whose shelter we had sought, now appeared as a menacing coastline of jagged rocks.

"The motor!" shouted Walvi. By the light of the single kerosene lamp below decks, Masa tried to start the engine. Nothing happened. Sea water must have come in through the exhaust during the *Tuntsa's* heavy rolling.

I rushed back on deck. In just these few minutes the wind had risen further. Karl and I threw out the second anchor. Spikes of rock along the beach loomed like evil giants.

But all our clumsiness, and the unorthodox adaptations necessary to rebuild the *Tuntsa* to hold us all on an ocean voyage, could not alter the soundness of her basic design. If she had been as blunt and flat as the average craft her size, the wind and water would by now have driven her aground. Her tapered bow and stern, however, gave the gale no grip. The breakers slid under us, and the wind lost much of its thrust. Even so, the rocks were constantly nearer.

Fearfully, I went back below. Masa and Arvi had taken off the motor head—eight nuts to unscrew—and were painfully drying out the cylinder with a little cloth. Every few seconds they would pour in a bit of gasoline and light it with a match, hoping to dry the chamber. Then they would replace the head and once more try to start the motor. Time after time, the sweat standing

out on their faces, they began again. Crank, remove
head, dry out—crank, remove head, dry out—crank,
remove head, pour in gasoline, light match. "Try it
again," Masa would say. His red hair stood up like a
brush. His eyes were deep hollows of shadow in the
flickering light.

May and Anna held the lamp overhead. I saw that
they were far from comprehending our danger. Kati,
who had been seasick all day, was still huddled in her
bunk. When my query to Arvi, "Any luck?" was answered by a desperate shake of his head, I turned to the
girls. "You had better go up and be ready to jump."

May stared at me. Anna laughed. We had teased them
so much in the past that they thought I must be joking.

"Well," retorted Anna, "we can swim, and this is still
Finnish land. You don't worry us one bit."

But May turned to her. "He means it," she said soberly.

"I'm afraid I do," I said. "Unless we can get the motor
started, it's a matter of minutes before we'll be on the
rocks."

"My God!" cried Anna. "Why didn't you say so? What
can we do to help?"

She and May hurried on deck with me and began to
work with Karl at pulling on the anchor chains. Kati
struggled up after us. But she almost immediately became too sick to stand. She crawled over to catch Tuntsa
and keep him out of our way. I still remember her slight
form curled up stoically near the lee rail as she held the
dog. Tuntsa was silent. So was she. It was, I think, as
keen a mark of courage as I was ever to see, for by now
it seemed certain that one more heavy sea would surely

give us the final push onto the rocks. The roar of breaking surf ahead was deafening.

Walvi shouted from his place at the helm. "Get Masa
and Arvi on deck. We're going to strike."

And then above the sound of breakers, we heard a
faint sputter. The motor had caught. The propeller was
turning. We had headway.

Inch by precious inch, the *Tuntsa* fought away from
the rocks. Our backs aching, Karl and I, May and Anna,
hauled in lengths of anchor chain until great heaps were
coiled at our feet and we could seize the anchors with
our hands.

The *Tuntsa* was safe.

We set our course for another island and cast anchor
much farther offshore. There we rode out the wind and
finally collapsed into exhausted sleep.

*

The next morning was calm, but we followed the
coastline closely all the way to Helsinki. In spite of our
caution, however, we were inwardly elated. Under the
worst of circumstances, and regardless of all our inept-
ness, the *Tuntsa* had shown that she was sound. And
possibly even better, she was lucky. As Karl put it,
"We've got work to do yet, but the *Tuntsa* is a *good*
boat." It seemed to us that we had only inexperience to
blame for our near shipwreck, and from now on all would
be well. Next time—within three weeks, we promised

each other—we would take another cruise, fill the water tanks for proper ballast, and get practice in selecting safe anchorage and handling our sails. Only Walvi was silent.

At Helsinki, we anchored in what was called the "Cholera Pool," unpopular waters, for it was believed that the Germans had thrown the bodies of their victims there during the war. We would have privacy for the work necessary before our final departure.

We faced formidable problems. Lack of money was now chronic. In all our households, we had sold almost everything we owned, but we still needed gas, oil, and food for the voyage. We had to buy a stove. And Walvi told us emphatically that we had to have an iron rudder to replace the old wooden one.

Walvi had said that, as our navigator, he would supply our navigation equipment: barometer, chronometer, sextant, compass, and charts. But ever since he had joined us in Valkom his manner had worried us. Now he told us that when he had left for Valkom his mother had been seriously ill. Now he had decided that he could not leave her.

I knew that my reaction was unreasonable, but I suddenly found Walvi's decision hard to accept. His mother was old, and Walvi was young. It was in him that the blood of his family would go on. Did not she—did not he—see the importance of that? Bitterly I wondered if this phlegmatic man had ever really intended to come with us. He had not gone to see the boat when we bought her. He had shown little interest in our labors during the refitting. Had he not simply enjoyed our company while discussing a trip he never actually intended to make? Possibly my feeling was unjust, but it measured the intensity of our disappointment. For without Walvi, the voyage became impossible. We were without a navigator, or navigation equipment. My three-months course did not qualify me for crossing the ocean. We knew our own clumsiness now, and we realized keenly that we dared not sail under any but an expert.

It seemed then that reasonable people would have given up. Probably we were simply not reasonable people. We decided that the worst problem was lack of money and determined to attack that first. Arvi suggested a carefully worded advertisement in the paper for an additional crew member. "If another person buys a share in the boat, we will have working capital again."

But I was dubious about using the newspapers. "The police are watching everything connected with the sea. Helsinki isn't Valkom," I told Karl.

We finally gambled, however, and placed the following ad: "Wanted: Someone interested in deep-sea sailing." We hoped the police would interpret it as a simple fishing trip, while to any minds busy as ours were with plans for escape, the words "deep-sea" would carry quite another meaning.

One man called. He gave his name as Lars Talvi. After a brief telephone conversation, he came out to the *Tuntsa*.

Short, slight, sharp-featured, with gray in his hair but a belyingly young face, he could have been a prematurely-gray thirty or a well-preserved forty. We learned later that he was thirty-nine. His smile showed poor teeth, yellow, broken, and misshapen. His speech and somewhat pedantic manner gave him the air of a professor, but his costume was incongruous. He wore over-long, drooping, light blue slacks, and, in odd contrast, a tight maroon sports jacket. If his face had not been so serious, and his words so exact and so oddly bookish, I would have been reminded of a clown just out of the circus.

"What kind of deep-sea sailing are you planning?" he inquired diffidently, as he stepped on board.

"What kind did you have in mind?" I asked.

"O-oh, some distant place—away from Finland," he answered, as he pushed the mizzen boom back and forth. "The farther, the better pleased I shall be."

I looked around. There were few boats near, but I knew by now how voices carry across water. "Why don't we go below?"

We sat on the bunks. Karl, Arvi and Masa looked at me. Apparently I was elected spokesman. I decided from the newcomer's appearance that I could be open. It seemed to me certain that no police agent could ever have thought either of such a costume or such a vocabulary. "We plan to head for the Canary Islands, stopping as often as we can along the way." I paused. "We're not coming back."

Looking into his face, I said, "We're headed for the United States."

The newcomer smiled. He looked ten years younger, almost boyish. "I hoped for something like that," he said enthusiastically. "It's what I have long desired."

He told us that he was recently divorced. Bitterly unhappy both with his personal life and the state of his country, he wanted to make a start in another land—as distant and as different as possible. It seemed to me that I knew how he must feel. In Finland as it was now, any personal problem seemed twice as severe as it would anywhere else. In the atmosphere of defeat, every private agony appeared hopeless. How could a person mend a broken life where most people felt as if there was no bearable future for anyone? Much of the population had simply taken to the solace of liquor. The Finnish people had always been hard drinkers, but never until the postwar years had drunken men been seen lolling about the streets. The more vigorous among the population were leaving. More were slipping away across the borders with every passing month.

I told our visitor that we would be glad to have him with us. I introduced the others—Karl, as calm and ceremoniously polite as if he were still at his desk in the insurance office; Masa, restless and running both hands through his red hair as he studied our new companion; Arvi, taciturn and non-committal. Lars would fit into any group easily, I thought. His smile was shy but warm. He poked around the boat, and seemed pleased by everything. I thought I had seldom seen a man less critical of practical arrangements than he. He made just one regretful remark. "No room for books," he said. "I will miss them. I'm a reader."

We told him he could have one entire two foot shelf in our precious cabinet, and he was delighted.

We checked Kati's record book and divided the total amount we had spent by five, the number of men in our

crew if Lars joined us. Lars pleasantly agreed at once
to furnish his share. Now we could get our navigation
equipment, gas, oil, food, iron rudder, regulation navigation lanterns, life preservers, a two-burner stove, our
general supplies, and still have a little left over. We decided to spend most of the extra money on tradeable
items to be bartered for supplies later, or sold for cash.
Just before our departure we would invest in stainless
steel knives, wrist compasses, and other items scarce in
the postwar world.

With our most urgent financial needs thus settled, we
turned our attention next to finding a navigator to replace Walvi. A veteran seaman, who had become our
friend shortly after we returned from Valkom, helped us.

This retired mariner, one of the few who roamed the
unfrequented piers fronting the Cholera Pool, had appeared on our first day in Helsinki while we were scrubbing down the deck. We heard someone stump along the
jetty and then halt abruptly near the boat. Out of the
corner of my eye, I could see a peg-legged, sun-browned
individual, wearing ragged clothes which hung sloppily
from a meager frame.

He silently watched us work for a few minutes, then
asked for a cigarette. We gave him a couple of packs and
finally some money. "Go get yourself a cup of coffee,"
Arvi called.

He did not thank us, just shuffled away. But that afternoon he returned and stopped long enough to throw
something on the deck. It was a package of salt-water
soap. It made our deck-washing much easier.

The next day he was back, and the next, and the next.

Soon he was always around—first watching, then making comments in sparse, heavily-spiced language, and finally giving us a hand. Bluff, inarticulate, immensely kind, and with all the nautical experience we did not have, he was a generous and likable person. We began to look forward to his visits. At last we decided he was safe and took him into our confidence. When he understood what we needed in a navigator, he put his intimate knowledge of the waterfront people to use and brought us a dockside character even more amazing than himself.

The man who came to the *Tuntsa* that day would turn out to be one of the most remarkable personalities any of us would ever know. He had a curl-tipped moustache beneath an intrepid nose—a really remarkable nose, harsh and straight and thick like a Roman General's, but turning up at the end in a way which gave his face an unorthodox look, inquisitive and almost impertinent. "I am not like the rest of men," his expression seemed to say, "and there is no use trying to make me anything else than what I am." His jaunty gold-braided skipper's cap was worn with an air. He had deep lines around his eyes and mouth. I guessed him to be sixty—a strong and husky sixty—with little loss in physical energy and none in the defiant habit of going his own way.

His name, he told us casually, was Baron Otto Alexander von Haart.

We raised our eyebrows. The family name was well known—one of the oldest in Finland.

"I'm a black sheep," he said without embarrassment. "No money, no roots. Besides that, I drink."

None of us could think of a reply. "We need a navigator desperately," I said at last, "but we can't pay."

Baron Otto Alexander von Haart waved a blue-veined hand as if to brush off a triviality of no consequence. "Money doesn't matter. What counts is the voyage."

"You know where we are going?" asked Karl.

Baron von Haart bowed. "I know. And if you need my services, they are yours."

It seemed too good to be true.

❋

"What do you know about a fellow named Otto Alexander von Haart?" Karl asked a friend, a merchant marine inspector whose acquaintance he and I had cultivated.

The man was at his desk. A harbor breeze coming through an open window threatened to reorganize a pile of papers. He put a heavy book on them, leaned back, and sucked meditatively on his pipe.

"He's an expert navigator," he replied at last, "one of the best." He paused and studied us. "Is he going to handle your boat?"

We nodded. Like several we had met since starting to make our plans, this man had gradually seen what our project must be, but never spoke of it openly. His sympathy, however, was obvious, and we had no fear of him whatever. An authoritarian country is like that. You may be denounced; but, also, there are unsuspected allies everywhere.

"You'll be in good hands," he said. "Von Haart is an

anachronism, you know. In another age he would have
been a Viking. In this time"—he shrugged—"well, for
such a man what is there? He has gone from one thing
to another all his life. He has the biggest heart of anyone
I know. Whenever he has money, he helps someone with
it—when he isn't drinking. That's his weakness. He
really soaks it up in port. But at sea, where he can't get
it, they say he is all right."

There was now only one final problem. We had to get
passports, and Karl had another friend he intended to
call on. His name was Loffe Karvi and Karl had known
him in the army. He seemed a most unlikely man to aid
such a project as ours, for he was now a member of the
secret police. Nevertheless, Karl was certain that inwardly he was as opposed as we to Finland's present
condition. Karl thought that Loffe's position was much
more to him than a military assignment or a way to make
a living. Unobtrusively he used it to help anyone he
could.

I was apprehensive, but finally we went to see him
one evening at his home. He was a tall, dark, thin man
with big, restless brown eyes and erratic gestures. As he
paced about his living room, he reminded me of an unin-
hibited antelope. My concern about the safety of asking
his help had been groundless. He did not even hesitate.
As soon as we told him our plan, he said simply, "What
can I do?"

We said we needed passports.

"I can get you sailor's papers," he said, "good in any
port for sixty days."

Less than a week later, we had them. He had gone to
considerable trouble and expense, not to mention the

risk. He had taken the two powerful secret police officials who had to sign all passports out to dinner, which
he followed with drinks, and during the course of the
evening observed, "Here's a bunch of passports for the
crews of. . . ." (he mentioned two steamers sailing the
following week). "Why not sign them now and save
time?" Mixed among the books were ours, identifying
us as "sailors," supposedly on one of the ships. The two
men glanced at the books on top, then signed the rest
without ado.

In our last few days in Finland we bought von Haart's
navigation instruments. Finally we set our departure
day: Monday, August 4. Weekends and Mondays were
particularly busy in the harbor. Many perfectly legitimate small craft were leaving. The officials could not
possibly check every one. The *Tuntsa* could slip out
among them.

The ironsmith finished our new rudder, and Arvi and
Masa installed it. Masa put into working order an old
airplane receiver he had contributed from his shop, and
we bought a used two-burner stove for the galley. Von
Haart was almost ecstatic over the *Tuntsa's* performance
on our practice cruises. He took the helm with such a
look of sheer delight on his weather-beaten face that he
looked like an ecstatic gargoyle. With our iron rudder,
our supplies on board, and our water tanks filled, the
Tuntsa steadied wonderfully. Von Haart tested her live-
liness in coming about, tried her on a broad reach to see
how much she wallowed in a following sea, and otherwise put her through her paces until the rest of us were
exhausted.

"What do you think of him?" Karl asked me privately.

"Our navigator?" I said. "I think he's a good man with a boat."

"There's something about him," said Karl. "I don't think I ever met anyone like him."

I laughed. "He is not as unusual as all that. Just one of those rundown noble families. There are a lot of such people these days."

But Karl was more perceptive than I. He shook his head. "I think he is extraordinary, somehow. It bothers me that we don't know how."

"I doubt if it is complicated," I said. "He has fallen in love with the *Tuntsa* and he likes the notion of our trip. Boats, drink, and adventure are his life. We can satisfy all but the middle one. In port I suppose he may get out of hand once in a while, but on board we can keep him sober. Perhaps there may be trouble from time to time, but I'm sure he will be worth it."

Karl nodded, and we left it at that. If we had foreseen, however, how much "trouble" von Haart could cause in port, or how often our lives would literally depend on his courage and ingenuity at sea, we might have continued the conversation about our enigmatic navigator with a good bit more feeling. But no one foresees the future, and for us it was probably a good thing; for if we could have known then what lay ahead for the *Tuntsa*, we might never have sailed from Helsinki.

*

Before we left, von Haart's widowed mother came down to bid us goodbye. She was an exquisitely regal little old lady of eighty, who looked every inch a descendant of queens—which, in fact, she was. She wore a well-cut silk dress under her short fur jacket, and an ostrich-plumed hat shaded her small, lined, kindly face. Several beautiful rings gleamed from her tiny hands. She seemed as out of place on the dirty waterfront as a diamond in a dust bin.

She was scarcely over five feet tall. But when she saw von Haart, she drew herself up as proudly as if she towered over us all and quickly went to his side. He rose from his seat at the wheel, where he was checking the compass, and bent down to the little woman to kiss her with unfeigned delight.

"Aiti (Mamma)!" he exclaimed.

Then, without preamble or ceremony, he looked at her jacket. With eyes suddenly shining, he said, "Give me your fur, Mamma! I can sell it and get some more money for the trip."

She smiled and patted his shoulder, "No, my son, you don't need it. You will be all right."

He seemed to accept the statement much as a three-year-old accepts his mother's comment that "the earth is round"—without further question or further thought.

She then looked around the *Tuntsa* and went below into the cabin. There she drew May aside. "My dear, will you look after my boy? Please see that he keeps dry and warm when the weather is bad. He is careless at times, and needs someone to watch out for his health."

May said gravely that she would try, but carefully kept her dancing eyes from the old lady's gaze.

I quickly took our guest back on deck, and we watched

her walk away along the pier. From the back she looked
like a young princess—head high, spine straight, and—
we knew—a faint, gentle smile on her face as she looked
straight ahead. Like her son, she was an anachronism.

But it was we who seemed unreal, not she. She was far
too vital. We went back to the mundane task of checking
our meager equipment with almost a sense of shock.

Our eating and cooking wares consisted of a coffee
pot, a frying pan, a pot for soup, old silverware, divided
mess trays, and aluminum cups. We had one spare blanket, sheet, and pillowcase each, plus a blanket, sheet,
pillow, and mattress already on each bunk. For water we
had the reconditioned tanks, and for fuel, a fifty gallon
underdeck container which fed to the motor. Twenty
gallons of kerosene in five-gallon cans and a half dozen
cans of oil were stacked below near the stern and on
deck near the bow hatch. Altogether it was only about
three days' supply if the motor was running steadily, but
actually we would use it only in harbors or for emergencies. Our tradeable goods: knives, jewelry, wrist compasses, watches, and so on were stored in boxes in the
hold. Hanging from the stays was an open-bottom canvas bag with smoked hams, sausages, salami, and salt
pork. Carrots, onions, and year-old potatoes (new ones
would spoil) were in bins below, and in the galley were
our few packaged and canned foods, loaves of hard rye
bread, condensed milk, saccharine, and the cheapest
coffee.

Our sole luxuries were a wash-tub, an old-fashioned
flat-iron and a phonograph belonging to Anna. Arvi and
Kati each had a camera. Lars had his small shelf of cher-

ished books—an odd mixture of Freud, Schopenhauer, and Tolstoy, plus a battered dictionary.

For navigation we had von Haart's instruments: a compass mounted on a binnacle near the wheel; the log towed astern for measuring the boat's total travel after each watch; and the sextant, barometer, and chronometer on his navigation table. The radio, logbook, nautical almanac, and scattered charts were also there, crowding the scratched, water-ringed wood of the battered surface of his work-table.

The girls stored the supplies neatly, and concealed any concern over their insufficiency. We did not tell them how seriously this same insufficiency extended into other essentials. We had done all we could with our slim resources and the scarcity of materials in postwar Finland, but our efforts were far from complete success. We had secured life preservers, but they were so old that they had been thrown out by another ship. We had picked them up and painted them for protection from the weather, and they looked like new, but three hours in the water would probably be all that could be expected of them. The dinghy looked as though it would hold two people, but it would do so only in a calm sea; heavy surf would swamp it at once. Furthermore, one of our economies was that Masa's radio was only a receiver. We had no means of transmitting in case of emergency.

As we prepared to leave, everyone was thoughtful. We had said our goodbyes the night before and we were leaving our children sadly. All were being kept by relatives until they could be sent for, and I knew from our own experience what sort of partings had been taking place. Although Eero usually liked to stay with his grandmother, he had somehow sensed our tension and burst into loud wails as we started for the door. May had hurried back. "It all right, darling," she murmured, rocking him on her lap. "You will come too! Soon!" To Eero her strained voice was even more disturbing, and he clung to her. By the time we finally wrenched ourselves away, May was weeping too.

But strangely joined with the sadness we were all feeling at leaving children and families, was our own eagerness to be gone. We had spent nearly six months working toward this moment. We firmly believed we were going to a better world, and that eventually we could send for those left behind. We had quite forgotten that we were all landlubbers except von Haart, that the *Tuntsa* was aging and not originally designed for the ocean, and that we had not had enough money even to buy food to last out the trip.

But when the actual moment came, and von Haart shouted, "Cast off!" I suddenly felt intense fear. Moving slowly past the great cargo ships in Helsinki harbor, the *Tuntsa* seemed a toy which would be crushed into driftwood by the giant seas. Only two weeks earlier a sailboat much like ours had successfully left Finland—only to shipwreck on the Swedish shore. Several of the crew had drowned. And they were experienced sailors, while we were landlubbers.

I glanced at the others. Masa was below at the motor. Lars was coiling the mooring line. Arvi had stationed himself at the mainmast. Karl was at the mizzen. May, Anna, and Kati stood gazing back at Helsinki.

Von Haart, at the wheel, saw our sober faces. He laughed. "Why, this is the adventure of your lives!" he exclaimed. "You've got the best boat in the Bay—and the best navigator in all Finland. Smile now! You're starting for America. And you'll get there too, or my name isn't Baron Otto Alexander von Haart!"

We straightened our backs, and the women turned away from the shore. In a few moments we were joking and laughing. Tuntsa went wild, barking and racing about the deck. The wind hustled us to the harbor entrance and onto the vast silvery platter of the Baltic, gleaming in the sun. Our sails filled. There was the smell of brine, the cries of seagulls, the exhilarating sound of water rushing to either side of the hull.

We followed the sea lane, and within an hour entered our own private world. Only a few boats could be seen far behind.

Then sudden, unwelcome company interrupted our progress. Bullets spat across the bow. A coast guard cutter was slicing toward us.

"Lower the sails," shouted von Haart. "There's no point trying to get away. They're too fast."

We were surprised, confused—and fearful. Had we trusted someone we should not have told? Had the authorities at last heard about us?

As the cutter drew alongside, its skipper called, "We're taking you in."

"What's wrong?" von Haart called back.

The coastguardsman shook his head. His stony face gave no clue.

There was nothing we could do. We tossed our line to the cutter, and were towed to a station facing the mole. A pacing inspector angrily leaped to our deck. "You imbeciles!"

"What's the matter?" asked von Haart with feigned calm.

"What's the matter?" the man repeated. "I'll tell you what's the matter! Another hundred yards and you would have been in the Russian zone! Don't you people look up boundaries before you start off joy-riding?"

"We didn't think. . ." Karl began.

"That's just the trouble—you didn't think!" the inspector barked.

"We didn't think it was that near," Masa said lamely.

"Another hundred yards and we wouldn't have been able to help you at all. The Russians would have confiscated your boat and everything you own. You. . ." the inspector gestured toward the three women at the bow, "and your wives would have been imprisoned."

The others looked as shaky as I felt. We knew there was a Russian water zone, several miles square, bordering the coast on the Porkkala peninsula, less than ten miles west of Helsinki, but we had not been able to get complete charts of the area.

"Show us the boundaries so we'll be sure this time," Arvi said practically.

"O-oh no!" the official retorted, "we'll tow you around the Russian zone so everyone will be sure." Then he eyed us suspiciously, "Where are you going, by the way?"

"Sweden," Karl replied.

"Show me your passports."

Six passports were passed to him (the women needed only identification certificates and were seldom asked to show them). The inspector stepped ashore and phoned from a unit on the pier. After a few minutes' conversation, he returned.

We faced him tensely. He said nothing, just handed back our passports. He jumped to the pier and signalled a sailor who stood nearby. They spoke together for the longest minute I ever experienced. Then the inspector called, "My men will take you around the limits and let you know when it's safe to go on."

They towed us five miles out to sea and around the danger area, then waved us on. Outwardly it appeared that we had been cleared. This actually was not the case, as we soon realized.

The cutter continued to follow us. In addition, a plane overhead was checking our position, for when Masa turned on the radio, we heard the pilot giving our location to the cutter. "Heading toward Sweden." He added, "Surely they won't go further in that pea-shell."

The cutter and plane continued to keep us under observation. But apparently their doubts won out. It was impossible to believe that anyone could be attempting an escape in such a tiny boat, and cutter and plane were still talking it over at nightfall. Then, without running lights, we became a part of the darkness, and we finally saw their own lights turn to go back. They had lost us.

We sailed on in the dark. Suddenly we found ourselves so close to a Russian lightship that we could see the crew silhouetted under the beams of their own mast beacons. This vision, fortunately, was one-sided, and we passed swiftly and silently, an indistinguishable part of the jet sea and cloudy sky.

Finally we cast anchor in the lee of a small sandy-shored island. We were all too keyed-up for sleep. Everyone stayed on deck. We made coffee and smoked. Von Haart, however, spoke sharply.

"You had better realize right now that the only way we're going to survive on this trip is to have some discipline. There'll be strict watch schedules." He outlined them: four hours at the wheel, eight hours sleep, four hours at the sails, eight hours off, then back to the helm again. "The women should arrange to have coffee for us at the end of each four hours, and food at the end of every eight."

At this point, however, we went into sudden reaction from the tension of the day. Everything struck as as funny, particularly von Haart's solemnity. We would nod at him; then someone would remember a joke. We would roar with laughter, try again to give our attention to von Haart, then remember another joke. Finally von Haart himself gave up and joined the story-telling. We exchanged war experiences. Sang all the Finnish songs we could remember. Told more jokes. Sunrise over the Baltic found us still at it.

That night our lack of sleep didn't bother us, but as the sun's rays slanted across the foredeck and von Haart barked, "Let's go! Teppo and Karl hoist the sails! Lars, up anchor! Masa, take the helm! Arvi, run the motor until we're away from the shore," we were suddenly dullards with ten thumbs.

As soon as we were underway, von Haart sent Masa, Karl, Arvi and Lars to their bunks. They stumbled down the ladder. I chuckled at the spectacle, but then found that I, too, was nodding. Von Haart finally came across me asleep in a tangle of rigging at the foot of the main-mast, and he had to let the *Tuntsa* con herself while he shoved me to one side, straightened out the mess, and set the boom so I wouldn't be hit in the head after a sudden shift in wind. It was typical of him that he let me continue to sleep.

Four hours later Karl relieved me, Lars relieved von Haart, and our second watch began. The sea was quiet. She was saving her vigor for what would be one of the worst storms of the voyage.

the JOURNEY BEGINS

sandbars and small boats

an impossible harbor

bay rum is a drink?

the hospitality of Sweden

unexpected salvage

we fall under suspicion

Denmark is different

By mid-morning our second day out of Helsinki, we had crossed most of the three hundred miles to Sweden. Ahead on the faint horizon was the Swedish coastline.

"We had better make our first stop at a town where we can get sea charts," said von Haart. (Sea charts were, of course, essentials we had not dared buy in Helsinki.) "We're already in waters where we need them."

Just then May stuck her head out the bow hatch. "How about some coffee?"

"Fine!" I said. But Masa and Arvi had to go below to help make it. Our stove had worked twice, then given up, and neither Masa nor Arvi had been able to fix it. So the women were at the mercy of the unwieldly, flaring blowtorch for their cooking, and we did not want them yet to attempt it alone.

Arvi steadied the pot on the stove while Masa aimed the torch toward the base of the pot. Masa kept his feet braced against the bunk and his elbows pressed on the table, lest the roll of the boat cause the torch to jerk up suddenly into his eyes. "Your face is brown enough without that!" Arvi told him.

The coffee resembled fine mud in looks, and bitter medicine in taste, but it was hot, brown, and wet. We drank it gratefully, warming our cold hands around the cups. The breeze was cool, and we were uncomfortably chilled, even with coats.

Several hours later, we neared a coastal resort where von Haart said we could get charts. Karl and I noticed, however, that he was frowning.

"What's the matter?" Karl asked from the mainmast where he was furling the sail.

"I think we have too much keel for this little harbor. Without a chart, I simply don't know, but that pier looks to me as though it were designed for small boats only."

"How far in do you think we can take her?" I asked.

Before von Haart could reply, there was a long grating sound. The *Tuntsa* lurched. Von Haart swore feelingly. We were aground on a sand bar.

Seizing eight-foot lengths of two-by-fours, left over from building the cabin, Karl and I shoved against the ridge of sand. It was useless. The heavy keel had ground itself in.

A motorboat sputtered alongside. "Stuck?" asked a cheerful voice. A lean man with a white cap shoved on the back of his head looked up at us curiously.

"It feels as though we're stuck for good," Karl said ruefully.

"How about a push?"

There were other small craft about. Our unexpected friend sounded his horn to attract their attention, and with two more boats hooked by lines to our stern, and one on either side of the bow ready to push, Karl and I got set to shove against the bar at a signal from our benefactor.

"One . . . two . . . heave-ho!" he called. The *Tuntsa* moved back a foot. A third boat joined the two at the bow. It was a laborious process before at last we were free. The delay consumed precious time. We were still uneasy about the cutter and plane of the day before, not to mention the Russian lightship, and we decided to put off stopping for charts at present. It would take too long now to lower the dinghy and row ashore. We set our course for Visby farther along the Swedish coast, and waved a grateful goodbye to our friends in their little boats.

The seas were peaceful all that morning, with a light steady wind. Masa and Arvi took advantage of the opportunity to fix the *Tuntsa's* troublesome exhaust.

Then, shortly past noon, we heard distant rumbles and saw thunderheads to the north. By mid-afternoon, the sky had the flat sinister look of dull metal, and the wind quickened.

"Bad weather ahead," said von Haart. "But I think we had better keep going. We're still too close to home to want to sit this one out in a harbor."

We agreed emphatically, and von Haart had us string a lifeline from bow to stern. The prospect of a storm seemed to stimulate him, rather than otherwise. He walked with a slight limp, the result of an old war injury which impeded the circulation to his legs, and he periodically depended on a cane, but it in no way lessened his vigor. He went clacking all about the ship, checking rigging and hatches, and instructing us cheerfully. "When she blows, keep hold of a lifeline. One hand for you, one for the ship. That's the saying, and it's a good one. O.K. boys. I'm going to sleep."

"To sleep!" we exclaimed.

He grunted. "Yes, to sleep. I'll need to be fresh later. Wake me up when it gets bad." And off he went.

Below I heard him directing the girls to lash things down in the galley. "You might also fix some sandwiches. You may not be able to eat them. But get them ready anyway." He left them in a silence as profound as ours.

On deck we felt deserted, though none of us was about to admit it. Arvi whistled a little tune, and with a fine show of indifference began to lash down the oil and gas cans.

Von Haart had given Lars the helm. Our first estimate of Lars as a good addition to our crew had been sound. He was quiet and a little shy, but conscientious and of us all probably the least excitable. He followed directions perfectly, as though he might rather dislike thinking for himself. We would find later that he tended to become paralyzed in emergencies.

By now it was quite dark. The wind was constantly shifting, keeping Karl and me busy readjusting the canvas. Arvi went below to get the smaller and heavier storm sails from their storage bag beneath his bunk. He put them below the after hatch, where we could get them quickly. The wind increased but stopped shifting, and we felt somewhat reassured. Let von Haart sleep, I thought. We were doing fine!

But as the wind rose to gale force and the *Tuntsa* began to heel wickedly, Lars seemed to freeze to his course, regardless of shifts in the wind. Suddenly the mainsail luffed wildly, swinging the heavy boom.

"Don't jibe!" I shouted to Lars. "You could take the masts right out of her!" He spun the wheel and the sails filled quickly. But Lars' face was covered with sweat, and Karl's was the color of plaster.

"Why doesn't von Haart come up?" he muttered. "If he can sleep through this, he could sleep through a cyclone!"

I looked at my watch. "He's been gone two hours," I reported indignantly. Indeed, it seemed to us as if von Haart were somehow to blame for the gale.

Lars' features were drawn. He was still not adjusting his course to the wind, and Karl and I had constant work trimming the sails. "I keep imagining I see sandbars," Lars finally said in apology. He went off at another tangent, and the *Tuntsa* slewed violently.

Just then we passed almost on top of two buoys.

Karl wiped his forehead on his sleeve and stared at me bitterly. "God knows what those mean. Rocks, probably."

The buoys emitted a steady "whoo-clunk" as we slewed by. The sound seemed right from the grave.

Karl and I had had enough. Together we dived below to fetch up von Haart. Curled in his bunk, he was sleeping like a child. Anna and May sat huddled together in silence in the galley. Kati was being violently sick. As we passed, she gave Karl an imploring look and crept miserably to her bunk.

We shook von Haart. "Blowing, is it?" he asked yawning. "All right. I'll come. Get me a sandwich."

My stomach turned over as Anna, clinging to bunks and lockers, silently brought him a plate. Kati gave him one revolted glance and turned her white face away.

"Eat!" von Haart said to us sharply. "Get some food in you while you can."

I told him about the buoys, and he laughed. "Channel markers," he said. But he scowled as he glanced at the barometer beside his bunk. Karl and I made a pretense of enjoying our sandwiches, but we both gave the greater portion to Tuntsa. The little terrier braced himself at our feet. He was apparently as immune to seasickness as he was to fear. He snapped up our offerings and tried to follow when we went with von Haart on deck. Anna caught him and took him into her lap as she returned to sit tensely with May in the galley. Kati now was too sick to move. May got a cold cloth for her forehead, but Kati pushed it aside and whispered to leave her alone. "I think I'm going to die," she said with an attempt at a smile. "I just hope it will be soon. Ugh." She clutched the sides of her bunk, then huddled by the wall.

On deck the gale had increased. I noted that even von Haart gripped the rail. Rain had started to fall in torrents, and the wind lashed it blindingly into our faces.

"Set the storm sails?" shouted Masa hopefully to von Haart.

Von Haart shook his head. "We have to see what she can do." He was scowling up at the masts. More than ever their height seemed to dwarf the *Tuntsa*.

"They told us in Valkom they were too high!" shouted Masa.

Von Haart glared. "I don't care what they said in Valkom! Those masts are fine."

"Storm sails?" shouted Masa again, hopefully.

But von Haart sternly shook his head once more. After Masa's remark about the masts, he felt the *Tuntsa's* honor was involved. Von Haart would not let us set storm sails now, no matter what happened. Still stubbornly shaking his head he went to reinforce Lars at the helm.

The wind suddenly increased. Karl and I grabbed the lifeline. A great wave deluged the deck and swept over us. It was too dangerous to try to turn into the wind. We could only run before the gale.

"All right!" shouted von Haart. "Drop all sail except fors'l and mizzen!"

Somehow, as we clung to the lifeline, Karl, Masa, Arvi and I went to the halyards, our freezing, wind-and-water lashed hands scraped raw and bleeding.

Karl shouted to me, "This is worse than the war!"

At this moment May and Anna lifted the hatch.

"We're drowning below!" Anna cried.

I went halfway down after them. Leaking oil from two smashed fuel drums and sea water seeping through cracks in the deck, had mixed with the ten inches or so of water normally in the lower hull and was soaking everything in its path each time the boat pitched.

"Start the pump," I said. "You know how." And I left them.

I rejoined Karl just as a massive mountain of water poured over the *Tuntsa*. The weight crushed us. It seemed to me we were going down—and down. Giant firecrackers exploded inside my head. Then as suddenly as the mammoth sea had struck, the *Tuntsa* stubbornly rose. I gulped air and heard the crash of pots, plates, books, and other loose objects against bulkheads below. Three distinct screams and one startled woof told me, however, that all down there were still very much alive.

Between breaking waves, I clutched my way to the helm. Masa had relieved Lars. He and von Haart together were wrestling the wheel.

Masa leaned toward me and yelled into my ear. "I'm sure glad I bought that life insurance from you. My wife can use it."

I saw that he was laughing. It seems impossible, but I began to laugh too. For once Masa's wild red hair was plastered down. It had taken a gale and a good bit of the Baltic to do it, but he looked as sleek as a gigolo.

The *Tuntsa* was slewing violently before the mountainous following seas. The tops of waves were blowing off, and solid sheets of water struck us, cutting our breath and making movement impossible until they passed. Hours went by with no let-up. Laughter was gone, and we became frightened to the point of numb automation, woodenly carrying out von Haart's shouted orders.

"Get below!" he called at last. "Gather everything you

can find and wrap it in bundles. Tie each bundle to the end of forty or fifty feet of line and we'll throw them out for sea anchors. It's the rolling that's dangerous. If it goes on, it will tear her apart."

But Lars now seemed frozen to the lifeline. His face was expressionless. Obviously he could not move. I followed Karl, gripping rails and rigging until we were below, but Lars remained clutching the line as though paralyzed.

Together Karl and I began to scoop up the loose clothing and other articles sloshing on the water below decks. May and Anna were at the pump. Even Kati, sick though she was, slid out of her bunk to help us, and within minutes we had two fair-sized bundles.

Back on deck we followed von Haart's shouted instructions. We fastened a long length of line to each bundle and secured the lines to the rail, one on either side, and well aft. The bundled end was then thrown into the sea, where it drifted quickly astern.

Then as the boat listed sickeningly to port, von Haart would cry, "Pull up on the starboard line!"

It worked. As we pulled on the bundle on the high side, the low rail gradually rose. Then as the *Tuntsa* slewed the other way, we released the slack on the first bundle and pulled on the other.

It was by then nearly two in the morning, and we were still running before the furious gale. But the *Tuntsa* now seemed to be mocking the heaving sea. She steadied and plunged onward almost aggressively. Slowly Lars unfolded his hands from the lifeline and went to help Arvi. Each tended one of the bundles, while Karl and I re-

turned to the sails. Masa and von Haart continued together at the wheel. The *Tuntsa* was no longer throwing her rudder out of water and was answering her helm
readily.

All at once, I felt strangely jubilant. It did not matter
that we were still in danger or that I was drenched and
stiff with cold. I flung my head back and almost welcomed the storm in my face. As I did so, my eyes saw a
tired bird vainly trying to sit on the mast. It lost its balance and fluttered to the deck where it lay still.

"Look!" I cried and pointed.

"Merciful God!" exclaimed von Haart. He left Masa
to wrestle the wheel alone and beckoned me to help him
set up a barricade of oil cans so the exhausted bird would
be safe.

Hours later—years, it seemed to us—the dark sky
began to lighten. Day was breaking and in the distance
we could dimly see a solid mass. It could only be one
thing. We were nearing Visby on the island of Gottland,
near the southeastern tip of Sweden.

Its harbor, however, had a very narrow mouth, and
by a freak of ill luck the wind now shifted and the gale
blew directly offshore. We would have to tack our way
in, and if we brought the *Tuntsa* too close in this wind,
she would almost surely capsize.

"It's impossible," said von Haart, glaring at the harbor mouth. "There are a thousand trolls back of this infernal storm! Here we've got a harbor, and the wind
veers to blow straight out of it!" He chewed his moustache.

"Dammit!" he said, "I'm used up. If I just had a drink! If I had a drink, I could coax her in, maybe."

Purposely, of course, we had no liquor on board.

"Anything with alcohol," said von Haart. "Anything at all!" Suddenly he left Masa at the helm and plunged below.

Minutes later, as the *Tuntsa* lurched in the wild sea, and Masa, reinforced by Karl, struggled desperately with the wheel, von Haart thrust his head up from the hatchway. In his hand, he was gripping Karl's bottle of bay rum. It was already half empty. As he emerged on deck, he tipped the rest upside down into his throat, and tossed the empty bottle over the railing.

"Now!" he said. "I'll take her in."

Just then, beneath my feet, I felt rather than heard the motor begin to miss. Masa and Arvi hurled themselves below. In seconds, Masa was back, shaking his head miserably.

Sea water had mixed with oil in the crankcase and burned out the engine.

But von Haart had brought the *Tuntsa* to bear. We were close to the narrow opening, and the seas were somewhat less. And we had been seen! From the edge of a pier a figure waved, and then ran into one of the wharfside buildings. People began to emerge and cluster on the docks. The wind swept out of the harbor as if driven by the forces of Hell.

"A thousand trolls!" muttered von Haart again. For it was obvious that without the motor, he could not now make the *Tuntsa* fetch the narrow entrance.

On shore the watchers continued to gather, oblivious to the rain streaming over them, and the gale forcing them to cling to posts and buildings. It seemed to me that I could almost feel their combined wills trying to pull us to safety, so resolutely did they stand gazing.

And as we gazed helplessly back, a pilot boat slipped away from a dock and headed toward us. When it had come as close as it dared without the waves ramming us together, the skipper shouted over a megaphone to stand by for a line.

A sailor with a coil of rope studied the rhythm of the heaving water. He tried a cast—missed. Missed again. It seemed forever before the weight at the line's end, caught on our cabin roof. We scrambled to seize it and hauled until we got the heavier towing cable. Masa made it fast to a forward cleat.

The pilot boat turned. The cable jerked and grew taut. But the other boat's motor was not strong enough to bring us both in. Together we were drifting toward shore.

"Let go the cable!" shouted von Haart. "They'll only go aground along with us. Let go!" We cast off the line. It was agonizing to watch the little boat whisk back without us.

Then over the screaming of the gale, we heard a deep, throbbing chug. In our concern with the pilot boat we had not seen that a large tug had also set out. Now it was just astern, a squat pugnacious-looking craft with, somehow, a determined expression as it wallowed toward us through the heavy sea.

Once again we attached a cable. And within ten minutes the *Tuntsa* was safe at a pier.

People crowded around us, catching our hands, helping us ashore. Over and over they said, "Thank God you're safe! Thank God!"

Behind us, on the deck of the *Tuntsa*, the bird took flight, circled briefly and flew to land.

The next morning the local newspapers came out with stories about our near shipwreck. Interspersed with sympathy and interest were comments upon, "those crazy Finns!" Stubbornness, recklessness, unorthodox action, and a sort of taciturn but furious determination is the reputation my people have in the countries surrounding us. The papers were delighted to write us up as examples of the national type.

As we looked beyond the tiny harbor and viewed the monstrous waves still hurtling shoreward, we wondered if perhaps it was not indeed a sort of miracle that we had reached safety, and if we were not, perhaps, a little crazy to dream of taking the *Tuntsa* on into the far more difficult waters which lay ahead. But not one of us mentioned turning back, not even Kati, who had yet to find her sea legs.

The gale continued to rage that night and the next morning. The *Tuntsa* lay at Visby, and we spent the day putting our "house" in order. Masa pumped out the bilge water which had risen nearly three inches over our cabin deck grating, and we had the formidable task of cleaning up the soggy mess in the cabin and making the deck ship-shape. The women tackled the quarters below.

Anna took the galley; Kati the midships section; May worked aft.

May's first job was to dry out the lower layers of potatoes in the stern hold so they would not spoil. Only when she had finished with the food did she turn to our personal belongings. And then her cry of despair as she opened the lockers could have been heard half-way to Helsinki, gale or no gale. Salt and dirt were encrusted over everything. Clothes, bedding, blankets, and—worst of all—the few really "good dresses" were sodden and ruined. The girls laid the things out to dry as best they could and bore the loss with sorrowful resignation.

On deck, the rest of us donned raincoats or heavy jackets and checked the oil and gas cans. Everything was battered, and two oil cans had been smashed, with half the contents lost. One gas drum was leaking. All three had to be laboriously hauled below and their contents transferred into new containers. Meanwhile, Masa went out to buy a new cam for the motor, taking von Haart and Lars with him to get sea charts. Von Haart returned promptly with a great roll of them under his arm. Heedless of the rest of us still working on deck in the rain, he left again at once.

"I'll be gone the rest of the day," he said enigmatically and went below for his cane. We stood staring after him as he stumped off down the wharf.

Lars meanwhile had not come back. Masa returned and he and Arvi went to work on the motor. Karl and I finished on deck. Still there was no sign of Lars. Von Haart of course was somewhere in a saloon—but Lars? Did our diffident, rather over-gentle companion also surrender to temptations in port? There seemed little else he could be doing in Visby on such a day.

At length the mystery was solved. Lars came back. He had indeed been struggling with temptation, but not what we had supposed. Lars had found a bookstore.

In the days that followed, and all during the voyage we would learn increasingly that books were Lars' addiction. He filled his personal locker half-full of them, and at Visby what had taken him so long was that he was buying a condensed encyclopedia. Now he settled down with it happily, looking up from time to time to give us bits of information. Masa, who was mending the foresail, learned suddenly that Billingsgate was a London fish market, licensed in 1699. I came below for an oil drum, and was told that the earliest fossiliferous geological system is especially well developed in Cambria, Wales, where in place it acquires a thickness of 12,000 feet. To Kati, still queasy with seasickness, Lars read that blackwater fever is probably caused by a specific protozoic parasite.

Masa finally had enough. "Lay off," he growled. "This isn't a classroom."

But Lars, whom we had begun to find often at a loss when confronted by an actual emergency, was perfectly at home in the realms of theory. His love of books was compensation for his uneasiness in the real world, and he just could not seem to stop instructing us. Later on, the habit made for considerable strain. Masa would turn on Lars and swear. Karl, whose good manners made him an easy target, would discover that even his patience wore thin during the long lectures. He would excuse

himself on some pretext—he was needed on deck, or he
thought he had left the basin running.

*

We stayed a full week in Visby. The girls repaired our
clothes as well as they could. All they had for pressing
was the old iron which Masa would heat with the blowtorch, first placing a sheet of metal between the flame
and the iron's surface to prevent it from turning black.
In spite of our dangerous shortage of money we sent
some things out to be cleaned. We had to! For the hos-
pitable Swedish citizens of Visby had begun inviting us
to dinner at their homes.

On the very first afternoon a highly-polished, chauf-
feur-driven sedan pulled up at the edge of the pier. The
driver bowed. "My employers would like you to dine
with them this evening."

Karl sprang to his feet. "We would be delighted."

That was just the beginning of Visby's hospitality.
For the remainder of our stay, seven days in all, eight
other island families invited us to lunch or dinner, sending their cars to pick us up and return us to the dock.
Knowing the crew of the *Tuntsa* became fashionable in
Visby. We were "those crazy Finns" who had almost
shipwrecked. We were an enigma to them, but they
liked us. Neither Lars nor von Haart was happy on these
social occasions, however. Arvi and Anna, Karl and Kati,
May and I would make small talk and enjoy ourselves,
but Lars was at a loss for conversation and von Haart,
who had not been sober since we arrived, had a way of

demanding a drink which he called a "Patagonian swizzle."

"It's a time-honored custom," he would explain. "Originated on the old trading route between England and Australia."

A Patagonian swizzle, which in the end von Haart would usually manage to mix himself, would turn out to be made in a brandy snifter. The recipe was quite simple: one jigger of every liquor in the house. After a swizzle, dinner bored von Haart. He would excuse himself and retire to refill his snifter. Often when we left, our host would find he had no alcoholic beverage of any kind left, unless of course he had been warned in advance by our hosts of the evening before.

It was the locking up of the bottles rather than our remonstrances which made von Haart finally excuse himself from further entertainment. We then divided into two teams: von Haart and Lars; and Karl, Arvi and I with our wives—a common-sense separation which continued in port throughout the voyage. Lars joined von Haart in going from tavern to tavern. He had neither the same capacity nor the same appetite, but von Haart's flamboyance, his yarns of old voyages, the fascinating and often fantastic acquaintances he made at each bar delighted Lars, who became very fond of him. After a round of the taverns, Lars would pilot them both to the pier. There they would sit, finishing a last bottle and arguing amiably. We would hear Lars repeating his favorite epigram to his oblivious companion, "Corruptio optima pessima"—the corruption of the best is the worst —before Masa and Arvi or Karl and I would come out to silence them and help them down to the cabin.

When we left Visby, there were almost as many people seeing us off as there had been seeing us in. Von Haart's and Lars' friends were particularly vociferous, creating an atmosphere of celebration. We watched the crowd blend into the horizon with genuine regret.

"It's not just that they're good cooks," Anna said. "It's that they think we are crazy, but they like us anyway!"

*

The sea was placid, and May commented wistfully that it was as quiet as a child after an outburst of temper. "It seems to be saying, 'Look how good I am now,'" she said and sighed. She was remembering Eero. We were all homesick. We felt the rightness of our going to America as intensely as ever, but we had not anticipated how increasingly we would miss our families. We felt particularly forlorn after leaving the hospitality of Visby.

In the perfect weather we had idle time. After solacing our homesickness by writing to all the friends and relatives we could think of, Karl and Kati, May and I settled down to cards on deck. It was a game for four people similar to bridge but more complicated and lasting much longer—at least four or five hours, and sometimes eight or ten. It was a comparatively new game created in Sweden and Finland and had been very popular when we left Helsinki. We were to play it a lot during the voyage.

In the evenings we read. Except for Lars, we had

brought mostly fiction. We had two sailing books, and one we particularly enjoyed belonged to Arvi. Written by a well-known Norwegian writer, Ehrling Tambs, and called *The Cruise of the Teddy*, it told how he and his wife had made a similar trip along our intended route, in a boat not much larger than the *Tuntsa*. As we sailed on, their story was to become our inspiration. Even Lars, who abhorred popular writing, dipped into it.

Otherwise Lars read only non-fiction. Glancing up from his book, he would praise the sciences, but rail against religions and philosophies—all of them, from Plato to Marx, Christianity to Islam. His favorite definition of philosophy was: "It is a general madness which in the shortest time possible is aiming to drive mankind to extinction."

Arvi and Masa kept busy puttering with the motor or the radio: cleaning, and adjusting them endlessly.

Kati and May knitted. Anna sketched. She had considerable talent, and her softly pencilled, dreamy seascapes were lovely.

Von Haart, usually required at the helm, or else to supervise the helmsman, had little idle time. Much of this part of the Baltic was heavily mined. The cleared area was fairly well marked by buoys, but because we were dependent on sail and had to save our expensive fuel, we were not always on the safest course.

On our second afternoon von Haart and Arvi were scanning the water to sight the next channel buoy when suddenly Arvi cried, "Look there!"

We stared at an unbelievable phenomenon.

We were now so far from the Swedish coast that not

even a suggestion of its line was visible on the horizon, yet not fifty yards to port was a sand bank. On it rested a partly-submerged vessel. It had obviously struck a mine.

"Slow down!" von Haart shouted. Karl and Masa spilled air from the sails. We rode the waves and looked at the wreckage. We were mesmerized by the rhythmic hiss of the sea's even sweep across it. Then, almost simultaneously, we glanced at one another. There were so many things we needed. And there was the wreck—no good to anyone!

"Merciful God," said von Haart slowly.

"Let's go have a look," exclaimed Masa.

We spent the rest of the day at the derelict, examining every square inch above water. By dusk we had salvaged several lengths of chain, pieces of pipe, and a miscellany of other useful and useless items. Von Haart spent his time looking for something else. We breathed sighs of relief when he emerged from below empty-handed.

He had been keeping a lengthy, descriptive log book ever since our departure from Helsinki. Besides nautical facts, he reviewed each day's events in a pithy, inimitable way.* After our search of the derelict, he wrote scathingly of his spiritless survey: "Ten bottles. All empty. What selfishness."

It was nearly dark when we finished on the wreck so, since the weather was calm, we decided to tie up to it until daybreak. It would be nearly impossible to find the channel buoys in the dusk and get back on the path

---

* This log was lost in the shipwreck.

through the mines. But remembering the time on the return from Valkom when we had almost been smashed during the night, we slept lightly.

It was well that we did so, for toward morning a wind sprang up and began to bump us against the side of the wreck. We were on deck in seconds. Karl cast off the lines. The rest of us seized oars and poles and pushed. As we got underway I leaned over the rail in hope of spotting a buoy. Instead I saw glowing plankton, a luminous, shimmering, shifting drift of blue and green. We were in shallow water. I shouted to von Haart.

He called to Karl at the mainsail not to take too much wind, and sent Lars and me to either side of the boat as lookouts. The cold, blue-green fire of the plankton was a magnificent spectacle, but we were less moved by its beauty than by the fact that it let us see the sandbanks so we could steer clear.

Twice we scraped bottom, and all but von Haart took poles and oars. We seemed to inch our way for miles in that weird, luminous sea. I would shout, "Shoal to port!" Then Lars would cry, "Sandbar to starboard!" Von Haart would adjust his course—often just as Lars and I cried together, "Shallow water just under us!" Intermittently von Haart dragged a handkerchief from his pocket and wiped the sweat off his forehead.

It was more than an hour after I first noticed shoals before the bottom fell away and we saw no more shallows. Von Haart swore feelingly and sat down for a cigarette.

In silence we lined the railings and looked for the channel markers. Dawn was streaking the sky when Lars saw a dark spot against the water to port. A few minutes later, the sun flashed over the horizon, the sea turned the soft and gradual pinkish silver which dawn has in the north, and we sighed with relief as we finally saw the white markers dancing in the light.

We were back on course and would be in Helsingborg before another nightfall.

As we cast anchor fronting Helsingborg, we were treated to an extraordinary vision of delightful, timbered houses spotted up the slopes, like vari-colored buttons against a tweedy gray-green material. Behind them in breathtaking beauty was the steep, sheer gray and black rise of the mountains. We were eager to go ashore, but immediately were confronted by temporarily immovable obstacles.

Helsingborg was a city with an enterprising press. In a short time a reporter, a photographer, and groups of sightseers crowded the pier and barraged us with questions. We came from Finland? Impossible! In that little boat? Where were we going with her?

In Visby we had already found it increasingly awkward to evade questions. The pretense of just taking a cruise was more and more hollow, the farther we got from Helsinki. We had discussed the matter and decided that we might as well begin telling the truth. No Finnish coast guard cutter could endanger us at this distance. There was no Russian zone now, with its Soviet ships. And we did not think we could be extradited, for thanks to Karl's friend in the Finnish secret police, our passports and papers were all quite legal and in order.

So we acknowledged that we were sailing to America.

The reporters began to scribble. The photographer took pictures. The crowd grew thicker. Von Haart struck an attitude, and not only dramatized our adventures and our project, but remarked in passing on our need for food and supplies. The next day, as the papers told our story, a steady stream of people began to arrive on the docks, bearing gifts and wishing us well.

If the rest of us were embarrassed by Swedish generosity, von Haart was not. With a warm smile, an irresistible handshake, and a beautifully dramatic "Thank you and bless you!" he raked in money, clothing, canned goods, and candy—all invaluable to our meager larder. We felt the most sincere gratitude.

Again, as at Visby, we were asked to a round of parties. Swedish hospitality was inexhaustible. Once more we divided: Lars went to the bars with von Haart; the rest of us attended the formal dinners, where the questions were endless and toasts to the incredible American voyage flowed like water.

We stayed remarkably sober under the circumstances —or so I thought. But on the last night in port, we found ourselves returning to the *Tuntsa* across docks which seemed to heave mysteriously and posts which seemed to bend and get in our way. We were just congratulating ourselves on getting safely back, when Arvi slipped on the *Tuntsa's* deck and fell overboard. Anna at once dove after him, and Karl followed. Tuntsa loyally leaped after, and the three in the water, finding Arvi in no danger and everyone able to stand on the shallow sands, began to laugh.

Masa and I were just hauling them one by one back

on board when von Haart with Lars arrived from his tour
of the waterfront taverns. He took one look at us, threw
back his head, and rocked with laughter.

"Ho ho!" he roared. "And how was the dignified social
occasion?" He looked at the usually impeccable Karl,
sprawled dripping wet against the rail. We were cold
now and the members of the impromptu swimming
party were shivering as if they were about to have pneu-
monia.

"Quite a celebration, eh? Here," he said suddenly, "I
have just what you need." From his pocket he produced
a bottle. It was a supreme sacrifice, for clearly he had
been planning to smuggle it on board.

May boiled water and we quickly made hot toddies of
von Haart's liquor. Tuntsa was dried and wrapped in a
blanket. As I dropped off to sleep, I heard von Haart in
his bunk still chuckling softly.

At daybreak I opened my eyes, but closed them immediately. The sunlight flooding through the overhead skylights seemed to pierce my eyeballs. My head felt three
sizes too large for my neck, and when I tried to rise from
my pillow, ungentle devils inside me seemed to be pushing weights about. I sank back. Karl, just awakening in
the bunk above called, "What's the mat . . .?" and finished with a groan.

Then we heard von Haart's step and cheerful voice,
"Come on! Get up! We've got a good breeze."

We staggered out of our bunks and stumbled about
wretchedly, cursing our throbbing heads, while the girls,
equally pale, made pots of coffee. Von Haart, however,

was never more cheerful, chuckling at our bad temper and enjoying his own well-being.

"You should get used to it," he said. "What you need is more practice. I'll make sailors of you yet."

We approached the Danish coast at night and were greeted by confusing yellow-white glares. The lights were so bright, it was impossible to make out any shapes behind them. Even von Haart could not get his bearings.

Then we felt the dreaded, familiar scrape of harbor bottom against our keel. Ship's bells clanged and horns tooted impatiently. We had gone aground in what was for this harbor apparently the center of the channel. Boats began to pass on either side, missing us by only a few feet. Apparently their drafts weren't as deep as the *Tuntsa's*. It was the lights of this heavy traffic which had confused us.

An hour passed. Two. Three. No one stopped. The angry bells and horns blared at us. We could not push ourselves free. Nor, apparently, could we make ourselves heard over the din of ships indignantly going about their business.

"Where's the milk of human kindness?" Masa asked at last. "Did we leave it all in Sweden? What's wrong with the Danes, anyway?"

Four hours passed and we were still aground. Then at last someone took pity on us and pulled us free. "He must have been a Swede," Masa commented bitterly, as we headed toward the harbor.

But just offshore, less than fifty feet from the break-water, we grounded again. This time there were no moving craft in the vicinity. We would have to wait for high tide.

Next morning, we floated free and went in under power. But a grim official met us as we stepped on the pier. He demanded our papers. He was a hard-faced, middle-aged man with as unpleasant an expression as I had ever seen. Denmark, overcome and occupied by the Nazis during the war, was full of bitter, angry people. Like the population of my own Finland, the Danes had grown close and hard, and had a chronic suspicion of strangers. There could not have been a keener contrast to the atmosphere we had just left. Neutral Sweden, virtually untouched by the conflict, was open-handed and generous—rather like a rich man with a guilt complex in regard to less fortunate neighbors.

"Your papers," the Danish official said, holding out his hand.

"What does he think we are—German spies?" May whispered indignantly to me.

"It wouldn't be surprising," I murmured.

The man stood turning over our passports. "We shall wire Helsinki for confirmation of your identity," he said coldly at last.

We glanced at one another. Masa's face had gone white under his red hair. Karl bit his lip.

"Where are you bound?"

"We are cruising," replied von Haart, drawing himself up. "I should think you would see that for yourself. What else would we be doing in this little boat? My two friends," he gestured to Karl and me, "had a bad time in the war—their nerves give them trouble. We have made up a little vacation party. I," said von Haart bowing stiffly from the waist, "am Baron Otto Alexander von Haart."

No one could do the grand manner better than von Haart. Even the sour face before us looked somewhat embarrassed.

"Are free men," said von Haart rhetorically, but with genuine anger, "never to be free? One would suppose we were still under the occupation! Need I point out the anxiety you are causing to the wives of my friends?"

The man appeared to come to a decision. He thrust the passports into his pocket but handed back the women's identity cards. "You may return to your ship," he said. "I will not notify headquarters. But I warn you not to leave the harbor until we clear you from Helsinki."

"You are still going to wire?" Anna asked miserably.

Von Haart kicked her ankle.

"Of course." He left us.

"Never show uncertainty," von Haart said sternly to Anna, as we went back on board.

"Uncertainty!" exclaimed Anna. "What's uncertain? They will wire Helsinki, and we will all be sent back." She burst into tears. May put her arm around her.

"I just don't think it will turn out that way," May said practically. "We have our passports. In Helsinki, too, we are supposed to be cruising. It all fits together. No matter what they may think, what can they do as long as our papers are in order?"

But Anna would not be consoled, and all of us had too much experience with the habits of police states to feel at ease. Denmark was a free country now, but bad habits die hard. The man was not a type we enjoyed.

"He had the Nazi mentality," said Lars. "I could tell. Psychologically the hold of an alien philosophy remains long after it is overthrown in actuality."

Masa growled, and uttered several remarks uncomplimentary to the Dane's ancestry, his antecedents, and his personal habits.

Then we returned to the *Tuntsa*.

The next day dawned. A reporter turned up and took the *Tuntsa's* picture, and briefly we felt that there was interest and friendliness, at least among Denmark's ordinary people. We posed willingly and with a sudden light-heartedness all the more pronounced because of our underlying foreboding. But then the photographer left, and the day began to drag. The official did not return. No one came near us. Hour by hour our tension increased. By late afternoon Masa took to climbing the rope ladder and hurdling stacked oil cans out of sheer nervousness. Karl got out the phonograph and played all our few records. Arvi wore Tuntsa out retrieving sticks.

Dusk came—and still no one approached.

"My stars," May said, "how long does it take to wire Finland?"

"It went by slow sailboat, and we won't hear for a month," said von Haart. He was imperturably playing solitaire. Masa looked ready to toss an oilcan at him.

To have left Finland successfully, passed Sweden, and reached the Danish coast—then to be stopped. It *couldn't* happen.

We were all seated on the cabin roof or sprawling on deck when on the morning of the third day, we saw the official reappear. We rose hurriedly. You could have heard a pin drop as he stepped on deck.

"Well?" asked von Haart.

"Our inquiry to Finland has been answered," said the man. He was unsmiling. We didn't breathe.

"You have been cleared," he said abruptly. "You may proceed, or come ashore, as you like." He left us.

"Damn sadist," murmured Masa. "Did you see that? He kept us in suspense as long as he could."

We went ashore briefly. None of us, even von Haart, cared to linger. We weighed anchor and left that cold little harbor with no regrets.

a **SETBACK**

becalmed

floating on fish

the Queen's yacht club

von Haart finds a friend

"corruptio optima pessima"

smugglers!

We hoped for a brisk wind to carry us swiftly through the Lim Fjorden Canal into the North Sea. But the whole coast of Denmark continued to seem malevolent. Less than an hour out of the harbor, we were becalmed.

"Start the motor," said von Haart laconically.

For more than two hours the *Tuntsa* continued at a laggard pace, pushed by our insignificant one-cylinder engine. We were depressed, for every turn of the grudging propeller lowered our meager supply of fuel. Yet no one cared to prolong our stay off the Danish coast.

Von Haart at the helm, however, was whistling brightly, and we had been on our sluggish course scarcely two hours when I had the uncomfortable feeling that he was both too cheerful and was giving the wheel too frequently to someone else. He would go below, and perhaps five minutes later come back to the helm, where the misery of our slow progress seemed to affect him not a whit.

After I noticed four light-hearted returns from the cabin and was convinced he was not going for coffee or water, I followed him. He was sitting on his bunk making an elaborate pretence of studying a chart, but while I watched him, his free hand dipped to the floor. He brought up a bottle from under his bunk, drank lustily, and perused his chart.

I approached him. "Von Haart, you promised not to drink while we were on the water."

"You call this water?" He gestured at the flat dull canal visible through the portholes and looked at me indignantly.

I picked up the bottle. It was not liquor at all but a clear compound of some sort, probably intended for alcohol rubs or some other external use.

"Von Haart," I said. "Please! You'll kill yourself. . . ."

He turned on his most engaging grin. "Ah, Teppo, it's 180-proof. It was the only good thing in all that cursed little town. I just had to buy it. It's my future-brightener . . . my soul saver . . . my heart-warmer. . . ." When I did not smile he urged, "Have some."

"No thanks," I replied curtly.

Apparently my look made him think I might take the bottle, for he seized it and tossed the remainder down his throat, then looked at me and smiled again, rather shyly, like a child faced with an adult who does not understand.

"Oh, von Haart!" I said helplessly. When he stood up, I thought he would be reeling, but he walked with perfect steadiness. We would find later that he could drink even straight alcohol and show little effect. He would deftly steer his course, tell his stories with no sign of a lisp, remain clearheaded, and mesmerize us all with his charm. Yet we knew that no man, even with such magnificent strength as his, could live long this way. And we were growing deeply fond of him.

There was nothing I or any of us could do, however. I followed him back on deck, and he took his place at the helm to stand patiently guiding the *Tuntsa* through the dreary calm.

We were making our way on water smooth as glass when a fishing boat passed us from behind. The captain, a hook-nosed mariner with his seaman's cap squashed onto the back of his head, momentarily surveyed our efforts, then turned his head to shoot a contemptuous stream of brown tobacco juice into the canal. Looking back, he drawled, "Want a tow?"

Instantly von Haart went forward for the mooring line and tossed it unerringly toward the other boat. "You bet we do!"

The skipper looked astonished. Von Haart's alacrity was probably the fastest movement, outside of fighting fish, he had seen in his entire seagoing life.

Von Haart stood smiling as the line tightened. I looked at him and shook my head. I had just seen him take a drink which would have left another man paralyzed. Yet his reactions were quicker than mine; he was quicker even than the energetic Masa.

We cut our engine, the fishing boat chugged forward, and the unexciting flat landscape at which we had been staring all day, seemed now almost to whiz by.

Von Haart sat down on deck to resume his solitaire. Karl and Kati, May and I got out our own cards. Lars fetched a book. Arvi and Masa went below to see if the brief run had exhausted their beloved engine. Anna entertained Tuntsa. His antics delighted us all; and the rest of us, including von Haart, finally gave up our other diversions to join in. Tuntsa retrieved, played tug of war, and participated in hide-and-seek. Only when Arvi decided to hide in the galley and Tuntsa, bounding about to look for his master, nearly wrecked the evening meal did the frolic end. By then, Tuntsa, who for all of us was replacing our children, was completely exhausted. He fell asleep on deck, and slept until we reached Thyboron, a fishing community at the canal's end.

We stayed in Thyboron two days. It was too small a town to have a suspicious officialdom. We visited a fish cannery, attended services at a tiny Finnish sailors' missionary church, felt homesick, mailed letters, and arranged most carefully for mail following us to be forwarded to Amsterdam, our next stop. Then we headed into the North Sea, dipping southward in our course.

The lowering of our fuel reserve during our trip through the canal had made us think soberly of our always chronic problem—money. At Thyboron the fishermen had boasted of the bounteousness of their waters, and we determined to try filling out our food supply.

"Here you can catch fish with any sort of lure," one of the Finns at the mission church had said. "A hook and line with anything that shines will get 'em."

So less than an hour out of Thyboron, we dropped anchor and Masa asked, "Well, what do we use for lures?"

"We look among Kati's treasures," Karl suggested, smiling.

Kati was a collector. Her under-bunk locker was full of odds and ends, usable or unusable: needles, pins, bits of broken jewelry, beads, buttons, paper, ribbon—anything. The strange and thrifty collection was often surprisingly helpful.

Within a few minutes, Masa returned with scraps of foil from old cigarette packages. I got hooks and lines from our storage cabinet. As we regarded our equipment, we did not really have much hope of success. Fishermen are notorious boasters. Probably the fishing off Thyboron was no better than anyplace else.

Nevertheless, Arvi and Masa rigged two lines with hooks attached at random intervals. We slipped a bright scrap of foil over each hook, made the lines fast to the after rail, and let the hooks drag well past our wake. We sat down to keep watch, expecting to have a long, dreary, fruitless vigil.

To our astonishment only seconds passed before we saw the first line tighten. With an exclamation, Masa hauled it in. Not one, but half a dozen shining, silver mackerel lay flipping on the deck. There was something primitive in our delight. We were not fishing for sport, as nearly all of us were accustomed to do on occasion, but because we needed food. I remember thinking that this was how the primitive coastal tribes must have felt when they had a catch. Masa gave a whoop of glee. Von Haart was already hauling in the other line, his cane leaning forgotten against the rail, his tough old face grinning. Behind us the water was boiling with fish. Masa had already rebaited and let the first line back out. We were in the middle of one of the great schools of mackerel which furnish the livelihood of the villages along the coast. I had never seen nor imagined such a sight. It seemed to me as if the swarming fish could now have carried the *Tuntsa* along on their backs.

✿

During our five days on the North Sea, we fished every morning, and ate fish in every conceivable way: in chowders—fried—and in a variety of special sandwiches which Anna invented.

After one such meal, May said to me, "It's queer we aren't tired of fish. The galley is beginning to smell like a trawler."

She was sitting at the table having a cigarette. The others were on deck, enjoying the daily diversion of playing with Tuntsa. This was a rare moment for us— being able to talk alone.

"Are you tired of fish?" I asked with a smile.

She laughed and shook her head. "No. But I don't understand why. Unless it's because fish just taste better at sea."

"Maybe it's because we need them," I suggested. "We're not eating them as culinary delicacies."

"So they are delicacies because we don't expect them to be," May said thoughtfully. "It's odd. I always thought people resented whatever they were forced to do."

"We are not being forced to do anything," I said. "We are here in the North Sea by our choice. If there was ever a situation that was not entered into by force, it's the *Tuntsa*.

"I know," said May. "And all during the war all of us were forced in almost everything we did. You know, it is extraordinary how well we get along together, all of us on the *Tuntsa*. We are all so different, but there are no quarrels—hardly even a disagreement." She paused. We listened to the laughter and the dog racing about overhead. "I think it's because for the first time in years, we are free—every one of us."

"Any regrets?" I asked her.

"I miss Eero, but that's all," she said slowly. "And soon we will send for him."

Masa shouted down the hatch. "Hey, come up, Teppo! The sun is perfect."

I left her regretfully as Kati came down to help with the dishes.

Dishes were washed in a bucket of sea water, with salt-water soap, then turned upside down on the galley table to dry. "We can save on seasoning," von Haart had commented dryly. It was quite true. The dishes were never free of salt smell and taste, and, though not unpleasant, it pervaded whatever we ate.

The day was perfect. The sun was on the horizon, ready to dip into the sea. The saucer-curved sky was cloudless. The waters rolled under a steady wind. We were on a broad reach, our best point of sailing.

We sat together and discussed some of our personal philosophies. Von Haart eyed the cane at his side and commented, "If life has taught me nothing else, it's taught me to walk slowly. I've become a patient man in my sixty-four years. I've learned to enjoy every day and take it as it comes."

"That's the way to be," said Masa. "Most people are too inflexible. They keep the same attitude winter, summer, fall, or spring. Plants and animals speed up, come out of hibernation when the weather or circumstances change. But not people. Either they won't—or can't change. The most important thing is energy." He ran both hands through his red hair.

Karl and Arvi grinned, and so did I. The speech was characteristic of Masa. He made restlessness a virtue. Yet without restlessness, none of us would have been on the *Tuntsa*.

On a reach, the *Tuntsa* almost conned herself. Arvi took out his mouth organ, and we began to sing. None of us were potential opera stars but we were loud.

Karl had the most pleasing voice. Masa was the most vigorous; von Haart was the most dramatic; Arvi carried the best tune. We did a good deal of singing on board. The women sang when at work. Kati, in particular, seemed always to be humming in her sweet high soprano. Anna possessed a husky alto and sang when she was sketching or looking at the sea. May preferred to join someone else, blending her lively contralto while others carried the melody. When there was a helper at the sails and duets would waft down into the cabin, she would go on deck to harmonize with them. Often those below would come up one at a time to join them, until we were all together. To us, as people temporarily without a country, the songs we knew were like tangible memories —fragments of the past we had left behind.

✲

The beauty of the sea was taking hold of us all. We were learning to love it and to understand the fascination it held for men like von Haart, who for reasons of temperament or circumstance were without roots. When you put to sea, you left ordinary life behind and would not pick it up again until the voyage ended. The water, especially during this part of our passage, was as mild and shimmering as a dream of a rosy future. But I remember a day when we passed a group of the enormous crimson jellyfish one sees in late summer in those waters. Some were three or four feet in diameter. Undulating in sinister rhythm they pulsed along just below the surface, each one trailing its network of stingers whose venom cripples and blinds.

We had been sailing eight to ten miles from shore, out of sight of the continental mass. Von Haart thought it best. "You get more wind." But now—as our fifth day on the North Sea grayed toward dusk—von Haart said it was time to shorten the band between boat and shore. "We'll be at Imunden by dark." Imunden was a tiny harbor town at the mouth of one of the canals that connected the North Sea with Amsterdam.

As we approached the windless area near the coast, Arvi started the engine. It throbbed agreeably, but the *Tuntsa* did not move.

Masa advised Arvi to shut it off. "We might as well anchor for the night. If it's the propeller, we sure can't do anything in this black soup."

At dawn, Masa peered over the railing, then directed me to hold his legs, while he squinted down at the propeller as Arvi ran the engine. "Something is wrong down there. The propeller's not moving."

I relayed the news to Arvi, who shut off the motor and came on deck to lend his practical know-how. He peeled off his shirt. "I'm going down to take a look," he said.

Von Haart regarded us boyishly and grinned. "I used to be quite a swimmer. I'll go down with you, Arvi."

He and Arvi plunged together. We watched the rising bubbles, then saw the two men surface. Von Haart was breathing hard. He held up his hands and we pulled him on deck.

He smiled, but his look was rueful. He pulled his jersey over his head. "I need a drink," he said to me reproachfully. "If I had had a drink I could have fixed that propeller myself."

Arvi, in the meantime, was feeling skillfully along the shaft. He spotted the trouble and came up shaking the wet hair out of his eyes. "The pin connecting the drive shaft and propeller has sheared."

Masa went over the side to check the size of pin needed. "We can fix it," he said with relief. "We can file a piece of steel rod to the right diameter, if it doesn't fit as is." Arvi nodded and the two went to find tools and materials.

Lars, Karl, and I took turns diving, and drove the pieces of the old pin out of the shaft. Arvi and Masa

would use them as a model for the new piece. When
they were finished, we took turns (this time, two of us
at a time) at driving the substitute pin into place. Within
two hours from the time we started our improvised repairs, we were again underway.

The *Tuntsa* moved slowly now because ahead of us
was a series of locks. Five or six ships were already lined
up, and we had to wait our turn. It took almost a day to
travel from Imunden to Amsterdam, although the distance was less than thirty miles.

Once in Amsterdam, we moored beside a large white
yacht and went into the sailing clubhouse. It was a lux-
uriously furnished, beautifully decorated place and since
no one told us to go away, we gawked at every room.
"Nicest club I've ever seen," said von Haart. "I wonder
if we should take our shoes off."

The next morning we discovered we had been in the
Royal Sailing Club and that our mooring-mate was the
Queen of Holland's private yacht. We kept our choice
spot, however, for the ten days we were in Amsterdam—
and no one paid us the slightest attention.

As always, our first quest was the post office. Most of
us had mail waiting. May had a snapshot of Eero. Wistfully we exchanged our information from home.

"The baby is getting so big!" May exclaimed. "We will
have to get to America fast, or he will forget us."

We were all homesick after our letters. Clutching our
mail, we walked in silence. Then the wonderful waterfront restaurants brought us back to the present.

With incredulity we bought butter, cream, and milk.
Finland was still in the grip of war shortages, and the

abundance of Amsterdam astonished us. We ate like greedy children. "We'll buy a gallon of milk and a pound of butter before we leave—for a special treat on the *Tuntsa*," Anna said.

"If this is the beginning of similar luxurious tastes," von Haart said, "we had better start selling our compasses, knives, and watches right away."

"We had better start selling anyhow," Kati, our boat treasurer, informed us. "Our money is just about gone."

So we tried hard in Amsterdam to sell our wrist compasses and knives. We concentrated on the harbor, trying to sell or swap advantageously. But no one was interested. Amsterdam was too prosperous.

By the close of our ninth day, we unanimously decided to move on. "Another port, smaller and poorer, might be better," I said. But I was feeling downhearted. We had counted on selling our goods, and the abundance at Amsterdam made me fearful. Was Finland the only place which still suffered from postwar shortages?

During the morning of our tenth day, we spent sparingly for food and a two-gallon can of ethyl alcohol to be used for lighting our blowtorch. Then we left the harbor.

To protect von Haart from his attraction to everything alcoholic, we immediately hid the big can of blowtorch alcohol and took out only a small amount, which we put in a glass jar. The girls kept vigilant watch over both. But von Haart with elaborate ceremony was soon very much in evidence in the galley, offering to help with the cooking, to put away dishes, anything. Each time, May or Anna or Kati would pat him on the back and explain that they would not dream of asking our captain to assist them.

Von Haart would then indignantly come on deck. "Women! I offer to help—is my offer accepted?—no, indeed! What appreciation do they have of courtesy?"

The rest of us merely smiled. That same night Kati woke to find him tip-toeing toward the glass jar.

"Looking for something?" she asked coolly.

Von Haart explained carefully that he had left his deck of cards in the galley.

"You are going to play now? By the light of the moon perhaps?" said Kati.

Von Haart went back to his bunk.

The best of men in every other way, he was quite helpless in the grip of his addiction. We had of course no hope of curing him or even of mitigating his habit. Indeed, after we had known him this long, the very thought of interfering with the course of a life of a man like von Haart seemed an impertinence. But we tried in every way we knew to slow the process down, and, when we were at sea, to keep him sober. For while it required enormous quantities of drink to unsteady von Haart, when it did finally happen he would drop over and lie wherever he fell like a pole-axed ox. Nothing could wake him. We knew that if this happened during an emergency, our little band of sea-going amateurs could well make some mistake which might cost the lives of everyone on board, including von Haart.

It was the morning after Kati woke to find von Haart tip-toeing toward the blowtorch alcohol that we were struck by an ugly squall. We were not quite in the Eng-

lish Channel, when the wind seemed almost to explode
upon us.

"Hits without warning!" shouted von Haart, wrestling
the wheel. "The Channel's like that. For God's sake, get
sail off, fast!"

But the wind did it for us. With a sound like a cannon
shot, the mainsail split in two, even as Karl, Masa, Arvi,
and I were fighting our way along the deck.

Relieved somewhat, the ever buoyant *Tuntsa* righted
herself, and we hauled down the torn canvas. Von Haart
put about for Ostende, and we proceeded under our
storm sails through seas which pitched us about like a
cork in a mix-master. It was during this storm that Kati,
always prone to seasickness and stubbornly gallant
about crawling into her bunk to get through her suffer-
ing alone, began to vomit blood. Karl was desperately
worried and would not leave her. It turned out that our
starboard tank had filled with seawater during the early
part of the storm and Kati, unknowing until she swal-
lowed it, had drunk brine. We were all busy on deck, and
as usual she had said nothing, but had gone off to be
sick alone. She was desperately ill, and when we finally
came into calm water off Ostende we decided to lie over
in harbor a few days to help her recover.

We were all the more pleased to stay when we found
that, unlike Amsterdam, Ostende was a ready market for
our merchandise. While Lars and von Haart patched
the sail, Karl, Arvi, Masa, and I roamed the beach and
sold fourteen of our compasses. This solved our immediate food needs, but it did not allow for the cost of
recharging the radio battery, which we had optimistic-

ally sent out on our first day. We had also ordered oil, which we needed badly.

One trait in von Haart which made him such a good companion was his optimism. He would never look at the dark side of any situation. Indeed, he would not admit that there was any dark side. Now he said reprovingly, "Don't worry about money—*never* worry about money; it isn't worth it. You will sell another dozen compasses and we will be all right. You'll see."

Karl rather diffidently pointed out that the proceeds from another dozen compasses would be far from the sum needed to settle our bills for oil and the battery.

"Well, something will turn up," said von Haart. "I promise you," he added cheerfully.

The "something" which finally "turned up" was a charming, gray-haired Belgian official and his wife, whose yacht had been forced into Ostende by the same storm which had turned back the *Tuntsa*. Our little boat, and then our incredible expedition interested them, and they struck up acquaintance with us. They were intelligent and perceptive people, and of course their favorite was von Haart. One could not be with him and fail to realize that he was an extraordinary being—as fascinating as he was baffling.

Von Haart, for his part, was as always perfectly aware of his charm and of the character of the people around him. On the day that the oil and the battery were to be delivered, he first urged us to go down to town to try to sell more compasses before the deadline of the delivery, and then announced that he would stay behind—his leg was bothering him. As soon as we were out of sight, he

invited the Belgian over for a visit, with the appeal that
we had been able to afford very few charts, and would
our wealthy friend perhaps temporarily loan some of his
own which von Haart could study?

The Belgian of course arrived with a great roll of
charts which he gave to von Haart and told him to keep.

"Why, I know the Channel like the palm of my hand,"
he said. "Please take the charts. You need them much
more than I." Then he settled down with a drink to
enjoy von Haart's company.

In the midst of their conversation, the oil and battery
arrived and the delivery man handed von Haart the bill.

"Excuse me," von Haart said to his visitor and opened
the drawer in the navigation table. He checked through
a cigar box there carefully, and furrows deepened on his
expressive forehead.

He turned back. "Look here," he said reluctantly, "my
friends took our money with them when they went out.
Do you think you could loan me enough to cover this
bill?" And, then, keeping the bill turned over, he named
an amount in excess of what was needed.

"Please—my dear fellow," said von Haart's acquaintance, smiling. "Let me pay your little bill for you. It will
give me great pleasure."

Von Haart bowed. "You are most kind," he said and he
meant it. The affection and the entente he felt toward
the Belgian were quite genuine.

The Belgian then, with a polite, "Please permit me,"
opened his wallet and took out a sum even larger than
the one von Haart had named. "Possibly this will allow
you to buy some extra supplies," he said.

Von Haart bowed again. "You are most generous."
Then he went on deck, paid the delivery man the amount
of the bill, and pocketed the rest. When he came back,
the Belgian invited him to bring us all to dinner that
night, conversed a little longer about other matters, and
took his leave.

When we returned to find the battery and oil on board
and the bills mysteriously paid, we were of course delighted because we truly had not seen how we were
going to get out of Ostende and on with the journey. But
when von Haart told how he had accomplished all this,
we were aghast.

"We must go over to the Belgian's yacht, explain to
him, and return the extra money this minute," said Kati
firmly.

"Dear Kati," said von Haart, "don't you understand?
You would be telling him nothing he does not know.
Also you would be robbing him of the happiness of doing a good deed. Look—suppose I had begged him directly to give us money to pay our bills so we could go
on? It would have been humiliating for us, and our hu-
miliation would have embarrassed him, for he is a very
good man. But, as it is, no one is humiliated, and everything is fine."

We looked at one another. Von Haart's ways were not
our ways, and we often felt as if he had turned things
upside down and we were all standing on our heads.
Finally, we agreed, and I don't think any of us could
have said in the end whether our point of view or his
was the "right" one. In fact, I still don't know. But, at
any rate, we went to the Belgian's yacht for dinner and

we had a wonderful time. Von Haart even refrained from swizzles. However, he went off with Lars afterwards to a little tavern he had found which pleased him.

In nearly every port, von Haart would pick out a waterfront place where he discovered a group he especially enjoyed. He would then favor that one over the others for his visits. In Ostende he usually concluded the evening with a stop at a quiet and singularly beautiful church, which happened to be nearby. He would go inside and sit in silence near the back. Then he would return to Lars, settle down beside him on the steps, and drink until the bottle was empty. Lars was a skeptic; von Haart a believer, with a simple, almost childlike faith in what he called the "goodness of the universe." Lars would argue with him and urge him to see the light of "scientific reason," but von Haart would brush him away with a smile and a wave of his hand. At last both would come reeling back to the *Tuntsa*, Lars a little sullen, but von Haart delighted with all the world. Lars' "corruptio optima pessima" bothered him not at all.

❖

We began the twenty-four hour trip to Dover in a light fog. Von Haart would not admit any danger, or even the possibility that the fog would ever become more than a mist. Shortly after midnight, however, it thickened into gravy. Nevertheless von Haart at the helm would not acknowledge that there was the least possibility of being lost, and sent below those on watch so they could get some rest. We were all somewhat apprehensive, but the next morning—right before our eyes—was a harbor!

"Dover!" called Masa jubilantly. "We came right to it."

We sailed blithely into the harbor and spoke with assurance to the customs officers.

"This is Dover, isn't it?" Karl finally asked.

They had eyed our small sailboat with its Finnish flag strangely when we first docked. Now they gazed at us with absolute astonishment. One official cleared his throat and answered. "This is Ramsgate." We were fifty miles north of Dover.

Chagrined by our mistake, we decided not to go ashore. We would do a few necessary things on board, then make an early departure. The girls carried clothes upon deck to air. The cabinets acquired a musty smell from dampness if we didn't do this frequently. Meanwhile, the rest of us fought over who would shave first. We had no shaving cream—only coarse soap—and our razor blades were never sharp. They were an expensive luxury and they had to deliver a round of six shaves each. We alternated for first use of every new blade.

Shaving was a torturous job which all of us, even Karl, put off as long as possible. From the start of the voyage, we had tried to think of every conceivable excuse for eliminating the word "shave" from our vocabulary, but the women did not cooperate. With sure, accurate memory they would remind us of when we last shaved, and threaten to stop preparing meals, cleaning the cabin, doing the laundry, or even talking to us, if we didn't move promptly to razor and soap. Not storms on the sea or work on the boat, or even seasickness could deter them.

"It is," said May, "a matter of keeping up *standards*. If we let that go, we might let go of *anything!*"

We did not agree, but nevertheless we knew that twice a week, we were to shave. Our morning in Ramsgate marked the beginning of our fourth day without a session with razors. "Move!" Anna ordered. She was the most vocal of the women, but all were determined. We shaved.

We left Ramsgate after lunch and sighted Dover at dusk.

The *Tuntsa* sailed partway into the harbor. Then her motor died. It was almost dark, so we signalled to shore with our flashlight. In Morse code, we reported that our motor had failed, and we wanted to enter. They winked back that we should wait until morning. This seemed strange. We had no choice, however, and grudgingly, we complied.

We dropped both anchors to keep the strong tide from carrying us out. Then we went to bed—all except Arvi. He puttered with the motor until midnight. To him an engine was a sensate thing—almost a person. Before I fell asleep, I heard him mutter indignantly to the inanimate troublemaker, "Pull yourself together, will you? So you're tired and getting old? Well, hold on until we get to America or . . ." the fervent pound of the hammer drowned out the rest. Next morning he said simply, "She's fixed, for now."

Then we went on deck—and saw the reason for the signals of the night before. Dover had two entrances.

The one we had approached in the dark was clogged by a tanker sunk during the war, and lying precisely where we would have tried to go through—if our motor had not failed. I felt like patting the old creature on her tin hood. Except for her contrariness, we might have joined the derelict at the bottom of the harbor.

This time the motor chugged us serenely into the proper entrance, and we spent most of the day trying to sell our knives, compasses, and other items in the city. It was as depressing as Finland. The people were shabby. Whole blocks were bombed out. Skeletal, half-fallen walls seemed like open tombs. Rubble filled great areas. Almost no reconstruction had taken place. It was as if the people had lost their will to recover. Faces were pinched, bitter, tired, and tense.

When we showed them our goods, they had no interest. "We've got no money, chum. Not much of anything else either." We couldn't sell a thing.

Anxious to secure English pounds because of their value in other countries, we decided to leave Dover and try another town. We would head south with plans to stop at a fishing village. Sailors and fishing skippers, like the dairy farmers around Amsterdam, had an immediate source of income. And compasses should appeal to them.

Our first stop at a tiny harbor village was successful. A dozen fishermen enthusiastically bought our wrist compasses. Encouraged, we decided to try selling in a bigger town—Brixham—a few miles away, on the Channel.

Once the *Tuntsa* was moored, Karl and von Haart took a bus into town, about a fifteen minute ride. There they inquired where they could find a watch repair shop, thinking that it would handle compasses and navigation apparatus as well as watches. And so it proved. When von Haart mentioned to the shopowner that we had fine wrist compasses to sell, the man ordered fifty of them.

They returned to the boat with the good news. It was a custom's violation of course, but in those days everyone smuggled almost as second nature. We would have to be careful, however. "I'll carry a suitcase," said von Haart, "to look like a traveling salesman." He brought up his old bag from the cabin. It did indeed look exactly like a realistically battered sample case.

We rode a bus to our destination and proceeded past a half-dozen boarded-up stores to the jeweler's shop. Karl and von Haart walked a bit ahead, Karl carrying the case because of von Haart's leg. The rest of us stopped at a grocery store next door and talked among ourselves, while our compass-carriers disappeared into the shop.

Within minutes, however, they came out accompanied by two men. One glance disclosed that something disasterous had happened. "What's wrong?" Arvi asked one of the two strangers.

"Smugglers," he said briefly.

This was terrible. Karl and von Haart arrested!

"May we talk to them?" I asked. "They are friends of ours."

My broken English was probably not understood, but no move was made to stop us when I addressed von Haart in Finnish. The English police have a special calm all their own. I did not realize until we started our excited conversation that probably nothing could have looked more sinister than a group of foreigners holding a voluble and incomprehensible discussion with a smuggler who had just been caught with the goods.

"What happened?" I asked Karl.

He said that the moment he opened the case, two detectives came up from behind, showed their credentials, and arrested him.

"They looked like customers and were even looking at watches when we came in," Karl said numbly. "How could I tell?"

"I trusted that storekeeper like my mother," von Haart added bitterly. "I bet he was in hot water with the police for something else and denounced us to curry favor. The scoundrel!"

Indeed, the storekeeper was guilty of what von Haart considered the one major sin. He had betrayed people who trusted him—a crime no honorable man would commit—whatever else he might do.

"All right there, chaps," the nearest plainclothesman now interrupted. "Come along now, the whole lot of you."

So we all went to the station together.

Once there, however, von Haart effected the most marvelous transformation. While the rest of us stood in uncomprehending silence, he made use of his excellent English to launch an explanation, in the course of which he brought out the worn and bulky wallet he always carried when ashore, and from among myriad old letters and soiled cards extracted Canadian citizenship papers and finally his Victoria Cross—both complete surprises to us. We had no idea he had ever been to Canada, or been cited in combat, or even that he had served in the Canadian army. The interview ended with the officers shaking hands with him.

They let us all go except Karl, who would have to stand trial the next morning. I had understood very little of von Haart's actual speech, but it seemed to have a wide range. It covered the *Tuntsa*, the American voyage, Finnish independence, and Finnish ignorance of English law, and I had the distinct impression that if it had been possible for British justice to free a man discovered in the actual act of smuggling, it would have been done for von Haart.

"He's a gentleman, that fellow," one officer said admiringly to another as we left. Apparently in England that was a sort of extra passport.

Von Haart instructed the rest of us to go back to the boat. He would stay in town and appear on Karl's behalf the following morning.

We returned reluctantly. Next day on board the *Tuntsa* Kati dabbed at red eyes throughout the whole long morning. May and Anna kept glaring at us, as if Karl's imprisonment were somehow our fault. We were all thoroughly miserable. I was sure that with von Haart to advise him, Karl would get the minimum penalty. But suppose they imposed a heavy fine? How would we pay it? Or suppose they sent him to jail?

But Karl came back in the early afternoon, unfined, unjailed, and unharmed—though considerably sobered by what had transpired. A German-speaking interpreter had been furnished him for the trial. Karl had made a von Haart-like speech about the *Tuntsa,* our need for food and fuel, and his confidence in British justice. At the end, the judge released him. Charges would not be pressed.

"I would advise you, however," the judge concluded dryly, "to leave England with all possible speed."

He also confiscated the compasses, a development which annoyed von Haart immensely.

"That's the English!" he said. "He was just—he was merciful—but, by jove, he wasn't going to have any more trouble. So now we're out of compasses. And there was a little shop around the corner from that other one where I thought. . . ."

"Never mind what you thought," said Karl. "Let's weigh anchor."

*

We set sail for Spain. Although we had scarcely enough food to last, we decided to go directly rather than follow the French-Spanish coast. In this way we would bypass the treacherous Bay of Biscay, where violent storms spring up suddenly and last for hours. Even von Haart did not care to take his amateur crew into it.

"But the way we're going is safe as a cradle," said he.

We were to find out shortly, however, that von Haart's predictions were not always infallible. That night brought a clear, brilliant sky, and von Haart kept his gaze on one particular star which he always believed predicted the next day's weather. As the moon rose, he would make his forecast. If his special star came close to the moon, a storm would mark the morrow. If it kept a respectable distance, the sailing weather would be good.

"She is behaving like a lady," he said at last. "Sometimes she snuggles right up to the moon, but tonight she is remote as a duchess. We could swim in the Atlantic, the sea will be so calm."

His star had correctly predicted our squall after leaving Amsterdam, but had overlooked entirely the gale which had crossed our path the second day out of Helsinki. This time it erred again. The next day a storm struck, and like the one off Helsinki, it reached gale force.

Later von Haart would scratch his head in meditation, when we teased him about these two false predictions. "I forgot to mention that this particular star has a blind spot when it comes to gales! She's infallible for ordinary storms, you'll see." He grinned and then added, "But I did say she was behaving like a lady last night, didn't I? Well, I suppose she was after some handsome male star and was miles from where she was supposed to be."

The storm did not turn into a life-and-death struggle for us because of two saving factors: it came up slowly giving us time to set our storm sails, and the gale-force winds struck from almost directly ahead. We were therefore able to tack back and forth close-hauled, rather than being forced to run before the wind. We also now had more experience in handling the *Tuntsa,* and she responded beautifully.

The constant tacking was exhausting work, however, particularly when the wind shifted to dead ahead.

"We had better turn back toward England," von Haart said after hours of violent battering. We came about cautiously, to prevent capsizing in the teeth of the gale. Soon afterwards, we had left the greatest force of the wind behind, although it still blew and rained fiercely.

We had sailed perhaps two hours on our new course when we sighted a pair of lights.

"A lighthouse out here?" Von Haart stared incredulously. "We must be near England, then, but I didn't think we were moving *that* fast."

Then, as we drew nearer, we saw that the lights were on an island. In order to approach it, we had to alter our course until the heavy winds were dead astern.

"It's dangerous," said von Haart. "Let's get around to the lee side."

The *Tuntsa* rolled badly, but with great care and von Haart's expert hand at the helm, Tuntsa's barking encouragement, and earthy language from some of us we reached shelter beside that miraculous piece of land. We anchored nearly three-fourths of the way around in a small bay. The *Tuntsa* was safe.

We were so exhausted, and so numbed from the cold and the wind-driven rain, that we wrapped ourselves in blankets, wet clothes and all, and fell asleep as suddenly and as heavily as if we had been drugged. Even Tuntsa curled up beside Arvi and slept as if he were dead.

At dawn we regarded our anchorage with some fear. Evidently there were tremendous tides in the area, for now, as the waters ebbed, we could see menacing rocks appearing along the shore, and projecting all around us. None of them had been visible earlier.

"Are we over shoals?" Arvi asked with misgiving. There was slack in the anchor line. We could not tell.

"We'll just have to wait for high tide. It will be all right. You'll see," von Haart said.

"In the meantime," Karl suggested, "shouldn't a couple of us row to that house on the shore and get some information?" It was still raining heavily, but the wind had gone down somewhat. Arvi and Karl together launched the dinghy.

Von Haart and I watched until the boat had made its precarious way through the choppy water and was pulled up on the beach. Then I turned to him. "I've been curious about something ever since we left Brixham. How did you happen to receive the Victoria Cross?"

A smile rippled from beneath von Haart's nose to mid-cheek and onward. He looked thoughtful. One hand stroked the worn smoothness of the wheel. "Oh, it was nothing," he said at last. "It was in Canada when the first World War broke out." He shrugged. "So naturally I joined the Canadian infantry."

"Naturally?"

"Yes, of course. When the noise stopped and Canada started to hang medals on people, I happened to be standing in the line where the Victoria Crosses were handed out."

I persisted, but it was all he would say. And it was all anyone ever got out of him. Von Haart did not care to talk about himself. He told lots of stories, but none where he appeared as hero.

Karl and Arvi returned in less than two hours. As they came on deck, they squinted toward the northeast horizon. "What do you see?" I asked.

"Nothing," Karl replied, "but the fisherman and his wife said we were within fifteen miles of Brest."

"Brest!" I exclaimed.

Brest is on the French coast just inside the arm of the Bay of Biscay, the very area we had been trying to avoid.

"It sticks out," von Haart explained. "It sort of got in our way, so to speak."

Actually, however, he was as amazed by our proximity to Brest as we were. He took off his cap and ran his hand over his head as if in wonder that it was still there. It was his gesture of amazement at the strange ways of a strange world.

It continued raining the rest of the day. Karl and Arvi had learned from the fisherman that there were no rocks directly under us, but if the wind increased we knew that we could be driven upon the shore. We had no choice, however. We could not very well put back onto the very seas which had forced us in. We dropped our extra anchor and settled down to keep sharp watch over our position. In spite of the precarious situation, the girls prepared to do laundry. Rain water was too precious to waste.

Because of our small supply of clothes, we had to wash some of them almost every day; and, in order to conserve our small supply of fresh water, we used sea water and salt-water soap except in port. This left clothes stiff, grainy, and smelling of brine. When it rained, we filled buckets and carried them below for the small pieces. Larger articles were done right on deck. Then we would all wear our soft, sweet-smelling, fresh-water-washed clothes as long as we dared—always hoping for another rain!

The next morning the wind had gone down, and we set sail for Brest. It was raining, and our voyage took all day because of the tricky bottle-neck channel from the sea to the city. We arrived in the early evening. We were exhausted, and ten minutes after the *Tuntsa* was moored, we were asleep on deck. The rain had continued until mid-afternoon, it was wretchedly damp below, and we preferred to sleep in the open rather than in the clammy air of the cabin.

We found Brest a paradoxical city. It had been heavily bombed during the war and, like Dover and so much of our own Finland, many areas had not yet been cleared of rubble. Drab, unpainted wooden barracks sheltered people who had been bombed out of their homes. Yet in spite of the desolation, the populace seemed friendly, happy, and optimistic. "We have to rebuild practically the whole city," one father of five children told us, "but today is such a beautiful day, and I'm so lucky to have all my family safe, that we're simply going to the park." This attitude was typical of the men and women we talked to. We did not know whether to attribute it to the natural light-heartedness of the French, or to the buoyancy of the people in this particular area.

Not only were the people optimistic and happy, they were eager to buy what we had to sell. Many had been frugal savers throughout the war. Now, convinced that easier times had arrived, they longed for new possessions and readily dug out their hoarded francs. In addition to much of our contraband, we sold most of our extra clothing. We would soon be in warmer climates and would not need jackets and sweaters. We even sold our second blankets.

Once we knew we had money to buy enough food, oil, and other supplies to get us to Lisbon, we proceeded to enjoy the delightful city. Anna sketched the picturesque trawlers with their nets drying along the shore. Von Haart and Lars drank deeply of the city's wonderful red wine and had long superb arguments about the universe. Arvi, Karl, and I worked aboard the *Tuntsa*—or bargained for various small supplies at ship's chandlers. Kati and May went wild just walking through the stores. They could not afford to buy of course, but the mere sight of the beautiful post-war merchandise enthralled them. May, whose father had been a wealthy lawyer, and Kati, whose family had also been well-off before the war, had grown up in comfort and luxury during their girlhood—that time before Russia overflowed our land, which to all of us who looked back seemed so remote and touched with magic. Kati's and May's delight in the displays in the stores of Brest was due to far more than appreciation of material things. All their memories, a whole way of life, seemed symbolized by the productiveness of these newly free, happy, and friendly people. Kati and May debated carefully, and finally decided that from their slender resources they would buy one small bottle of perfume.

Perfumes were amazingly cheap, and the girls went from store to store sampling each fragrance. They probably visited every perfume department in the city, and each counter was loaded with little atomizers containing samples to be sprayed on hand, arm, or behind the ear. Finally, they made their decision and bought a tiny bottle of Chanel No. 5. Then they hurried back to the *Tuntsa* to show off their purchase.

We trouped back aboard that day with the gayety of a parade. Anna brought out the phonograph and put on a dance record. Kati and Karl, May and I, Anna and Masa (Arvi did not dance) whirled happily about the deck, while Arvi took out his mouth organ, and improvised accompaniments which ran merrily up and down the scale. Even Lars did not go below to get a book but danced with May, while von Haart advanced with a low bow and invited Kati to be his partner. His battered cap and old jacket were shabby as ever, but his straight back and precise steps (specially when Arvi put on a waltz) made one think of Saint Petersburg under the Czars. To this day the sound of music makes me remember that day in Brest. I seem to smell the faint odor of Chanel No. 5 and the strong tang of salt air, and hear the sound of seabirds.

Toward the end, Anna tried to get Arvi to dance. He would not, but went on changing records and playing his mouth organ. Like May and Kati, Anna had also spent the day looking wistfully through the stores, though she had gone alone because she liked also to visit the art shops, while Kati and May did not have her interest in them. To Anna, whose years of fashion editing before the war had given her a sensitivity to clothes second only to her love of all the other beauty she tried to capture in her sketches, our life on board was particularly bleak. If the displays in the stores had been hard for Kati and May, they had been for her a veritable ordeal.

Now, after once more fruitlessly begging Arvi to dance, she suddenly cried, "Oh, why does everything have to be so dull and ugly? Why do I have to wear these . . . these. . . ." she looked down at the faded slacks she had worn all day in town, and words apparently failed her. "And now you won't even dance!" Her eyes were shining with unshed tears. She looked around wildly and saw the record player with the record still spinning its loud careless music. She seized it and hurled it at Arvi's head. Arvi ducked, and the record player, with a rasp as the needle scraped across, sailed over the rail. There was a splash, a bark from Tuntsa, silence from Arvi, and a sob from Anna as, without looking to see whether her missile had hit Arvi or what had become of it, she rushed below.

We ran to the rail. Our cherished record player had sunk in water far too deep for recovery.

Kati and May spoke almost together, "Don't blame Anna!"

May added, "I know just how she felt." She looked at the rest of us, and Arvi in particular, as if daring us to make a hostile comment.

The fact was that no one was inclined to—Arvi least of all. It was Anna who loved music more than any of us and to whom the record player had meant the most.

Few of us were immune from occasional lapses in self-control. They seldom came at sea, where we had to cooperate for the safety of the boat, but occurred usually during the first or second day in port, as a reaction from the long hours and the crowding aboard the *Tuntsa*. Even under the best of conditions, food became monotonous, personal care was difficult, someone was always stumbling into someone else, and privacy had to be forgotten. Sailing was a new, unpredictable business. Salt

spray and musty cabins and daily privation wore upon
the women. Luckily, squabbles were relieved by von
Haart's wit and Tuntsa's game-provoking antics and his
heart-melting snuggling and affection for each of us. In
a short time we would gravitate together again, united
in our mutual, burning interest to move one step closer
to our goal.

The day after the loss of the record player, Anna was
her energetic, pleasant self once more. She and Kati and
May started to clean the cabin together, and not to be
outdone, we men scrubbed the deck and then decided to
scale off the *Tuntsa's* barnacles. It cost money to have
the boat hoisted onto a trestle. Our problem was to get
the hull out of the water without having to pay. Finally
we asked the harbor captain for advice.

He told us to moor lengthwise at the shore end of the
pier and explained that the tide rose or fell ten to fifteen
feet, so the harbor bottom had been built up in steps. By
lashing the *Tuntsa* to the pier at high tide we would get
her on the top step, where at low tide the hull would be
exposed. The iron keel would rest on the cement block
bottom, and if we lashed the *Tuntsa* firmly enough she
could not careen. Then the barnacle-cleaning would be
comparatively easy.

Next morning, while we were scaling and painting,
von Haart slipped away on one of his customary excursions. He had made friends with the crew of another boat
in the harbor, and with Lars he and they began a round
of the taverns. The procedure was customary with von
Haart in every port, but this day was particularly mem-
orable because long after dark when he and Lars re-

turned to the dock, it was low tide, and with the *Tuntsa*
lashed so closely, he and Lars lost track of where the pier
ended and the boat began. After several uncertain
marches up and down, round and about, they figured
they had arrived on deck, jovially slapped each other on
the back—"G'night, ol' pal. Shleep well!"—and curled
up on the end of the pier, where we found them still
snoring in the morning.

While cleaning the *Tuntsa*, we met the crew of the
Kiruna, a Swedish ship repairing a leak sprung during
the same storm as the one which had so astonishingly
snared us off Brest. An American vessel, the S.S. *Sea
Hunter* berthed just behind the *Kiruna*. We were visiting aboard the Swedish ship when the first mate of the
Sea Hunter dropped over and introduced himself as
"Mike Kelly, U.S. citizen and world roustabout." Our
experiences and our project captured his sympathy and
he told his shipmates about us. With typical American
generosity they immediately took up a collection of
canned food, cigarettes, line—all sorts of things. But we
had to figure out how to get it all back to the *Tuntsa*.
Customs officials were constantly pacing the docks.

"We'll find a way," Mike promised. So we returned to
the *Tuntsa*, where soon we heard a loud "Hello" from the
pier.

We were being visited by two of our friends from the
Sea Hunter. We noted that they wore exceptionally
bulky windbreakers. One said loudly, "We'd like to see
what your boat looks like below deck." As soon as he was
on board, he lowered his voice and added, "We have
stuff in our pockets and under our coats. The whole crew

will be coming over in twos and threes. If anyone asks
why we're here, we're sightseeing. Take us below." For
the benefit of the watching customs officials, he waved
his arm toward the cabin.

During the next hour we ceremoniously ushered
nearly a dozen groups onto our deck and then down to
the cabin, where they left coffee, butter, canned food—
riches of all sorts. We were overwhelmed and tried in
return to show them everything on the *Tuntsa* which
might interest or amuse them—the galley, the stove, the
blowtorch, our bunks, the storage cabinets—all the rest.
Their faces showed disbelief, surprise, wonder, shock.

"Gee," exclaimed the second mate with a shake of his
head, "I don't know how you've managed to stay afloat.
And how you'll ever make it to America, I can't imagine."

His companion nodded, "Neither can I, but I sure wish
you luck."

When the last group returned to the *Sea Hunter,* they
had left behind them almost fifty cans of food and twenty
cartons of cigarettes, which in the world of postwar
shortages were worth almost their weight in gold as a
means of barter.

In spite of all this abundance, however, von Haart
felt he had to have one last visit with the cook of the *Sea
Hunter.* About eleven that night we heard von Haart and
the cook, both singing with the happiness of extreme
inebriation, fumbling with the painter of our dinghy,
which bobbed next to the pier off our port side. Somehow they got into the little boat and rowed a wiggly
course to the *Sea Hunter.* Twenty minutes later they
rowed back. We could see from deck that the bottom of

the tiny boat was covered with cans, poorly hidden under a tarpaulin. Apprehensively I looked around. Custom inspectors paced the pier throughout the night, and at that very moment, a lone figure stood at the far end of the jetty.

Von Haart and the cook, silent now, but no less fumbling, slowly began handing boxes up our rope ladder to Masa, who flattened himself against our rail to receive them while Arvi and I hurriedly shunted them toward the hatch. We kept our faces turned toward some imaginary object on the opposite side of the deck while our hands grasped cans and boxes. Below, the girls got everything out of sight as quickly as possible.

Then the lone figure on the pier turned and slowly paced toward us.

By now more than half the dinghy bottom was cleared.

But as von Haart reached for a last box, the tipsy cook took that moment to stand up and wave us a warm farewell.

He lost his balance. Von Haart swayed. The dinghy flipped over and the cook, the remaining gifts, and von Haart all tumbled into the dark water. Suddenly sober, they struggled to right the dinghy, while cans, potatoes, carrots, and loaves of bread floated away, merrily bobbing along with each swirl of the swift harbor tide.

The customs official was two ships distant when the dinghy somersaulted. I was thankful for the night and the swiftness of the current which carried the retreating food almost instantly out of sight. As the man passed, all he saw was Masa nonchalantly making fast the dinghy astern of the *Tuntsa*. The cook and von Haart had hurdled the railing with the help of the rope ladder and had already been hustled below, where they were huddled in blankets, for they were half frozen from the icy water. The rest of us sat with them, listening with bated breath to the approaching footsteps of Masa, then the steps of the man on the pier as he started his return trip from the end of the jetty.

Some one else was walking with him. They walked slowly. They stopped, seemingly at our gangplank. I heard muffled conversation.

We sat in absolute stillness. My throat was so tight, my body so tense, that I ached all over. We would be jailed, I thought miserably. It would be worse than England.

Long after I heard laughter and then dimming footsteps on the pier, my mind still refused to recognize that we were safe. At last, slowly and with great effort I relaxed. I had to start with my toes and then gradually release every muscle. Von Haart grinned triumphantly. Wrapped in his blanket, his hair plastered to his head, his high cheekbones and intrepid nose unusually prominent, he looked like an Indian chief who has just brought off a successful raid.

"Didn't I tell you it would be all right?" he said to the shivering cook.

The cook, like ourselves, was speechless.

The following day we said a grateful goodbye to our friends and set sail for La Coruna, in Spain.

We faced the Bay of Biscay before us and the hazy foreshadowing of all the ports still ahead with unshakable confidence. Von Haart's "it will be all right" was more than ever contagious. But soon all our confidence—and all his skill—would be sorely tested.

the **PULL** of the **SEA**

fog

a world all our own

we insult the Portuguese navy

Masa leaves

von Haart's windfall

a swim with the sharks

a Russian ship

we meet a whale

Fog hung over us for two timeless days. The only change from day to night was the blackening of swirling mists. We were alone, suspended in an eerie vapor which seemed to have no top or bottom, front or back. Nothing but the lapping of water against the *Tuntsa's* hull prevented us from surrendering entirely to the impression that we were afloat, not on the sea at all, but in some nameless sky.

The sails hung slack. Only the steady hum of Arvi's and Masa's motor told us we were in motion. It ran almost constantly, filling our solitary, strange world aboard the *Tuntsa* with oily, acrid exhaust fumes. For direction we had to depend entirely upon the compass.

The clearest, most tolerable area was on deck. No one

could endure the engine fumes in the cabin for more than a few minutes. Finally we turned our living schedule upside down. We slept on deck during the day when the warmth of the invisible sun made it bearable to be motionless. At night we carried the blowtorch, coffee pot, coffee, bread, cans of sardines, and a large can of drinking water on deck. That, together with the hanging meat from the mast, was our sustenance. Then all night long we would huddle together awake in our blankets and talk, or walk up and down to warm ourselves. Or we did what routine chores we could by the light of our kerosene lantern, swinging from the mast and casting ghostly luminous swirls into the protoplasmic mist enveloping us.

On the afternoon of our second day, I went over to von Haart seated at the helm and pulled up a packing crate to join him. He nodded without speaking. I looked beyond him and tried to see the water, but I could not see as far as the rail lifeline, so dense was the vapor. Above I could see the mizzen boom and only a few inches of sail.

It was unreal, yet attractive—that strange special world, populated only by ourselves.

"It's getting you, isn't it?" said von Haart placidly.

I looked at him without understanding, and he explained. "You're feeling the pull of the sea. You are— aren't you?"

"Yes," I said, and we both sat savoring the silence and our isolation.

I was aware suddenly that my senses—all of them— had grown uncannily alert. War had made me keenly conscious of surroundings—had made me listen, look, smell, touch carefully—simply in order to keep alive. But this was an entirely different sort of awareness. I felt completely safe—in a very strange way.

I considered the significance of smells: the dry wood of the cabin; the wet oakumed planking of the deck; the salty, fibrous odor of rigging and sails—each distinctive.

I went over my memories of ports. Each memory was different. Visby had a tourist air—an odor of new shoe leather, an impression of crowding figures. Dover reeked of coal and oil—the fuel of the big ships. Ostende smelled of drying shrimp and sole; Thyboron, of freshly-caught cod and mackerel.

Even the sea had its special pungencies, all individual —heavy; or sharp and salty; or sour and full of sea-vegetation; or smelling of clams and mudflats at low tide.

But this was only a part. No matter in what port we anchored, there were the great ships perpetually taking on and unloading cargo. There was the aroma of coffee, spices, bananas, mahogany logs, sugar . . . one suddenly began to wonder where they came from, and where they were headed, and how it looked there. I found myself wanting to see those lands.

I glanced at von Haart. He was watching my face.

I had a strange, unexpected longing—to voyage indefinitely, to make new friends forever, to see a line of new places which would never end. I realized quite suddenly that, for this moment at least, only part of me still wanted to go to America. The rest of me wanted to voyage—just to voyage—forever.

I shook my head as one does coming out of deep water.

Impossible thoughts! Not go to America? Of course I would go to America! Hadn't we planned for years? Was I not bringing true my father's dream? My son, his grandson, would grow up there.

I, a wanderer?

Impossible! I had May, and Eero.

I looked at von Haart almost indignantly, as if he had somehow deliberately tempted me to a sort of treason.

Arvi came over to us. "We were talking about the sea and its effect," I said.

"What effect?" He leaned against the mast and looked down at me. I tried to explain what von Haart meant by the "pull of the sea."

He gave me a longer look. "You too, eh?" he said at last.

"You know," he went on, "for me it's been like being born again. I feel as if a whole new life stretches ahead out there." He nodded at the mist. (For Arvi, usually so taciturn, it was an incredible monologue. I could only stare, as he a moment earlier had stared at me.) "A new life," he said. "And you can do anything with it, anything you please."

We were all silent, filled with our individual yet shared meditation.

I wondered if some of our crew would find the "pull of the sea" so overpowering that they would never again be able to settle down. I had swayed for a moment. As for von Haart, he had long ago made his decision.

But the next morning, a brisk wind lifted the fog, and we sighted a dim mass in the far distance: the Spanish coast.

According to our calculations, La Coruna was dead ahead. We had intended stopping there, but after our fog-bound drift, the fine wind was too exciting. We sailed on to Lisbon. As we passed La Coruna, we saw an awe-inspiring sight—the great Hercules Tower whose very age is unknown, except that it dates from remotest antiquity. The whole coast around La Coruna is incredibly ancient. It was known to the Phoenicians some three thousand years ago. Today the great tower remains. Once a fortification, it now serves peacefully as a lighthouse. We sailed by in silence, wondering how many seafarers, in boats even more primitive than ours, had looked up at those weathered stones. A mile north in the curve of the peninsula was the ancient harbor, an ugly brown patch of rocks where white surf was breaking heavily.

The tide was ebbing, as in mid-morning we approached Lisbon, and we had to use the motor. Our progress up the seven-mile stretch of bay to the city was so slow that we barely moved. It was nightfall before we found an entrance. There were few lights, and except for the dim red and green glow of our port and starboard lanterns both the still water under us and the silent darkness ahead were like ink. Finally a great shape loomed before us, and dimly we made out that it was an immense battleship. Afraid to go farther in the blackness, we moored the little *Tuntsa* humbly to the battleship's anchor buoy. But at once sailors came to the rail above, and began to shout. I could not guess whether we were offending their sense of propriety, or breaking naval regulations, or whether we just seemed ridiculous. In any case, it was clear we were not wanted. We cast off and moved on gingerly until we found a pier. Masa tossed out the lines, and Lars looped the *Tuntsa* securely to a piling.

Almost immediately, however, four uniformed men appeared and began a furious diatribe in Portuguese. We could not understand.

"What's the matter?" Masa asked, bewildered.

A mixture of Portuguese, Spanish, German, and sign language finally got it across to us that we had blundered into Portugal's naval harbor and were subject to a large fine. Karl, who spoke the best Spanish, finally convinced them that: (1) we were not spies; and (2) we had come into the harbor by error. Possibly however, the most important point of all was that: (3) we had no money. Once the officers understood this, their attitude changed. People without money—any money at all—are people without significance. They cannot even be spies. They are—nothing.

So we were let go, and we anchored in the harbor, where the following morning after some delay, we were allowed to go ashore, and by the mercy of some unknown official no fine was inflicted. We could not have paid it anyhow, but there was always the jail!

*

Lisbon is a beautiful city. Pink, blue, green, and yellow adobe houses rise above the blue water in a great mosaic of color. Red-tiled roofs jigsaw up narrow, crooked, steep streets behind the waterfront.

But Lisbon was marked for us by a major disaster. Masa left us.

Like many men of superabundant energy, Masa's temperament led him from peaks of excitement and enthusiasm into moods of deep depression. And at Lisbon our situation was enough to depress anyone, regardless of temperament. We could not sell any of our merchandise, and Karl and I spent all of a first exhausting ten hour day trying to interest sailors in our remaining compasses. Then I attempted to sell a German pistol, a souvenir of the war, but no one wanted that either. At last May insisted that I take one of her rings. It did sell—but for one tenth its value, and I was ashamed to go back and tell her how little it had brought.

"Never mind," she said. "You'll have better luck tomorrow. It will be all right, you'll see."

I told her wearily, "Now we all sound like von Haart!" But I don't think I ever felt more tenderness toward her than in such moments. May and I had always had a good marriage, as had Kati and Karl; and for us as couples the voyage was deepening and strengthening the bonds already existing. It was becoming an affection and an understanding so deep that May and I, Karl and Kati, had hardly to speak to understand one another.

But Masa had no such help. He and Arvi had nursed our miserable engine through long days and nights, and now it critically needed parts we had no money to buy. Furthermore, our fuel was almost gone, and our oil was low. Masa became more and more quiet as each day passed, and we sold nothing. His enthusiasm, energy, talkativeness—all were suspended. It was rather like having a merry-go-round pony stopped in mid air by an electrical short-circuit. Finally one day he returned from a trip to town and told us that he was leaving. He had signed on a Dutch freighter to Panama. From there he expected to get a ship bound for the United States and then work until he had saved enough money to send for his family.

"I just can't go on with the *Tuntsa,*" Masa said, running his hands through his red hair and looking at Arvi unhappily, and then at us. "You're wonderful—all of you. But I can't go on with it any more."

"All right!" said Arvi. "If you're sure you want to leave, go ahead and leave." He spoke stiffly. The friendship between him and Masa had been close.

"I wish you would all give it up!" Masa blurted. "It's hopeless now—you must realize that yourselves. You'll never make it."

"We've got to go on," said Karl simply. "There's no choice."

For us that was true. Lars and von Haart could sign up on a ship, as Masa had done. But Karl, Arvi, and I, with wives, could not even get aboard. And with only sailors passports, we would not be able to get the papers needed for legitimate passage on a regular steamer, even if we could somehow earn the fare. Masa's wife was back in Finland and had a job she could live on. Our wives were with us and would suffer our fate, whatever it might be.

Masa left the next day. When the moment of actual parting came, we could sense his regrets, but he had made his decision and clearly intended to stick with it. He shook hands hastily, not looking at us, and particularly not at Arvi.

"I'm sorry. I wish you luck," he said, and was gone.

Karl, Arvi, and I watched him nearly sprint the length of the pier. I remembered ruefully that it was Masa who had first had the idea we could sail to America. Now he was giving up. Was he right? Was it indeed hopeless, as he said? There seemed good reason to suppose that he was.

Lars and von Haart had already gone off for one of their days ashore, but so far in Lisbon von Haart's rounds and his stories of our expedition had brought no gifts at all.

"Von Haart and Lars may leave too," I said.

Arvi shook his head. "Von Haart won't. I'm sure of it."

"We've become his *noblesse oblige*," said Karl. "As for Lars, he won't leave von Haart."

That afternoon von Haart again returned empty-handed. All he had was a five-gallon jug of cheap wine from a group of sailors who had enjoyed several hours of his sea stories. He shared it with the rest of us—an enormous generosity, for he could have downed it all himself in a space of minutes.

"Let's set sail," he said. "Fuel or no fuel, let's get out of this place."

"Do you think we should try it?" May asked dubiously. Kati looked frightened. Anna was scowling.

"It will be all right. You'll see," said von Haart.

Anna stalked below in eloquent silence.

Before leaving we decided to check a last time for mail. We could not risk missing any of the precious letters following us from home. But the post office was some distance away. And we had no money for streetcar fare. But von Haart had a plan. And although Karl, Arvi and I were skeptical, we followed him.

As a streetcar came toward us, von Haart instructed us. "See where the conductor is; then get on at the opposite end."

We did so, and while the conductor was moving through the crowded car collecting fares, it progressed several blocks.

Finally the conductor arrived at where we stood. Von Haart looked at him. "Fares, please," the conductor said.

"We don't have any money," von Haart replied.

"Then get off!" the conductor replied, outraged by these stupid foreigners. "Get off at the very next stop!"

Von Haart's plan worked admirably. Six streetcars and six "get off's" later, we reached the post office.

During our on-again, off-again progress through the city, Arvi spoke to Karl about the possibility of selling the *Tuntsa*. It was impossible of course, because stranded in Lisbon we could neither have earned enough money to go on, nor even to get home. But the very mention of such a thought made von Haart stare at us with stricken eyes. To him, selling the *Tuntsa* would have been the equivalent of selling one of her crew.

Lars said loyally, "It's impossible for foreigners to get working papers in Portugal anyhow. I've read that lots of times."

At the post office von Haart took a list of our names over to the clerk and waited for the man to check mail being kept to be picked up. Only one letter was handed to him. It was registered and postmarked from Switzerland. And, oddly, it was addressed to von Haart, who never bothered to write to anyone, and of us all was the only one who did not receive and devour news from home.

"Who knows I'm here?" he muttered to us as he produced his identification papers for the clerk. We sat on a bench while he opened the envelope. Inside was a draft for fifteen hundred Swiss francs* made out to Otto Alexander von Haart. He looked bewildered.

Then he read the accompanying note. "Hmmm . . ." he murmured. He explained to us that he had a distant cousin with exactly the same name, for whom the check was apparently intended. There were von Haarts scattered all about Europe of course, for it was one of the oldest and most famous families. Even so, it was certainly a coincidence that von Haart's cousin should also be about to arrive in Lisbon, and it was quite impossible to convince von Haart that the coincidence did not represent divine Providence.

"Cousin Otto doesn't need money," he said. "We do. Destiny has guided us. And when I think I almost lost faith!" Von Haart shook his head in self-reproach.

"Don't be silly!" Karl exclaimed. "Nothing guided you. It's an accident. That's not your money."

But von Haart simply got up and started briskly down

---

* Approximately $350.

the street. We looked at one another, spread our hands helplessly, and followed.

He entered the first marine supply store and ordered all the gas, oil and general supplies we needed, then bought a case of the best cognac and several boxes of fine cigars.

That done, he said thoughtfully, "Now I must be polite" and sent wire to Switzerland thanking his cousin's parents, and requesting twenty pounds in English money to be sent to Otto Alexander von Haart at Gibraltar, our next port of call. Then he signed his name. Not to make the most of such an opportunity, he said, would be insolence to the powers above.

We left Lisbon that afternoon, and since von Haart had been so generous, we told him it was all right to drink on board. He was drunk all the five days to Gibraltar.

We had good weather, but it was eerie to be sailing with him. He drank slowly, quietly, continuously, almost solemnly until he fell into unconsciousness. Then he would wake and start again. We watched with sadness, disquiet, and a sort of awe. There was no singing or joking or story-telling as there was during his visits ashore. The unwonted opportunity of five whole days with a case of brandy was clearly an important matter, not to be wasted. Once I went below to see how he was, and he looked up at me seriously. Apparently he wanted to explain.

"You know why I drink, Teppo? It's not to get away from anything, but to go toward something. Drink opens your heart. You love your fellow men, because you see them not as they are, but as they could be. Man is immortal, Teppo. God is good. The universe is good. If man had not turned his planet into a hell which is tightening down harder on all of us every day, we would live in the paradise God created. Look at the sea sometime when you get up in the morning, and it will tell you that. Perfect peace *could* exist—perfect understanding, perfect love. That's what I see when I drink. The world as it is falls away, and the world as it could be begins. I see it all so clearly. God, Teppo," he said slowly. "Merciful God. Can you understand?"

"Yes, von Haart," I said. I went on deck.

I did understand—while he was talking to me. And later, sometimes, I have felt I understood. But when I emerged into the open air, the understanding I was carrying with me at that moment suddenly overturned. Either von Haart's thinking or the entire world was upside down. And surely it could not be the world?

There was a steady breeze, and as usual when the wind was good we reefed our sails at dusk—with special caution now because we knew we could not rouse von Haart. The *Tuntsa* seemed a strange caravansary— carrying the unconscious von Haart and his strange vision of paradise and us with our dreams of new life. Karl and Arvi, Lars and I in alternate watches were on deck all night. It was pitch black except for occasional phosphorescence. Spray flew through the red and green glow of our running lights. There was no sound but the rush of water past the hull, the hum of the wind in the rig-

ging, and the occasional rattle of gear as we came about
or altered our point of sailing. We missed Masa. Without
his constant talk and brisk energy, we felt even more the
"pull of the sea."

It was during this part of the voyage that we had our
first brush with sharks. Ever since leaving Helsinki we
had longed to swim off the boat in fine weather. Von
Haart had never permitted it.

"There are sharks even if you don't see them," he said.
"They're in league with the devil. They know the minute
you plunge in, and they come from all over."

But now von Haart was below, and more than ever our
parched bodies ached for the consolation of being en-
folded by the clear blue water. No morning ever looked
more innocent. The sky was an angelic blue with
shredded clouds like lace. And on board we could take
nothing but saltwater sponge baths from a tiny basin.

Anna sat moodily by the rail. "Let's have a swim," she
begged Arvi.

Since the incident with the record player, Arvi had
taken pains to be more attentive to Anna's moods.

"What harm can it do?" he said to Karl. "I'll stay on
board and keep watch."

So in the spirit of children out of school we tiptoed
past the sleeping von Haart and got into our bathing
suits.

"It's a scientific fact that sharks never attack on the
open sea," Lars told us. "It's only in harbors, or where
there's been garbage."

"There's been garbage all over the Atlantic," said
Arvi a little tartly. He missed Masa, and toward Lars he

seemed to have taken on some of Masa's sharpness of tongue.

"Never mind," said Karl peaceably. "We haven't thrown over any today anyhow."

Arvi let down the rope ladder and remained at the helm. The rest of us had a frolic in the water, with the *Tuntsa* sailing around us.

Then there was a cry from Arvi.

I turned to look where he was pointing. There was no mistaking the thin gray sliver with its ugly peak suddenly circling us. And Kati, our weakest swimmer, was farthest from the boat.

Arvi brought the *Tuntsa* about, and in a din of flapping canvas picked us up—all but Kati and Karl. He had swum to her and was splashing around like six people to frighten the creature off. Arvi threw Kati a line, and Lars and I pulled it in hand over hand, with Kati in the curve of Karl's arm as both clung to the end. Karl pushed her ahead of him up the ladder, and in seconds they stood white-faced and shaking on deck. I was boiling with irrational fury and went below for my German pistol. I fired twice, and after the second shot saw a small hole in the fin, like a round bubble with sky and water on the other side. I fired frenziedly then and must have scored a direct hit, for the water suddenly roiled. Our shark was being attacked by another, attracted perhaps as much by the commotion as by blood.

Arvi put the *Tuntsa* back on course, and we left the struggle behind, but I counted four separate fins before we could no longer make them out—while Kati, who had been closest to danger, assured us solemnly that she had counted six, even while she was still in the water.

"It was full of them," she said shuddering. "Just full of them!"

Through it all von Haart serenely slept. We never told him.

❋

It was dusk when we finished our thirty-mile course through the Strait and passed by the Rock of Gibraltar. As we entered the harbor, we heard the silvery sound of a bugle and watched the British flag being lowered. To the west we could see the bright lights of the city. But we were too tired to go ashore. Anna and Arvi, Karl and Kati, May and I, and Lars all went to our bunks and slept like mummies until daybreak.

Von Haart had finished the brandy. Now he gradually became sober, and as in almost every port, he soon met someone he knew. Our second day in Gibraltar, he greeted an old friend, an English ship chandler named Joe. They exchanged enthusiastic back slaps and salty language; and he, Lars, and the chandler made the usual tour. At the end of it Joe insisted that we use a rowboat of his instead of our own little dinghy while we were in port.

"You'll drown yourselves in that thing," he told us.

"We haven't yet," replied von Haart cheerfully.

We accepted the loan gladly, however, and the next night we had all returned to the *Tuntsa* after an evening in town and had just stepped on deck when we heard a hail from the pier.

Three strangers stood there.

"What do you want?" Karl called.

They wanted a lift back to their ship which, they told us in English, was "anchored about a mile offshore."

"Why not?" I decided. I was feeling expansive after the dinner to which von Haart's friend Joe had treated us. It seemed only right that we should be generous too.

My passengers were a chief engineer, a first and second mate. There was no mark of nationality I recognized. I assumed they belonged to an English merchantman, since that was the language they used. I was far too unfamiliar with English myself then to know whether it was being fluently spoken or not. I could barely make out a few words.

Then as we neared the ship I was deeply shocked. It was a Russian tanker!

The chief engineer must have seen my look. There is something about fear. It can almost be smelled. Russians get to be particularly good at detecting it, because it is an emotion they so frequently evoke—simply by being Russian.

"Where are you from?" he asked with sudden curiosity.

"O-oh, I'm Portuguese—a Portuguese sailor," I said. With my deep tan and black eyes I hoped I could pass.

They invited me on board for coffee and sandwiches.

I hesitated. It did not seem a good idea. On the other hand there was something about going boldly on board a Soviet ship and sitting around with a Russian crew which I found immensely attractive. What fun to go into the lion's mouth and come out to tell about it!

I accepted.

But as I got on deck and was looking curiously around (it seemed to me a sloppy ship—there were coils of line, buckets, paint, even drying clothes) I noticed also that the rowboat looked poorly secured and I mentioned to the engineer that it was not mine, and that the water was choppy.

"Okay, okay," he said reassuringly in English. He ordered one of the seamen to watch and see that it did not drift off.

With this assurance, I went below and was enjoying excellent coffee in the galley—an old-fashioned, chromeless area with large wooden cabinets—when the seaman suddenly rushed in. "The boat's gone!" he exclaimed.

"Gone!" I cried. I rushed to the deck. The rowboat was adrift and already some fifty yards away.

I stared, scarcely believing the full horror of the disaster. Then I started to take off my shoes and shirt.

The chief engineer seized my arm. "You can't do it. The sea is too rough!"

I continued peeling off my clothes. When he saw I still meant to try, he said firmly, "We throw our garbage over. There are sharks."

I changed my mind then. I remembered our experience of the other day. Better a Russian tanker than being eaten alive.

The three men went to the captain for permission to lower one of their lifeboats and go after mine for me. Russian captains, however, are not apt to be moved by the plight of stray Portuguese fishermen. And they are strictly responsible for all equipment. He refused at once—as I had thought he would.

All I could do was hope that morning would bring help. The first mate gave me a bunk, but I was in no state for sleep. Neither did I dare draw more attention to myself by going on deck and roaming about in the dark. I sat on the edge of my bunk and decided that if I felt the ship commence to move I would rush up and throw myself into the water—sharks or no sharks. The crew was waiting for orders to sail. They already had steam up when I came aboard. I was panic-stricken. My best chance of escape was to hope she would remain anchored until dawn, when I might be able to get a ride on one of the fishing boats coming into the harbor. If only she did not get her sailing orders before then!

With the first ray of light I was on deck waving frantically to fishing boats. They were too far away. A wave from a large ship simply seems companionable. It does not occur to passers-by that anything is wanted. The fishermen cheerfully waved back—and continued on their way.

I became more and more desperate. The Russian sailors were rising and bustling about. So far they had paid little attention to me—just nodded as they went down to the galley or to their posts.

Seven o'clock. Eight. Nine. No boats came near enough to hear my shouts.

Then, at five minutes before ten, a trawler appeared. I called frantically, and the helmsman heard. The deck of the Soviet ship had been deserted when I called, but now a crewman approached, and I wondered if for some capricious reason (the Rusisans can always find one) I would now not be allowed to leave at all. As the crewman came nearer to where I stood at the rail, I turned

my back on the approaching boat and pretended simply
to be admiring the fine morning. The crewman nodded
to me. I nodded back, my chest so taut that I felt as if I
might suffocate.

The crewman went below.

I let out a sigh of agonized relief and turned back to
the rail. The trawler was now almost below me.

"Can you take me to the pier?" I cried in English.

Even as I spoke, I jumped overboard. I swam clumsily, fully clothed, to the trawler.

I didn't look back at the Russian tanker until we were
well away. No one had come to the rail. I was safe.

As I stepped onto the pier and thanked the fishermen,
Arvi saw me from the *Tuntsa* and picked me up in the
dinghy. On the deck of the *Tuntsa,* the others crowded
around me. Tuntsa jumped into my arms and licked my
face. Kati's eyes were red, and so were May's. Lars
grinned broadly, Karl shook my hand, and Anna
pounded me happily on the back.

"What happened? Where were you?" demanded
May.

After I told my story, I gave von Haart a worried look.
"Now, how on earth can we ever pay for the rowboat?"

He shook his head. "Don't worry about *that!* The thing
is that *you* are safe. The women have been wild with
worry. May thought you had drowned. If she had known
you were on a Soviet ship, she would have gone crazy.
Just thank your guardian angel that you got back. I'll
attend to the rowboat."

He left for shore immediately. By the time he returned
that afternoon, everything was settled.

He had gone to Joe. He and the English chandler immediately rowed together out to the Russian tanker, where Joe spoke heatedly to the captain. An established citizen of Gibraltar, with friends ashore who knew where he had gone, he was in quite a different position from the unknown wandering sailor of the night before. The captain agreed almost at once to pay for the lost boat.

The following morning, von Haart, who had been indefatigably checking the post office, found a draft for twenty English pounds duly forwarded from the parents of his rich cousin. He came back jubilantly, and he was determined to leave at once. We felt dubious about the whole matter, but there was little we could do. We were ready to sail in any case. So we weighed anchor and left Gibraltar that same afternoon. Our course was southwesterly, down the African coast—a passage which was to be one of danger and indecision.

Dangerous because the entire African coast was one long strip of jagged rock, unrelieved by lighthouses; indecisive because we would soon approach Casablanca— and we could not make up our minds whether or not to stop.

Casablanca, being one of the world's greatest black market centers, was certainly no place for impoverished voyagers to buy supplies. On the other hand, perhaps our own goods would be specially saleable. We argued back and forth.

Lars had now found an unabridged encyclopedia, twelve volumes, in a shop in Gibraltar and was devouring them voraciously.

" 'Casablanca,' " he read aloud, "hmm . . . 'one of the

most colorful of all Moorish ports' . . . 'built by the Portuguese in 1468' . . . 'wool and grain center for Morocco'
. . . 'anchorage five to six fathoms. . . .' " He followed us
about, reading diligently.

I don't think he particularly cared whether or not we
made the stop. Casablanca was more vivid to him in the
book anyhow. But he enjoyed instructing us. And with
Masa gone, there was no one to force him to keep quiet.
One by one we finally fled, leaving him in the cabin
alone, reading, and muttering bits of information into
space.

Meanwhile, the *Tuntsa* had found a playmate—a not
too welcome one to us. We gathered at the rail to watch
our first whale. It was a blue, rubbery-looking creature,
rather small compared to those which we would see later
—this one was a mere twenty feet or so. The white hull
of the *Tuntsa* seemed to intrigue him so much that we
began to wonder if he perhaps mistook her for an albino
lady of his own species. He would surface with a great
swoosh of water from his shiny rounded back, look up
coyly from one round eye, blow and harrumph out of the
spout on his round head (he was round all over—if he
had been smaller, he might have been called "cute") and
disappear with a lively twist of his flukes.

"He's doing a rhumba," said May.

Von Haart was not amused, however, by the antics of
our undersea visitor. "If he takes it into his head to
scratch his back on the keel, that will be the end of us,"
he said grimly.

Just then the blue snout, round eye, rounded back,
flirtatious flukes, appeared on the other side within three

or four feet of where we stood. And we felt a distinct heave in the deck beneath our feet. Von Haart gripped the rail and said nothing.

Karl wiped his forehead.

The creature surfaced again, this time wearing a geyser of water like a small festive fountain.

"Go away!" shouted Karl, waving his arms and staring down into one round eye, which seemed to look back merrily. "Get out of here! Go!"

Anna giggled.

"Don't talk to him!" Kati begged earnestly. "He thinks we want to play."

Lars then came on deck with his encyclopedia and added to the tension by reading to us out loud about whales. "One of the most interesting of all animals . . . erroneous to suppose it a fish . . . a mammal like a cow or a horse. . . ."

"Not like any cow I ever knew," said Anna.

Then, to our immense relief, our rubbery friend began to lose interest. Perhaps, I thought, it was Lars' reading, and he was as bored as we. In any case, we left him behind, frolicking still and heaving up his great back in curving humps, as if saying farewell.

"I need a drink," said von Haart, and looked at us bitterly. The brandy was gone now, and we had put him back on his promise of sobriety while at sea.

As the *Tuntsa* sailed on we saw a wreck. A cargo ship had smashed against the cliffs—probably not long ago, for her stern section was still intact. As we passed, we heard the steady crunch of her hull against the wall of rock. Blended with the pounding of breakers, the sound was hollow and deep, like the echo of a shout down a deep well. We shivered as we came abreast of the gaping hole torn into her forward hull, and we sailed swiftly by, as if the sight might have some magnetic power.

Our third day out of Gibraltar was uneventful—beautiful weather with a fine wind. We took to play-acting among ourselves. Anna began it, speaking to Lars as "Mr. Professor," while Lars called her "Manager of the Royal Household." Soon we all took it up, saying: "Mr. Karl!" "Messrs. von Haart and Arvi, please!" "Mesdames May and Kati!"—all with appropriate bows and flourishes. Only Tuntsa did not enjoy the game. He could always sense when anyone made fun of him, and now when he would hear "Mr. Tuntsa" or "Mr. Canine," he would raise his nose and leave our presence with offended dignity.

The game grew, however, and became a pleasant relief in the never-ending grind of labor necessary to keep the *Tuntsa* shipshape and efficient. We began to devise special titles for every job and treat each one as if it were a special honor. If I was to scrub the deck, I was called Manager of the Deck Cleaning Department. Von Haart would say with a poker face, "We don't demand . . . we don't ask that you do this . . . but as Manager of the Deck Cleaning Department, it seems to us that you should scrub the deck today." And somehow, it was less onerous. Anna was Royal Housekeeper; Kati became Master Chef; May, President of the Dishes; Karl, Supreme Commander of Sails; von Haart, Commander-in-Chief of The Helm; Lars, Professor of Knowledge and Self-Improvement; Arvi, Captain of Engine Repairing;

and Tuntsa, Master of Ceremonies and Supreme Entertainer to the Royal Household. Titles were exchanged or assigned according to whim, need, or who appeared first after a task presented itself. This practice was to continue throughout the voyage.

At meals, over our salt pork, sardines, potatoes, or rice, the game took another form. As we sat down to our rationed portions of uninteresting food, we would exchange remarks on the "excellent steak" or "fine caviar" or "splendid pastry." When we tired of this, we would guess what native specialties we could afford in our next port, or what we would order for our delicious first meal in America. The notion that a delightful, luxurious dinner might be just ahead took the edge off one of our greatest trials—the monotonous, limited food supply; just as the game of giving one another ceremonious titles made it more bearable to be penniless, rootless nobodies, without prospects or significance, or even a home, except for the cramped little *Tuntsa*.

It would not always be so—that was what our games said to us.

On the morning of the fourth day we sighted Casablanca. Graceful spires of purest white rose on a hill above a light mist clinging to brilliantly blue water. It seemed a place of most enchanting mystery. We looked at one another, and Kati put her hand on Karl's arm.

"Please—let's take just one look!"

And so we decided to stop—not for the sake of what we might be able to sell, or find to buy for our voyage, but simply because it was an exquisite sight, and we could not resist its beauty.

the **AFRICAN COAST**

Casablanca

von Haart takes French leave

a palace in ruins

von Haart's return

the Tuntsa *is crippled*

bargain day in Safi

the amorous fish canner

our mast is sold

we sail on

The waterfront of Casablanca is almost unimaginable for anyone who has not seen it. The allure of the city viewed from the harbor vanishes as soon as one steps ashore, for the harbor area is part of the Arab quarter and is completely cut off by high walls and a maze of tortuous alleys which separate it from the gleaming white buildings we had glimpsed from the *Tuntsa*.

By the waterfront little arches lead into dirty alleys, which end in more arches—then still more cobbled alleys, all enclosed by high walls of weathered crumbling stone and all littered from wall to wall with refuse, alive with flies in the tropical sun.

And the children! Ragged, sharp-featured, sharp-eyed Arab children swarm like the flies. They gather around

each traveller to hold out pitifully thin arms and cry,
"Baksheesh! Baksheesh!"—a shrill cacophony of begging
childish trebles more like the wailing of wild birds than
human voices.

A little boy about nine held out a tiny puppy to Kati.
I saw that the puppy was blind. A second glance made
my heart contract, for the child was blind also—looking
up with eyes perfectly white in his dark pinched face.
"Buy," he begged, holding out his puppy, a limp little
wad of bones barely alive. "Buy."

Kati's eyes filled with tears. She held out her hands
helplessly to tell the children we had no money.

Yet they would not leave us.

Here were people whose monstrous poverty made
even the *Tuntsa's* shabby crew look affluent.

All along the wharf were peddlers. Their loose flowing
robes and bearded faces made me think of illustrations
from a book of bible stories I had had as a boy. These
were not shepherds, however, but merchants. Rugs,
brasswork, leather—every conceivable type of shoddy
product of hand labor was for sale. Apparently we were
mistaken for English sailors, for an old man with a tray
of leather bedroom slippers kept following us and crying, "No charge-a for look! No charge-a for look!"

But we did not dare look. Compassion would have inspired us to buy everything on his tray. And we knew we
must not spend any of our small remaining funds so
foolishly.

The walled alleys were actually narrow streets between tenements whose balconies nearly touched overhead. There was not a blade of vegetation anywhere,

and all along were small shops with dark interiors like little caves. As we went farther from the waterfront, we saw that there was actually merchandise of exquisite quality—porcelains, brocades, and oddly carved silver.

Karl and I had brought with us some of our compasses, and we tried to sell them in several of these more prosperous places. No one was even remotely interested. Finally an ornate, silver-mounted, antique hand gun of my father's attracted the cupidity of a gesticulating shopkeeper. Excited by the only sign of a sale we had seen so far, Karl and I began to bargain eagerly. I finally sold it for a thousand Moroccan francs. In American money it was about two dollars.

We gave up then, and surrendered to the impulse simply to see the contradictions of this fantastic city. We visited the European quarter—immaculate white houses with walled gardens and a profusion of well-watered and manicured bloom visible through securely locked grilles. We also saw—from afar, for we dared not go into it— the Arab shanty town sprawling down one side of a hill: shelters made of old boxes, fragments of timber, rusty corrugated iron; and swarming with hooded human creatures whose misery made the waterfront quarter seem prosperous by contrast. Finally, footsore and heartsick, we went back to the *Tuntsa*, determined to weigh anchor and leave as soon as possible.

✿

But we went ashore again that evening, and while von Haart and Lars visited the taverns, Karl and Kati, Arvi and Anna, May and I went into a native café. There were quite a few tourists, including some whose expensive clothes showed that they must be off a smart ship or had come from the French quarter to take guests slumming. May, Kati, and particularly Anna looked at the fashionably dressed women and self-consciously smoothed down their own shabby dresses, which they had clumsily pressed with our blowtorch-heated iron. We ordered glasses of cheap wine and sat at an inconspicuous corner table to watch the entertainment. It consisted entirely of a succession of scantily clad, solo dancers—"daughters of the Nile," as they are called along that coast—creatures of exotic reputation, said to be mysterious *filles de joie,* exquisitely trained initiates of erotica as well as of the dance. Almost nude, except for a trailing head veil, and a transparent skirt belted as low as possible, the dancer would circle close to the spectators and rotate her hips in such studied and difficult gyrations that the sensuality of the motion seemed to be disappearing into gymnastics. At intervals the dancer would also move her head, face stiff and eyes front, with a dislocating sideways jerk—almost as if the head were taken off, set four inches over toward one shoulder, then four inches toward the other shoulder, then center again, at which time an unprepared spectator would be amazed to find it still attached to the neck. I could see that the hip exercises might be expected to produce erotic feelings in the audience, but what effect was supposed to be achieved by dislocating the head, I simply could not imagine. The music was a slow, mournful, discordant wail of reeds and strings. To the Arabs sitting about and staring from under their burnooses, the spectacle was no doubt delightfully suggestive, but our little group of Finns seemed to miss its charm. We were quite aware that we were in one of the world's most exotic ports and that we ought to feel something, but the remark I remember best is May's. "Like the American cinema," she murmured to me.

No doubt that was the trouble: while the Arabs mentally related the scene to imaginary harem debauches or the houris of Paradise, we had the wrong frame of reference. It sometimes seems to me that the cinema has rather taken the flavor out of travel.

Kati touched my arm. "Look," she said.

In a corner against the wall was a little girl of six or seven, dressed in a shabby loose garment. Gazing intensely at the dancer, the child was moving her own head to one side, then to the other. She could do it, too.

"Let's go," said May suddenly.

We left.

Meanwhile von Haart and the faithful Lars were making their usual rounds. By now of course von Haart had another objective on these expeditions besides filling up with the alcohol without whose periodic intake at each port he could not have gone on. The gifts and kindness of our early hosts at Visby and Helsingborg, the generosity of the American sailors at Brest, and the interest in our voyage of almost everyone we met, had long since cast von Haart in the habitual role of gift-getter; and no head of a foundation or fund-raising university president ever canvassed more energetically than our navigator when he was exerting his talents on behalf of our

shabby little expedition. In every bar he would tell the
ever-lengthening story of our adventures, our goal of
reaching America, our lack of money and indeed of everything except determination, and then would finish
with fond and sincerely grateful reminiscences of how
he and the American cook had smuggled the canned
goods aboard the *Tuntsa* under the noses of the French
customs officials at Brest.

Von Haart was an inimitable story-teller. His audience
would soon be roaring with laughter. He could count on
the fact that under their rough exteriors, they were usually warm and sympathetic people. That was, in fact,
the only kind he liked and the only kind he drank with.
They seemed to gravitate to him, and he to them, by a
sort of inherent recognition. In every such group, too,
he could rely upon national pride. Had the Americans
indeed done so much to help the *Tuntsa?*—whatever
nationality the listener belonged to, he was apt to feel a
competitive challenge.

In Casablanca it was the Swedes. With lavish generosity, the captain and crew of a Swedish vessel restocked
our depleted larder. They moved whole crates of stores
across the harbor to us, in spite of customs inspectors on
their very decks. There were three of these inspectors.
While the crates of the generous donors to the *Tuntsa's*
expedition were being lowered over the sides, one inspector was kept in conversation with the captain in his
cabin, the second was constantly being sent for to check
some item of cargo below, and the third (for it was impossible to get them all off deck at once) was assigned to
von Haart, who in his fluent French drew attention to

sights on shore or to a supposedly unique and colorful fish, which von Haart would pretend to spot just as a crate was rushed up and dropped over the other side of the ship to Lars, Arvi, and me waiting in one of the ship's boats with some of the crew.

It was tense work and, even with von Haart's ingenuity, it was a miracle no one was caught. Afterwards von Haart went ashore to celebrate. We had no objection, for he deserved his reward, but when he continued to celebrate for three days in a row, the crew of the *Tuntsa*, provisioned and ready, began to feel growing impatience. We all hated Casablanca.

Finally when von Haart staggered back aboard on the evening of the third day, Karl issued an ultimatum. "We'll sail tomorrow. If you are not here, we will have to go without you."

Karl did not mean it of course, and when von Haart merely nodded pleasantly and said, "You may have to," we thought he did not mean it either. He rolled happily off to his bunk, and we all went to bed and slept.

But at daybreak the next morning we woke to find him gone again. Even Lars had not seen him leave. We had set ten o'clock as the time to weigh anchor, and we hoped he had simply gone ashore to say goodbye and would come back. We waited until half past eleven.

Finally Lars said, "Look—he's in some bar and has forgotten. I'll go get him."

"We'll all go," said Karl grimly.

So he, Lars, and I went ashore, while Arvi stayed with the women. In some ports we felt that Tuntsa was sufficient protection, but Casablanca was not one of them.

It was a long march. The squalor and the misery of the place seemed more oppressive than ever. Finally, in the eighth bar, as we pushed aside a beaded curtain and peered into the dark interior, we heard von Haart's voice raised in laughter and found him with three of the Swedish sailors. Von Haart appeared not a whit surprised to see us. He waved at us to join them. "Have a drink, have a drink," he urged.

I shook my head and said irritably, "We are sailing today, you know. We've been waiting for you."

He shrugged. "Oh, that. Come on, have a drink."

My irritation turned to anger. "No," I said. "Karl told you we were going to sail—with you or without you. Now which is it?"

He nonchalantly waved his hand. "Go ahead. You can get along very well without me. I'll see you in Safi."

My heart sank. There was no doubt that he meant it. Von Haart, as long as he was conscious at all, was never so drunk that he did not know what he was saying. And once he got going as he was now, he could lose all sense of time. I felt that he might be in Casablanca for weeks, even months, and not know it. Not only did it seem wrong to leave him, but how could we take the *Tuntsa* on without him? It was at Safi that we would start the longest and most dangerous stretch of the voyage—the part everyone said we could not survive—the Atlantic crossing.

"I'll meet you at Safi," repeated von Haart. "I'm not ready yet. Now go!"

There was something about von Haart. He could, when he needed it, put on an air of command which made one feel like the prince's stable boy. Karl flushed with anger, turned on his heel, and walked out. Lars looked at von Haart pleadingly. I had a moment's wild notion that perhaps I could carry him off bodily, but the bulk of the three Swedish sailors, all glowering and obviously determined not to lose their drinking companion to mundane fools like ourselves, made me decide it was hopeless. Besides, I was experiencing some of Karl's anger. There was no doubt about it. We were being snubbed. At the moment we were simply not worth von Haart's time. He had something better to do.

"Listen," I said. "Casablanca isn't an amusement park. You'll get yourself in trouble—maybe murdered."

Indeed it seemed highly probable. The thought of him dead drunk and alone in this place filled me with dread.

He waved his hand in my direction like a king dismissing a servant. I glared.

"Come on," I said to Lars.

That afternoon we sailed without him.

"Will he catch up, do you think?" Lars asked wistfully as we cast off.

"How can he?" said Karl. "He hasn't a penny left from the twenty pounds he got in Gibraltar. How would he get to Safi—even if he wakes up in time and finds out what day it is."

Lars looked sad, but both Karl and I were still too angry to care. Only Arvi, who had not seen von Haart on shore, ventured to be hopeful. "I somehow just don't think he will leave us," he said.

"I don't either," added May. And Kati nodded.

"If he is really gone," said Arvi, "we will have to get another navigator at Safi."

"How?" I asked.

"I don't know, but we will have to. We need one right now."

That was certainly true. The sinister west coast of Africa is almost unmarked for navigation. Huge cliffs rise from ugly surf breaking over jagged rocks. Giant boulders from landslides jut into the ocean, many hidden just below the surface, waiting to sink their crags into any passing hull.

By day, we could sail at a safe distance from the rocks, but after dark, with no lighthouses along the coast, it was difficult to tell where we were. Our only guide was the sound of the huge combers crashing against the cliffs. If the resounding roar was not muffled and distant, we knew we were too close to the rocks, and we sheered off quickly.

✺

On our second night out of Casablanca, Lars had the four to eight watch at the helm. The wind was steady and he had said he could manage without a helper at the sails. It was pitch black in the cabin when I was half-awakened as Karl sprang from the upper bunk. I heard him mutter, "Something's wrong!" He reached out to shake me, but I was already on my feet. On deck, Tuntsa was barking shrilly. Karl and I bounded up the ladder.

Lars was sound asleep, deaf to Tuntsa's excited yelps. Indeed, the little dog's barking could scarcely be heard over the deafening roar of breakers from the cliffs. It was the sound we dreaded, and now we could not only hear but see the towering combers. White spray seemed to leap half-way up the black sky. We were five to ten minutes from deadly shipwreck.

Karl shook Lars awake while I sprang to the wheel and swung it over hard. There was no time to come about. I jibed the *Tuntsa*, throwing her boom viciously across, with a jar that seemed about to take out the mainmast. The suddenly refilled sail cracked like cannon shot, but it could scarcely be heard over the pounding surf, and as we swung around I saw formidable rocks jutting from the water not more than a hundred yards off our bow.

Arvi, who had run on deck seconds later, gave a look of horror, and rushed back below to start the motor.

Karl and I struggled to keep the luffing sails filled with wind. In our panic, even the little we knew seemed to escape us. Our hands fumbled. We acted like novices. The wheel bucked as each comber dropped the rudder back into the water. Then, as the motor started, Lars and I clung to the wooden bronco under our hands and held our breath.

The motor took hold, and we made headway. We left another cluster of rocks a few feet to starboard.

We did not resume our original course toward Safi until we were at least five miles out. By then the sky was brightening with the promise of a beautiful clear day. The breeze sprang into our sails and rounded them caressingly. Everything seemed to reassure us. The wind shifted to come over our quarter, and we found ourselves on a broad reach, the *Tuntsa*'s best point of sailing.

We had originally chosen Safi as the chief port of call on the African coast because it was a major fishing center. We wanted to clean the hull of the *Tuntsa* at the last possible moment before the critical Atlantic crossing, and it would be easier and cheaper to do the job where such operations were an every-day occurrence. Dozens of sardine factories fringed the harbor. The odor was unmistakable, particularly to people so familiar with it as we. Canned sardines had long been the cheapest staple in our diet. We ate them incessantly—and we had come to hate them.

"Oh no!" moaned Kati, sniffing the air. "Not again!" Kati's problems with seasickness made her dislike sardines even more than the rest of us. There were limits to even her heroism.

We dropped anchor inside the rocky breakwater and decided to have a lunch of cheese sandwiches and coffee while waiting for the harbor officers to inspect our passports before giving us clearance to go ashore.

Hour after hour passed. No inspectors. We scrubbed the deck, polished our meager brass, re-lashed cans of oil and gas. The girls washed and ironed. They aired our clothes, hanging them in fantastic patterns on the rigging. Finally they began to clean the cabin. Night came. Still no inspectors. We sat fuming. No one felt like talking. What kind of harbor was this?

During the night the sirocco sprang up. This hot, oppressive, dust-laden wind from the Libyan desert, sweeps in gusts across Algeria into Morocco and spreads a layer of sand over everything in its path. It cloaked the *Tuntsa* with gritty dust, and it punched at the hull. In response the boat pitched and tossed. We would wake from fitful sleep to hear the deep, grating sound of buoys pushed down, resisting, and then springing upward with sharp, sonorous wails. The heat was stifling. Our throats were parched. And the thought with us all was of course the same. What could we go on without von Haart?

We rose the next morning after practically no sleep, ready to throw sand in the face of anyone who dared smile. I heard an eloquent oath from on deck and went up to see Arvi standing dejectedly by the hatchway. A half-inch of sand covered planking, rigging, brass, and even little Tuntsa, who had chosen that night to sleep on deck between two oilcans and now emerged looking like a small, sand-colored sheep dog.

He bounded up, shaking sand all over us. "Stop it!" Arvi shouted angrily. But Tuntsa was not disposed to go on wearing an overcoat of pure grit and bounced perseveringly about until he had shaken it all off—most of it onto us. I emptied half a cupful from each trouser cuff.

While the women cleared the cabin all over again, Karl started to sweep the deck. Lars and Arvi followed with buckets of sea water. I was helping Karl get the worst of the sand off the cans and cabin roof, when I saw a rowboat approaching.

Had the harbor officials finally noticed us?

Two men came aboard and introduced themselves.

Omar Bedinon was a Moroccan with a bit of French blood, a typical harbor official, brusk, a little contemptuous, and—like so many who drift into such positions—the bearer of a hungry ego feeding upon the official duties which made it natural to be playing god with other people's destinies. He was a benevolent deity, however, and cleared us rather quickly, though I recall think-

ing vaguely that von Haart (uppermost in all our minds
at that time) might not have cared to drink with him—
at least not for long.

François Dupré, the port police officer, however, was
an entirely different type. He was a man about forty,
whose slender athletic build and dark sensitive face
made him appear at first glance considerably younger.
I guessed, immediately, from the way he looked over the
Tuntsa, that he liked boats and understood them. It
turned out that he had not been born in Morocco but had
come from Paris, and was a former sailor. While Bedinon
checked our papers, Dupré played amiably with Tuntsa,
admired the boat, and chatted with the women. A true
Frenchman, he delighted each one by making her feel
that she was the most beautiful creature who had ever
crossed his horizon. Anna roared with laughter at his
outrageous compliments; May's eyes danced with fun;
and Kati, whose tiny figure and sweet nature often won
her more masculine attention than she welcomed, smiled
and took off her glasses. Kati's glasses were her shield.
If embarrassed by reporters or photographers or an apparent would-be wooer, she would quickly get them out
of her pocket and slip them on. When meeting strangers
she nearly always wore them. But with old friends and
people who made her feel at ease, she took them off.
François Dupré was a man who simply admired all
boats, all beauty, and all women. One knew at once that
there was such safety in the number of the little Frenchman's devotions that he was quite harmless—an aspect
which made him even more beguiling.

A strange man to be port police officer!

After Bedinon left, Dupré stayed aboard and gave us his help and official sanction in lashing the *Tuntsa* to the end of the pier as we had during our stay in Brest. She had sailed miles since then, and badly needed another cleaning. Held firmly by the pier, her hull would be exposed by each receding tide.

While waiting for the tide to go out, our new friend took us ashore. Safi was a pleasanter place than Casablanca. There were beggars, but there did not seem to be the same desperate pressure of population, nor the same dire poverty. The streets seemed picturesque rather than horrible. Seated at little outdoor tables, Arabs were selling tangerines, sun-warmed and delicious under their puckered orange skins. Beside them were hot, cooked sea-urchins which one broke open and ate from their shells with little spoons. The flavor was pleasant and resembled an odd sort of mushroom. There were dates for sale, too, but they were piled in dark, sweet, juicy heaps, which were crawling with flies, and we shunned them. Veiled women, in black from head to foot and with just their eyes showing, glanced at us curiously. The red fezzes of the merchants made spots of vivid color. Safi was an outpost of the French Foreign Legion, and we saw soldiers in white kepis setting off dark, tough, desert-parched faces.

Dupré played the host for his adopted town and showed us its chief monument, the palace built by Mohammed XVII, which with its succession of intricately decorated courts resembled an exquisitely frosted cake. The palace was beautiful, but I found it depressing. It seemed to me to express a mentality at once grandiloquent and brutal, magnificent but full of savage, wild, unfillable desires—a temperament which it seemed to me must have been rather like the Russian. But here all the magnificence and accomplishment had died long ago, and its counterpart was heir—the helplessness of these embittered people, paralyzed by centuries of wrong and poverty. There were lizards sunning themselves on the ruined walls and flicking their forked tongues in and out as if in mockery of such puny strivings as the *Tuntsa*'s. What liberty could there ever have been here?

I was glad when François took us back to the babble of the markets, and we could return on board.

We were up at six the next morning to begin work on the boat and start our rounds of scraping the exposed hull. Teetering uncertainly in the dinghy, Lars and I were removing stubborn goose barnacles, while Karl prepared to follow with deterrent paint, when there was a shout from the pier.

"Hello, my friends!"

There, leaning on his cane, stood von Haart!

We climbed to the pier and crowded around him incredulously.

May, Anna, and Kati came up from below to stare unbelievingly before they ran to him with cries of delight. Anna laughed and pounded him on the back. How had he managed to get from Casablanca? Would he go on with us?

"Naturally," said von Haart. "I never had any other notion. I told you so."

"But how did you get here?" exclaimed Karl, while

Lars glanced triumphantly at the rest of us over the vindication of his friend.

"I went to the Swedish Consulate."

"Oh?" said May.

"You remember our Swedish friends? I really only went to tell the consul what wonderful help had been given to us by the Swedish people at various stages during our trip. But while I was there, he got quite interested in us, in the *Tuntsa,* you know."

We nodded. We knew; we were perfectly familiar with von Haart's ability to attract sympathetic attention and hold it like glue.

"Then I explained that I had accidentally missed the boat's sailing for Safi."

"Accidentally!" said Karl.

"Of course. And so the consul paid my train fare."

"Naturally," I said helplessly. "Of course. What else would he do?"

"That's right," agreed von Haart pleasantly. "He was a gentleman."

Karl clutched his forehead. "Von Haart," he said, "you're hopeless!"

"Exactly," replied von Haart. "Now I must go find the post office. I am expecting a letter from Switzerland."

"Switzerland!" exclaimed Arvi. "My Lord, you didn't go and wire in your cousin's name for more money?"

Von Haart simply raised his eyebrows. When he did this, they went into peaks which always made him resemble a cheerful visitor from the nether regions.

He and Lars departed together.

"Are we better off?" asked Karl as we watched them

leave. "Or worse? Suppose he gets us all thrown in jail?"

"More comfortable than the bottom of the Atlantic," observed Arvi laconically.

"Well," said May, "it's just a good thing we know a member of the port police!"

Our words, however, belied our feelings. The truth was that we were happy and relieved beyond measure at von Haart's return. The lassitude with which we had been scraping barnacles gave way to earnest vigor. Karl and I took the dinghy diligently round and round the *Tuntsa* as the tide ebbed. Arvi went below to overhaul the engine and clean out the bilges.

In a short while, however, he called to us in a voice which told us immediately that something was seriously wrong. Karl and I hurried up the rope ladder onto the deck and followed Arvi below. May, Anna and Kati stood in tense silence looking down where Arvi had removed a section of the galley deck grating over the lower bilges which lay just above the keel. In the dark water were floating splinters and chunks of wood.

"She's rotted," said Arvi. "It's gone clear through."

"Impossible!" I exclaimed. "We know the hull was sound."

"*Was* sound," said Arvi. "It isn't now."

Karl and I felt under the water and stuck our knives into the timbers. Pieces of rotten wood crumbled out and popped to the surface.

I tested the entire keel line. Everywhere it was the same. All wood immediately above the keel was rotten. With a little effort, I could have thrust the blade completely through.

I sat back on my heels and stared hopelessly. "What shall we do?"

In the end, we went ashore and telephoned Dupré to ask if he could recommend a good ship's carpenter.

He could and did, naming two. One came in the late morning, the second in the early afternoon. There was little difference in price, and none at all in diagnosis. The *Tuntsa* had rotted all along her lower hull.

The second carpenter, a round little Frenchman, took off his cap and scratched the back of his head thoughtfully. "It means tearing out the bulkheads and the planking and putting in new. Then there's caulking. And reattaching that iron keel. It's a big job, messieurs." Like the rival bidder that morning, he then named a sum which made us shudder. It seemed like buying the *Tuntsa* all over again.

"We will let you know," said Karl.

We were on deck bidding him goodbye when we saw von Haart and Lars approaching. In our stress I had forgotten von Haart's hoped-for letter from Switzerland. Had it come? And had he spent the money? One glance told the answer to both questions. He was resplendent in a brand-new white linen suit. In silence, we watched him come aboard. He and Lars had bought drinks, and then in a state of unthinking joyousness he had gone out and spent almost the entire remainder of the check on the most handsome tropical suit he could find.

With long faces, we began to tell him about our discovery of the *Tuntsa's* rotting hull. I just made a start, however, when he gave me a reproachful look and sat down on an empty crate.

"Now, see here Teppo. No problem on earth can be as gloomy as your face!"

I assured him that this one was. With interjections from Karl and Arvi, I described the condition of the planking above the keel. To my surprise he got up at once and followed us below. We removed the grating, and he stood viewing the bloated yellowish floating splinters and shaking his head with an expression of reproach and sadness.

"Shouldn't be that bad yet—it can't be," he muttered. His tone was that of a man confronted by symptoms of grave illness in a cherished friend—one who had not been taking proper care of himself.

Removing his new white coat and handing it to Lars to hold, von Haart stooped like a doctor at a bedside and tapped tenderly all along the area above the *Tuntsa*'s keel. Finally he stood up. "She's got to have it all out, every inch of it," he said sadly.

"Dear Chief Surgeon," said May. "How shall we pay for the operation?"

Von Haart looked down regretfully at his white trousers and the coat over Lars' arm. "Well, for one thing," he said, "my suit will have to go back."

It turned out, however, that the tailor would not take it back. Von Haart and Lars finally sold it second-hand. It brought far less than its value; and still less came back with them to the *Tuntsa*, for von Haart stopped and bought two enormous bottles of absinthe.

"I need to think," he explained. "This is my fuel." Without waiting for comment, he went below.

"Look, it's *his* money," said May defensively. "He's

not supposed to contribute anything but navigation anyway."

"His cousin's money," I corrected.

"All right. But *he* stole it—and *we* didn't. It belongs to *him!*"

Karl raised his eyebrows. It was an example of the lopsided reasoning von Haart regularly inspired in his partisans.

Next morning Lars, who shared the forward cabin with von Haart, told us that when he himself finally fell asleep, von Haart was still sitting propped up in his bunk, taking long swigs of the potent liquor and staring fixedly into space.

❄

Von Haart slept late but came on deck apparently quite sober. He sat down on the packing case by the wheel, and looked up speculatively into the *Tuntsa*'s rigging. "I know how to get the money to repair the hull," he said.

"How?" asked Arvi skeptically.

"We can sell the mizzen-mast."

"What!" Karl and I exclaimed together.

Von Haart grinned. "Don't be so overcome. The *Tuntsa*'s a fine ship. She got along with one mast before, and she can do it again. That mast will fetch a good price. They haven't any timber like that," said von Haart proudly, "within a thousand miles."

The idea, which had appeared preposterous at first,

began to seem quite reasonable. The *Tuntsa* would lose
speed and maneuverability, but she could proceed perfectly well with one mast. We even convinced ourselves
that she might be improved.

"In coastal waters," said von Haart, "we needed to
maneuver, but in the Atlantic if there's one thing we will
have plenty of, it is sea room."

The chief obstacle to the plan was that even just taking the mast out would cost something, and we had no
money at all. Von Haart looked at Karl and me and shook
his head reprovingly. "For a pair of insurance salesmen,"
he said, "you two always amaze me. Go out and sell
somebody on doing it for us."

"You mean taking the mast out free?" asked Karl.

"Of course."

We discussed it further, but there was simply no alter-
native.

"I've sold some hard prospects," said Karl as we started
out, "but I never had an assignment like this one!"

Von Haart and Lars left to cover the town; Karl, Arvi,
and I each took a portion of the waterfront. We searched
all that day. To the thrifty French and Spanish fishing
skippers whose trawling winches might be large enough
to lift out the *Tuntsa's* mast, the notion of doing something without pay was ridiculous.

Meanwhile, the girls, quite unknown to us, embarked
on efforts of their own. We returned at noon to find them
holding a sort of impromptu waterfront auction and being practically swamped by shouting Arab hagglers.
Looking frightened but thoroughly determined, Kati
stood in the midst of a milling throng on our small after

deck collecting worn franc notes, while Anna in the role of saleswoman, held up the items of merchandise: old shirts, slacks, our extra sheets. Karl moved in swiftly, for the turmoil of the bargainers looked more like a riot than a sale, and in Casablanca, the hostility of much of the native population had often been overt. We soon saw, however, that these young Arabs of Safi had nothing in mind but the sudden and unexpected prospect of buying European clothing—at rock bottom prices.

Karl finally marshalled them sternly off the boat, but they were too delighted by their purchases to care. A young boy told me proudly, "I shall look like *un étranger très riche*—a most wealthy foreigner."

I thought somewhat wryly that the youth had chosen the wrong people to satisfy that particular ambition.

"Don't *ever* do such a thing again," Karl exclaimed to Kati. "Don't let *anyone* on board while we are gone!"

But Kati was too busy counting profits to do more than smile.

May said to me, "We're absolutely not going to stay here, Teppo—no matter what has to be done to raise money. Can you see us having to settle in Safi? I would be one of those women sitting in a doorway and weaving baskets."

Indeed the prospect that we might have to stay in Safi did not seem impossible as we gathered somberly that night. No one had found either a buyer for the mast or any way of getting it out.

The following morning we went to search again. Karl left Kati reluctantly, and the auction of the day before was not the only reason.

The charming port police officer, François Dupré, had introduced us to some of his French friends, and in the atmosphere of gallantry which flowed from François like champagne, one of them, a well-to-do sardine canner, had become enamored of Kati. Poor Kati, who hated sardines and was anything but a flirt, suddenly found herself beseiged by the most lavish proposals. The smitten sardine king came to call frequently. Would she tour the town with him? He had his car on the dock. Would she come with him to a dance that night? If so, he would lavishly provision the *Tuntsa*. Kati, who would usually just have retreated behind her glasses, began to change her ways. She did not exactly encourage the sardine king, but she did not precisely discourage him either. Our plight was too desperate.

"I think she hopes that in the end she will be able to appeal to his better nature," May told me.

"Pooh!" said Anna. "He isn't going to give something for nothing any more than the rest of these Frenchmen."

As if by poetic justice, it was on this day that we were to find Pierre Cantin, the French fisherman who was to take out our mast—a man whose generosity would put all such thoughts to shame.

Cantin was skipper of the *Céleste*, one of the best trawlers in Safi. A bronzed, muscular young man, he was on his deck when we approached and was supervising the unloading of what appeared to be a particularly enormous catch of fish.

"Had good luck today!" he called to us jubilantly, and I thought that a man who could so greet two strangers must have an extraordinarily warm nature.

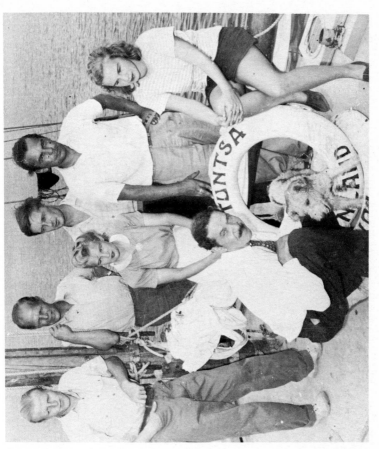

The *Tuntsa's* crew shortly before the end of the voyage. From left to right, Olle, Arvi, Kati, Lars, Teppo and May. In the foreground is von Haart with Tuntsa.

Helsinki harbor, our port of origin. Above, a scattering of the small racing craft for which Finland is famous. Below, the waterfront, with a crane resembling the one for which the *Tuntsa* had to wait because her turn was pre-empted by ships ordered by the Russians.

The *Tuntsa* docked at Aalborg. Seated, left to right, Kati, Masa, and Karl. Standing behind Kati are Teppo and Anna, and in back of her is Arvi. May is leaning on the boom while Lars looks over her shoulder.

The *Tuntsa* in one of her many guises. Each time her hull was scraped she was repainted black or white according to what paint was available or cheaper.

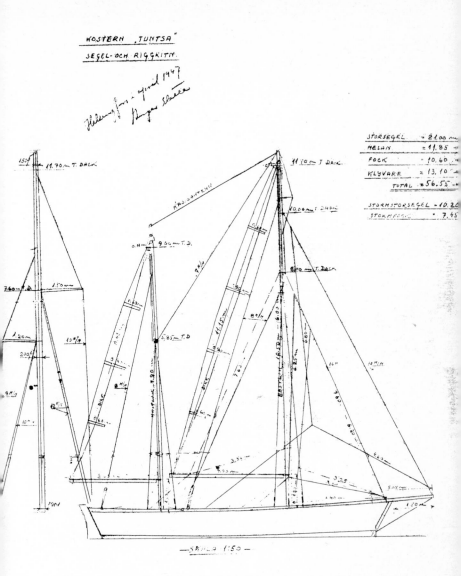

The water-stained and faded original blueprint of the *Tuntsa*, saved from the shipwreck. It does not show the iron keel which was added later.

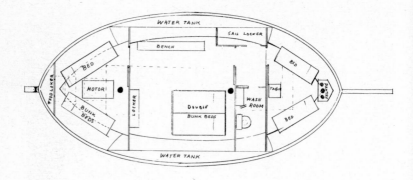

Two diagrams of the *Tuntsa* below deck. Arvi and Anna slept in the after section; Karl and Kati had the upper bunks amidships; May and Teppo slept below. Von Haart, in a single bed, and Lars were up forward, and Masa (later Olle) had the bunk above Lars.

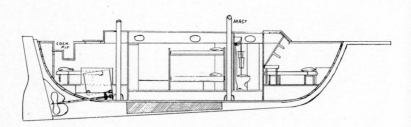

Above, May reads a letter from home. The somber lighting of the picture evokes the loneliness they often felt close around them when reading about the children left behind. Below, May and Teppo just after leaving Lisbon.

In Casablanca. Above, from the left, Lars, one of von Haart's friends from the Swedish ship that provisioned them, May and Teppo. Below, Kati and May.

Karl nudged me, "This one is in a good humor," he murmured.

The truck full of gleaming fish drove away and the young man turned to us. "Come aboard," he invited. "I am Pierre Cantin." He said it with the same pride as if he had announced he was king of the harbor.

We stepped aboard his ship. The *Céleste* was beautifully kept, and the crew was smiling and quiet as their captain showed us around. He was proud of his ship, and I liked the way any crewman he spoke to called him, "mon capitain." If this was a man to be liked, he was also a man who was respected.

He took us below and gave us mugs of delicious beer from an icebox in a shiningly neat cabin. We told him our story. He did not interrupt but listened with increasing soberness.

"You've come this far in your boat, and now you have to sell part of her to sail on with the rest of her—is that how it is?" he said when we finished.

"That's about it, I guess," answered Karl.

"And you can't pay *anything* for taking the mast out?"

"No, monsieur, not anything. We barely have food."

Pierre Cantin was silent. He looked at us narrowly. I could imagine that in the past his expansive nature might have led him into generosities he later regretted. He was appraising us carefully.

"Well," he said at last, "let me see your boat." He rose and followed us—unsmiling.

We led him along the dock. When we pointed out the battle-scarred *Tuntsa*, he stood stock still in astonishment.

"You got here from Finland in *that?* And now you're going to sail her to America?" For a moment he appeared to be speechless.

"Listen," he said at last, "if I can help you, I will." He shoved his white captain's cap on the back of his dark head, and regarded us with a changed expression. "What a thing you're doing!" he exclaimed. "Mon Dieu, what a *thing*—why, you can remember it the rest of your lives. I envy you," he finished abruptly.

We led him below at that, and introduced him to May, Anna, Kati, and Tuntsa, all in the galley. He shook hands with our wives, then bent his huge frame and shook Tuntsa's paw—quite seriously.

Karl took up the grating amidships. We let him test the rottenness of the hull at the keel. "It's just as bad all along the bottom," Karl said. "We can't take her into the Atlantic like that."

Soberly Cantin nodded. "You're perfectly right. She would go down in the first storm."

"We looked all yesterday," I said, "for a trawler with big enough winches to get out the mast. Yours is one of the few we think might be able to do it."

The young man suddenly gave the shy smile of a delighted parent who hears praise of his child. "If any boat can, she can," he replied. There was a charming touch of swagger about him as he made for the hatch. "Get a buyer for the mast, and I will take it out for you. That's definite," he said when we stood on deck.

We thanked him in chorus, trying earnestly to express our gratitude. Our French had never seemed clumsier, but we got him to shake hands again all around. Then,

however, he jumped to the pier. His own generosity embarrassed him, for he strode away without looking back.

"A fine man," said Karl.

We could only nod. Anything we could have added
would have been inadequate to express our feelings.

When Kati's sardine canner came to call after we left
again that afternoon, the climate on board the *Tuntsa*
had changed considerably. Kati had put on her glasses
and let her lovely hair be disordered by the wind. However, the sardine king's blandishments only increased.
Then Anna sat on the rail beside him and chuckled.

"We got someone to take out the mast, you know."

But the sardine king was too smitten and too confident of his own charms to grasp the nuance.

"Is that so?" he asked indifferently.

"Yes," said Anna with satisfaction. Whistling cheerfully, she wandered off to sketch at the bow. She and
May were indefatigable—and maddening—chaperones.

There remained the problem of a purchaser to buy
the mast. Once more, we had a discouraging mission. At
last Lars and von Haart picked up a rumor about a man
whose boat needed repair. We went to visit him toward
sundown. Von Haart led our little delegation, but the
man was a Spaniard, so Karl was appointed interpreter.

The boat was the *Queen III*, but a less queenly ship
could not have been imagined. She was a battered vessel
which had obviously seen more than a normal share of
storms. The owner, a dark man in worn and dirty dungarees, was reeving fishline into a winch.

Karl made some polite introductory remarks about the
weather, the fishing, and paid some compliments to the

superiority of the general state of affairs in Safi over Casablanca. He received perfunctory replies.

Von Haart gave Karl a sharp nudge. "Ask him if he would like to buy a good strong mast."

"All right, all right," murmured Karl. "But I have to get him in the right humor for a sale."

"Perhaps Arvi should play the mouth organ?" inquired von Haart derisively.

He had a point. Unlike Pierre, the Spaniard was not a man of feelings, but a man of business. He went on reeving the line as if we had not been present.

"Do you want to buy a good strong mast?" Karl asked finally in blunt desperation.

"Might be," replied the Spaniard.

"Would you like to come have a look at it?"

"Might be," said the Spaniard. After a moment, with the first sign of interest, he added, "What's the size?"

Karl gave him a complete description—height, diameter, type of wood—plus a strong salestalk on the advantages of Finnish timber. "Like to see it?" he finished pleadingly.

The Spaniard rose slowly, spat over the side, and wiped his hands on his faded dungarees. "Might be," he admitted.

He followed us to the Tuntsa, where he silently checked and rechecked the mast from butt to yard—from time to time spitting into the water to show he was not impressed.

"How much?" he asked after a twenty-minute survey.

We quoted an outrageous price.

He turned as if to leave. We reduced the price. He came back. After an hour of fervent haggling, during which we all took to spitting over the side to indicate vexation, we finally arrived at a settlement. It was not generous, but it was more than we had hoped.

After we told him the mast would be removed the next day and left on the pier for him to pick up, we left him, and jubilantly trooped over to Pierre's trawler to tell him the news.

Pierre proved to be almost as excited as we. "Now you can go on. What a fantastic adventure! You know, I have a mind to come with you. But"—his face fell—"I'm a married man."

"Tutt, tutt! Too bad," said von Haart, who obviously found Pierre delightful.

Pierre gave him a look. For a moment I half expected him to say in all seriousness that he was going to join us. "What a story it would be to tell," he murmured. "Mon Dieu, what a story!" Then he cleared his throat. "For me it is not possible," he concluded gruffly. "Now, let's see. I have to leave tomorrow night with the tide, but if you get right at it, you can strip your boat of her canvas and tackle and get the boom off in daylight. Then if you can strip the guy wires, we'll get at the hoisting at dawn tomorrow. Otherwise you would have to wait the four days I'm at sea." He eyed us teasingly. "Just a little job, eh? Hardly enough to raise a sweat."

"Don't worry about us," Karl retorted. "We'll get ready for you, even if we have to work all night."

Pierre stood looking after us as we left. There was no doubt of his envy. If he could have known what awaited the *Tuntsa* and her crew on the Atlantic, he might have felt differently, however.

As we approached the *Tuntsa,* Karl suggested, "Let's

go aboard and tell the girls we have to give up and stay here. I'll tell Kati I've taken a job cleaning sardines. . ."

"I'll tell Anna we found someone to buy the *Tuntsa*," said Arvi.

"And I'll tell May we have no choice but to rent an adobe house and weave baskets," I added.

It seemed great fun. Only von Haart looked dubious.

We ambled down our gangplank with long faces, and short, hesitant steps. May came swiftly to meet us. Anna and Kati crowded behind, obviously concerned by our looks.

Hardly had Karl begun to explain that we had had to sell the *Tuntsa* and would be forced to stay in Safi than Kati started to cry. May stared, and Anna clenched her fists. We had not realized how the tension must have been building up for them. While we hurried about negotiating, they had had to sit on board and wonder what our fates would be. The auction—the sardine king—all had been symptoms of sheerest desperation.

Karl put his arm around Kati. Arvi hastened to reassure Anna. "It's all right, May," I kept repeating. "We sold the mast. It's all settled. Really!"

May told me later that it was ten minutes before she could realize that we would not have to stay in Safi after all. "And then I could have killed you!" she said. "My heart seemed to have stopped."

Indeed, she had turned perfectly white, and so had they all.

We worked until past midnight stripping the after rigging and clearing the area around the mizzen. Then we slept for a short five hours, and at dawn moved the

Tuntsa outboard of Pierre's trawler and tied up to her at the deep end of the pier. Von Haart tossed our anchors out as far as he could, fore and aft, and cinched them tight so that we would roll as little as possible.

Pierre was on deck waiting for us.

"Ready to go, I see," he said gazing approvingly at our smiling but exhausted faces. He contemplated us. "Some job, eh? Well, we'll have her out for you in no time. Mind you take care, though. She will want to swing vertical when she comes out of the socket, and again when she clears the deck. She might rip it out."

It was a danger of which we were already keenly aware.

"Get a couple of nooses with fifteen foot tails to hold the butt when we lift her," Pierre continued. Karl and von Haart quickly obeyed.

Under Pierre's supervision two of his crew secured the lifting rig around the base of the mast and snugged it in below the iron band supporting the boom. Another inserted the winch cable's big hook into the loop at the end of the rig. Meanwhile, the rest of us worked feverishly to detach the guy wire shackles. As the mast was lifted free from her base, we would have all we could do to steady her tip.

Again we marvelled at the efficiency and the atmosphere of solidarity on Pierre's ship. One could tell that far from grudging their captain's generosity, his men took it as evidence of power, and felt its reflected glory. "Oui, mon capitain," they said. "Non, mon capitain." A battleship could have envied them their discipline.

The winchman started the diesel. He maneuvered the

lifting boom until the hook had a straight lift upward.
He took up the slack in the cable and looked to Pierre,
who signalled to take a strain. We were ready to hoist.

Pierre's thumb jerked up. A loud splintering was
heard. The *Tuntsa* lurched protestingly. We strained on
our balancer lines, anticipating the weight when the
mast would come clear and the tip would start to fall.
The diesel roared again and . . . nothing. The motor had
conked out from the load.

I let out my breath and relaxed. Arvi went below to
inspect the socket. The diesel was started again, and
revved up from half to three-quarter power.

Arvi reported, "No real damage. Try again."

We resumed positions, and Pierre once more gave the
signal. This time the mast grudged out of her socket.
Lars, Arvi, and I were almost thrown to the deck by
the tremendous jerk on our balancing lines, but we managed to anchor our feet at the edge of the cabin and
kept the tip of the mast from swaying. Von Haart and
Karl strained at the nooses around the base. Pierre mo-
tioned to us to hold her while he inspected the winch.

"Only about a five foot lift of cable left. The mast is
about four foot six below the deck. She should just clear.
Let's find out," he said briefly.

He signalled to lift slowly, and more and more of the
butt grated slowly through the deck. We leaned on our
balancer lines and held our breath.

The big hook on the winch snugged up to the block
of the trawler's lifting boom just as the mast cleared the
deck by about two inches. With all of us straining on

our lines, we gentled the big spar into a vertical position.

"Ha!" said Pierre happily. "Look at that!"

Indeed it gave one a surge of pride to see the huge mast obedient and responsive to our puny efforts. Gradually the winchman swung it around until we were able to rest it gently on the dock and let go our lines.

Von Haart stepped back, tipping his head to one side in the manner of an artist admiring a newly completed masterpiece. Suddenly, just as Lars gave a shout of warning, he stepped backwards right off the dock and into the water. He came up wearing an expression of outraged surprise and reaching for his cap, which was floating miraculously over the spot at which he had gone down, marking it like a buoy.

We burst into roars of laughter and hauled him sputtering and swearing onto the pier. The girls, who had been watching in breathless suspense while we maneuvered the mast, laughed hardest of all.

Pierre had us to lunch. Our wives joined us and by their thanks to the crew, and their obvious delight at being able to go on again, made our gratitude easier to express. We ate as we perched on the rail, or wherever we could make-shift a seat and balance a mess tray. Von Haart came up from below lugging a case of beer no one knew he had, and we toasted one another exuberantly.

"Next time, you'll look where you're walking backwards," May laughed.

He raised his glass to her. "I didn't mind the water as long as none got inside me. Water is the cause of all stomach trouble. Rusts the insides."

"Ho," said May. "I think if you hadn't sneaked a little beer before the work started, you wouldn't have slipped."

But von Haart was forever deaf to all arguments of that kind.

Two evenings later we got the rest of our mast money from our laconic Spaniard, and von Haart assigned us our tasks.

All the cabin grating was carried on deck. We lashed the *Tuntsa* lengthwise again at the shallow end of the pier and pumped out the bilges. Even with the money from our mast, it was still impossible to hire a carpenter. We would have to do the work ourselves. Lars, Karl, and I began cutting into the hull from inside. We cleared away only the debris and rotting wood which came loose easily, plus enough to give us a smooth working surface. The lumber and supplies were delivered, and we began the more arduous part of our struggle.

Arvi was named Technical Consultant, and von Haart was Works Examiner. Arvi would quietly suggest, "I would do it this way." He would argue with von Haart and settle on the method, and then the rest of us would do the actual work, for von Haart was very busily engaged in finishing off another case of beer, a gift from Pierre.

Arvi removed the mizzen socket and smoothed over the top, while the rest of us reinforced the hull. I worked amidships, Lars in the galley, Karl aft. The women brought us coffee. We must have drunk gallons of it—hot, black, and strong. We were in high spirits and sang at our work—all the Finnish songs we could remember. We were going on!

The next morning we started caulking with oakum and pitch. Old rags were used to stuff some of the wider, deeper seams. Sheet metal covered these areas, and a final heavy coat of tar completed an inner seal. Carpentry and tarring took us a full week.

For the time being, we would make no changes in our remaining sails. Von Haart decided we should test them for balance and handle them at least to the Canaries. The truth was that he was proud of the *Tuntsa's* tall rigging. Having had to sacrifice one of her spars, he was in no mood to cut down her remaining elegance, though later he would wish that he had done so, for the *Tuntsa's* beauty was almost to cost us our lives.

✿

It was time now for the *Tuntsa* to leave. Refitting was completed, and we all had our various reasons for wanting to get away. Von Haart longed to be at sea again. The rest of us were ready for a change, and Kati in particular was eager to leave Safi behind. The persistence of the amorous fish canner was exhausting her patience. Bewitched by her strange eyes and blond beauty, he could not believe that he would not finally prevail. In vain Kati wore her glasses, tied her glorious hair into a tight bun, appeared in overalls—a fish canner of Safi is a man not easily discouraged. Kati, who believed the best of everyone, hoped that when he saw we were actually about to sail, he might send some of the supplies he had offered.

Anna laughed, "Kati," she said. "Oh, Kati!"

"You're all wrong," replied Kati sturdily. "I'm sure he'll send something. You'll see."

He did indeed send something. Two days before we were to sail, we received one small box of sardines.

Karl wanted it thrown overboard, but Anna restrained him. In spite of von Haart's best foraging efforts, we would be severely rationed between Safi and the Canaries. Anna put the sardines carefully away.

Before sailing we decided that we would have one more expedition ashore together, and a last look at the colorful Arab markets, whose like we would probably never see again. So we wandered off to gaze for the last time at the veiled, black-clad women, the white-robed men, the haughty, swashbuckling French legionnaires, and the scattering of tourists each trailing his or her separate wake of pathetic waifs crying, "Baksheesh!" and holding out hands for pennies—a scene we would carry on our hearts for the rest of our lives because of its desperate poverty, even though Safi was so much better in that respect than Casablanca. We roamed the markets with a feeling of shame. In some obscure way we felt responsible. Was it because we were leaving without having been able to do anything for these people? But what could we do? We could not afford to buy the wares on display—the dates, breads, brasswork, cloth, pottery, parrots, and so on.

Finally Anna stopped. There was a man selling turtles.

"Tuntsa needs company," she explained, groping in her purse. "And he won't eat much—he's a very small turtle. I'll name him Ahmed."

So leaving the delighted turtle seller behind, we went off to the boat, where Anna introduced Ahmed to Tuntsa. The little dog reacted with curiosity and enthusiasm, but Ahmed would not cooperate. When Tuntsa tried to nuzzle him, the little turtle pulled his neck and legs into his shell until the dog lost patience and turned away. But then, as Ahmed prepared to crawl, Tuntsa saw him and came racing back to turn him over. Ahmed thrashed wildly. Tuntsa nosed him right side up with exuberant yaps and watched with interest while his new plaything traveled several feet.

Barking excitedly, Tuntsa jumped within an inch of Ahmed, then lay down and regarded the little turtle with interest. He extended his paw; Ahmed snapped as decisively and strongly as a small turtle can. Tuntsa yelped, turned tail and raced to the wheel where he nursed the nip on his leg. The surprise attack and resultant wounding of his pride made Tuntsa ever after regard Ahmed with respect. Henceforth the midget turtle was allowed plenty of crawl space. Tuntsa would caper around him, but not touch him.

Ahmed, his status established, seemed to delight then in hiding both from Tuntsa and from us. He would peek out as we approached, then crawl behind an oil can or coil of line. Seconds later, he would peer out again to be sure we knew where he was. He would inch across the deck, turn around and eye us, allow himself to be picked up, then when put down again, would be off and out of

sight. If we gave Tuntsa too much attention, Ahmed
would reappear to crawl about enticingly, while Tuntsa
in exacerbated jealousy would thrust himself into our
laps.

Since that time, many people told us that turtles have
no intelligence. We have never doubted the perceptive-
ness of these people as far as turtles of this continent are
concerned, but they never knew Ahmed, our African
turtle friend!

The afternoon after purchasing Ahmed—on Friday,
December 5, the day before Finland's Independence
Day—we prepared to sail out of Safi.

At the last moment, just as we were getting ready,
there was a hail from the dock. There stood Pierre.

"Wait!" he shouted. He was holding an enormous silver tuna. He jumped to our deck. "That's for you," he
said, thrusting it at von Haart. "You people have been
a good luck charm for me. Ever since we took out your
mast, I have been practically swamped by fish. I wanted
to bring a thank offering."

Von Haart replied that we should be doing the thanking, not he. Proudly he showed Pierre our reconstruction, and the young Frenchman ran his hand over the
patch covering the socket where the mizzen had been.
"I shall like to remember," he said soberly, "that I had
a share in getting you to America."

"Come with us," invited von Haart.

For a moment Pierre stood absolutely motionless.
Then he shook his big head and laughed. "I'm a married
man. And you are a tempter, eh? A real tempter." He
laughed again, and von Haart smiled. With his cap on

the back of his head, his brows arched quizzically he indeed resembled an amiable Mephistopheles.

The big fisherman stood on the pier to watch until we were out of sight. His hands in his pockets, his heavy shoulders a little stooped, there was about him a singular air of wistfulness. We waved as long as we could see him.

It was a beautiful day, the sky was a rich blue over a green and azure sea, and the pastel colors of Safi's harbor seemed to fade into grays behind us like some magic land. After our next stop at the Canaries we would be leaving the hemisphere of our birth, and passing quite definitely into what we must consider the other side of the globe. I recall being glad that the day was so lovely, and then suddenly seeing with a sort of chill, over von Haart's shoulder as he stood at the wheel, a pair of the triangular fins we all so disliked.

After a while, Lars wandered on deck with his beloved encyclopedia. "Sharks," he read aloud. "By some sailors, their following of a vessel is considered an ill omen."

"Oh, *do* be quiet!" exclaimed May, looking up from our cards.

Anna had paper and pencil and was sketching the receding coast. I saw that the dreamy expanse of water in her picture showed no sign of fins at all.

the BEAUTIFUL ISLES

three and a half months at sea

porpoises

waves like skyscrapers

the man with the gun

an unwilling bargain

a night on a dark beach

We were four hours out of Safi, on a calm sea with a brisk wind over the port quarter. Our mast now seemed too high and von Haart admitted it would probably require some changes when we reached the Canaries, but he pointed out that in this weather the *Tuntsa* handled beautifully. She did indeed. I even imagined I was a sailor at last.

I called to Karl. "We're getting good! How long since you've fouled a line?"

Karl smiled. "Years, it seems. . ."

But von Haart scoffed from the wheel. "How high can you point the *Tuntsa* into the wind? Could either of you feather her through good hard gusts? On the Atlantic, is it one of you two who will keep the boat riding the back of a wave without getting into the trough?"

I would learn some day not to brag near von Haart. "Well, at least you have to admit we're much better than our first day out of Helsinki," Karl said.

Von Haart laughed and nodded. "You had ten thumbs, blind eyes, two left feet, and acted drunker than I've ever been. I'll never forget it. There were times when I thought you and the rigging could never part company, you got so tangled."

We all chuckled at the memory.

We had been sailing three and a half months now, and somehow our increasing confidence in ourselves and our boat steadily added to our confidence in the rightness of our goal. We would get to America. Our dream would come true. On that blue and smiling sea, all good things seemed inevitable. The endless horizons made the *Tuntsa* seem the center of a great vault, with benign arches flung up to infinity, and openness and freedom on every side. The whole world was ours to move in as we wished. Our voyage toward liberty seemed almost incarnated by our movement over the endless waters, with no visible limits anywhere. Anna's sketches were full of light.

Arvi reclined on the deck and played his mouth organ in soft contentment. Tuntsa sat at his feet, intrepidly gazing at the horizon before us, motionless as a carved figurehead of a dog. Ahmed climbed to the top of a coil of line and sunned himself. Karl and Kati, May and I played cards, interrupting the game only to adjust the sails and congratulate each other on our seamanship. Von Haart at the wheel conned his beloved ship and gazed up proudly at her fine tall spar; and each time I looked at him, I thought of Vikings.

But the sharks of Safi had either adopted us personally or were passing us along a chain of their Atlantic comrades. Anna might persist in drawing her scenes without fins, but to the rest of us they were all too visible. When I rose from the card game to get a reading from our log mounted on the stern bulwark, I looked down directly into the face of a monster. He seemed to be grinning, three rows of sawlike teeth exposed. There was a small piece of scrap lumber by the after rail. Moved by a fury I could not have explained, I hurled it down upon him; and was not comforted when he seized it with a curious sawing motion of his great jaws and disappeared beneath the water. Curiously, though we all watched, not one of us, including von Haart, commented on the incident.

We took a log reading at the end of each watch to determine the distance we had traveled. We occasionally got false readings because the *Tuntsa* was moving too slowly or some obstruction was interfering with the free movement of the rotator at the end of the line, which was some fifteen fathoms long. Soon after my spiteful episode with the shark, I returned to find the log clock's dial not moving at all. This was strange, because we were advancing at a lively clip through the water.

I leaned over and pulled the line. It was unwontedly light, and almost immediately a short end broke the surface. "Something's cut it," I muttered. The "something" was of course one of our underwater escorts. To sharks the rotator no doubt looked like a new variety of fish.

It was all quite simple, but I suddenly felt as if the sea were infested by demons, all watching us, and all waiting their chance.

Von Haart, however, merely shrugged. He refused to replace the log, assuring us that he could get to the Canaries by celestial navigation and his inborn sense of direction. And such was his persuasiveness, and our confidence in him, that we were content once more. I quite forgot my notions of demons. We sailed on, and I was as irrationally carefree and unworried as I had been unreasonably apprehensive. Moods are strange at sea.

The hours passed, and with them came again the magic pull of the endless waters. We sat dreaming on deck, surrounded now not by sharks, but by a school of porpoises, who with humorously benign expressions poked their heads above the surface and seemed to caper into the air purposely to get a look at our strange craft.

Lars read to us from his encyclopedia. "It is said that porpoises have been known to nudge a drowning man in the direction of his boat," and our new mood made us so ready to believe it that we looked over to smile at the rotund creatures as their intelligent-looking pointed snouts broke the water. To us they seemed to smile back. The sea and its denizens were our country now, the *Tuntsa* was our home, and all on board were our compatriots and our dearest friends.

There was frantic excitement on the day we lost Ahmed. We had adopted the habit of carrying the little turtle below with us while we gathered for mid-morning coffee in the galley, and somehow he crept out of sight. No lost child ever caused greater consternation. Tuntsa ran about whining. Anna was near tears. We searched frantically all morning. No Ahmed. In the afternoon we renewed our hunt until dark, and in the middle of the night I woke to find Arvi pattering about the cabin with a flashlight.

"I thought I heard him," he muttered, and went shame-facedly back to bed.

Finally in the morning we began in the galley and moved methodically on toward von Haart's and Lars' quarters aft. Every box was lifted. The cupboards were opened. Blankets were unfolded and shaken. Our under-bunk lockers were sorted piece by piece. No Ahmed. By late afternoon we reached the after cabin. Again, we checked over, under, between, and around every conceivable object. Only the potato locker remained.

We began removing potatoes one at a time—potato after potato. Half-way down, two eyes and an olive shell caught our attention. Anna gave a cry of delight. Ahmed clambered onto an adjacent potato and gazed up sentimentally. He was lifted out and taken on deck, where he was petted and fondled by everyone in the party, and reprimanded like a disobedient infant.

After that, when we went down for coffee, Ahmed reposed for the interval in an empty tin—which he hated.

"Like Eero in his playpen," said May to me. "Remember?"

Indeed I did remember. Sipping my coffee and feeding crumbs to Ahmed, I began to plan that as soon as we got Eero to America we would buy him a little turtle as a pet.

*

On our third morning out of Safi, the dancing, rippling waters around us gradually ceased smiling. The white clouds which had floated over the *Tuntsa* like lazy bubbles, turned to lace-edged tatters, and were then invaded by a little black cloud, which hung in the sky and drooped tentacles like a tiny squid. Wind came from all directions in succession. Von Haart would no sooner finish instructing us to trim the sails, when they would be suddenly flapping again, leaving us to wallow helplessly without way. Then, all at once, there was no wind at all. It was deathly still, and the *Tuntsa* hung between sky and sea, as unreal as a ship in one of Anna's drawings. The black squid of a cloud began to swell above us. It grew as if it were swallowing the sky, bloating itself on some monstrous dark fluid as it did so.

"Get the mainsail down!" shouted von Haart suddenly. "Get everything off! Lash down the cans! Hurry! Arvi. . . ."

But there was no need to finish. Arvi had already plunged below to start the engine. In a minute a steady sputter began to pulse under our feet. At Safi, Arvi had overhauled his engine as never before. Without Masa to help him, and with the prospect of the most dangerous portion of our voyage ahead, he had nursed the machine's primitive anatomy until its antique parts now meshed like a new Swiss watch. But nothing Arvi could do with his miraculous hands could avail against the demons of the sea. Huge waves began to rise above our deck. Soon they were as tall as trees, then as large as buildings, and finally as huge as skyscrapers—great on-rushing walls of water, tons of it. The *Tuntsa* rose on top of each foaming mountain and fell into every black valley with a dizzying drop. With von Haart I clung to the wheel. The propeller was seldom in the water, the engine throbbed uselessly, and the *Tuntsa* rose and fell until we were nearly senseless. And as she slid down each of the steepening waves, she began to career as if she would go over.

"That damn mast!" von Haart shouted in my ear. "She's making us top-heavy." We hung on top of a veritable Alp of ocean, then cascaded down the other side. "I'll get six feet off that spar. See if I don't," cried von Haart. It was the only time I remember ever having heard him criticize the *Tuntsa*.

We rode that infernal storm half the night. My hands were burned raw from the brine-stiffened lines, my body ached. The storm seemed a creature with a brain, alive and malignant, and bent on our destruction. The noise was deafening—the howl of wind in our naked rigging, the thunder of cascading water. But it was exhilarating to feel the *Tuntsa* climb each surging mountain. The darkness was so filled with spray that it resembled snow. I suddenly remembered our white-clad ski troops sweeping down the mountains to strike the enemy and be gone before his rage could grasp us. It is when one is closest to death that one most realizes the triumph of life. Von

Haart spun the wheel to balance us on the back of a wave, and he laughed out loud as we forced it to carry us. At that moment I felt that the *Tuntsa* must be immortal, for if this did not destroy us, surely nothing could.

Karl and Lars got on a rag of storm sail finally, and it steadied us somewhat. We began to sense that the worst was over. Kati was desperately ill, and May stayed beside her, but Anna in an old coat of Arvi's came on the water-washed deck and worked at the sails beside Arvi to relieve Karl, who flung himself onto his bunk in a stupor of exhaustion.

And then, incredibly, the sea went down just before sunrise. The horizon flamed like a Burma ruby and became a sudden kaleidoscope of color—a wildly beautiful, moving luminescence, with great jagged banks of swiftly flowing purple cloud. We gazed at it in awe. Midway on the curve of the horizon as it arched to the southwest over the suddenly gentling sea was a sliver of green.

"Tenerife!" exclaimed von Haart, wiping his forehead, and putting his cap back on at a jauntier angle. "Beautiful Tenerife. The jewel of the Canaries."

We lined up at the rail to look our fill. Tuntsa crawled on deck and sat on his haunches. Karl woke in the new stillness, and brought up Kati, white-faced and unsteady. We stood together, still wet and shivering, but watching that astonishing sunrise and feeling unspeakably grateful to be alive. It amazed us to see that the school of dolphin, which had been with us before the storm, had apparently clung to us through the terrible night. Perhaps it was a different group entirely, but, anyhow, there they were, ten or fifteen of them, sharp-snouted and smiling, breaking water and eyeing the *Tuntsa* as if in mutual congratulation.

We reached the island in the late afternoon. Near-at-hand, its beauty was breath-taking. Relaxed on the lap of the now quiet ocean, it was a free-form wavering line of still blue inlets, fringed with green palms and splashed with great pools of red and blue flowers upon green-yel-low hills with tops hollowed out by old volcanoes. In the harbor, white sailboats darted about like lambs upon a blue pasture. The haze of the late day surrounded the *Tuntsa* as if enclosing us in a hollow transparent bubble, which magnified every beautiful thing before us and brought it into reach while still leaving us the free and perfect isolation of the sea. Distant mountains seemed near at hand. The flower-clothed foothills seemed no farther away than the *Tuntsa's* own rail, as it moved gently up and down. It was a vision of peace and prom-ise for storm-tossed voyagers.

Or so we thought.

We had scarcely come into the harbor and were pre-paring to drop anchor, when a gray dory shot out from shore. It circled us purposefully, and we could see a uniformed helmsman squinting at the name on our prow —*Tuntsa,* the brass lettering we had put on so proudly in Helsinki and had newly polished before leaving Safi.

Four uniformed men swung aboard, and the first one on deck brandished a machine gun, swinging it about in all directions.

"Don't move! None of you are to leave this boat!" he shouted in Spanish. His companions spread out across the deck, as if expecting us to leap the rail in a break for freedom.

The leader shouted again. "Which is Otto Alexander von Haart!"

Von Haart stepped forward. "I am Baron Otto Alexander von Haart," he said coldly, and emphasized the title.

At once two men moved swiftly and roughly grasped him by the arms.

"You are under arrest. We are taking you in for theft."

The official with the gun turned back to us. "All of you will be watched closely," he barked, and fingered the trigger warningly. "You will not leave this boat!"

Von Haart was jostled onto the rope ladder and pushed roughly into the dory. Once in it, the two men relaxed their grip somewhat, and he shrugged himself loose, calling back to us in French. "Don't worry. It will be all right. It's a family matter. I'll be back at once. You'll see!"

The man with the machine gun scowled and remained on our deck. He seated himself on the packing case beside the wheel, and glowered at us. We had not improved matters by speaking a language he did not know.

We looked at each other, dumbfounded. Theft? Family matter? What had happened?

Then Karl groaned, "Of course! It's that money he's been getting in the name of his cousin."

Silence dropped across the deck.

This was serious. It would be easy to prove the fact that von Haart had taken the money. He would probably be jailed. And so might we. After all, we had all more or less willingly let him spend the money on the boat and on us.

Kati voiced the thought we were all having. "Oh, why did we let him do it? He was a fool. How awful!"

"Perhaps," said Karl quietly, "only a fool would navigate a boat like this for seven other fools like us."

It was the closest I ever heard Karl come to quarreling with Kati. Her face flamed. In truth, I think we were all ashamed. Just a day or two earlier I had been looking at von Haart as he stood at the wheel with the endless sea behind him and I had thought of Vikings. But now I was thinking of him as a man who stole, a no-good, one of those fellows for whom there is no place in society. It was of course an image which a man like von Haart easily evokes. But in his case, everyone who met him knew better, and we, who had sailed with him for months, perfectly understood his true quality. Our treachery now was inexcusable. Furthermore, our anger and fear were very much motivated by selfishness. Our longest stretch of open sea lay between the Canaries and the West Indies. Without von Haart we had no navigator—we must give up the dream. Suddenly I wondered if we had ever been worthy to dream it at all.

No one cared to speak. Kati went below. The rest of us sat on deck, and kept our backs ostentatiously to the man with the gun. He laid it across his knees, and put his right hand on the stock. Anna took up Ahmed and stroked his shell meditatively. The little turtle drew in his head and lay still as a pebble. The difference between our sensations and the freedom from which we had just come, sent us all into shock. Our solitude on the open

sea and its vast distances had made molehills out of
mountains. The endless horizons had made us feel free.
But the feeling was ridiculous. Surely there were never
people more helpless than we—at the mercy of the elements, at the mercy of the sea, and in each port friend-
less and unknown.

The morning passed. At noon Kati came up bringing
sandwiches and coffee, and she offered some to our guard.
He refused. He also refused to let her go back below, or
to let anyone leave the deck again. He jerked the gun
up menacingly.

"He thinks we may poison him," said Kati, dismayed.

"Not at all," replied Anna. "I don't think he suspects
anything. It isn't that. He is enjoying himself. He likes
making us do what we don't want to do."

We were silent. It was a psychology with which we
were only too familiar. When we left Finland, it had
seemed like a tide overflowing the world. It was what
we were fleeing.

The guard indicated that he would accept a drink of
water. Kati fetched it. Apparently he found it foul-tast-
ing, though our tanks always gave less trouble than
those on most boats, and thanks to the lining suggested
by our friend in Helsinki, our water was notably fresh
and sweet. The guard, however, took a sip, made a face,
and threw the rest contemptuously overboard.

It was late afternoon before the gray dory returned.
May saw it first. There were three men but it was too far
to identify them.

We gathered at the rail as the boat approached. The
guard with the gun stood up. I thought von Haart was

one of those in the boat, but I refused to believe it. Already I had made up my mind that he would not return.

For our unspoken treachery to our good genius, that would be the punishment—we would lose him.

But he was in the boat. And he was smiling. He waved a sheet of paper. We stared.

He came on deck alone. The man with the gun leaned over to listen to the two in the dory, and then descended the rope ladder without a backward glance. The dory moved away.

Von Haart spoke first. "I have greetings from Madrid, welcoming us to Spain." The paper he was flourishing was a telegram.

"Oh, please," begged Kati. "Don't joke, von Haart. Tell us the truth. What's going to happen?"

"I *am* telling the truth," von Haart said. "This is a telegram from Spain saying how delighted they are that we have arrived. Here—read it."

He handed the paper to Karl, who read and passed it back. "The government of Spain," he said in a dazed tone, "is pleased to welcome us to the Canaries."

The tension left us, and we laughed with childish abandon. Von Haart settled himself on the cabin roof and leaned against the mast. "I told you not to worry." He closed his lips firmly and looked as if he intended to say no more.

"You tell us what happened!" exclaimed Lars, "or we won't let you have a single drink ashore. Not one! Not until you tell us. That's a promise."

We were all crowding around him, trying to express not only our happiness at his return, but also our sincere

warmth and affection, as amends for our previous reaction.

Von Haart lifted his hands in mock horror at Lars'
threat and replied quickly. "Well, it was perfectly simple, actually. Just required a bit of tact. I wired my
cousin and told him that charges had been pressed
against me for taking family money and suggested that
he clear me. My cousin and I have always been good
friends. We were boys together. We exchanged tele-
grams and he understood at once. If he had known it was
I getting the money, he would never have made charges
in the first place—although," said von Haart naively,
"I really can't imagine why he didn't guess." He went on
briskly. "Anyhow, he thought it was a thief. He didn't
realize it was I. The poor boy was really never very
bright. I'm sure he is extremely sorry. He sent me his
best wishes at once, and he also wired the Spanish authorities, urging them to extend to us the courtesies of
the Islands. So now . . ." von Haart got to his feet, "let's
go ashore." He hesitated. "There's just one thing. I can't
get any more money in his name. He was quite firm
about that."

"I can imagine!" said Karl a bit grimly.

"It's a beautiful place," went on von Haart. "La Luz,
they call it. Means 'light.' It's the capitol city of Las
Palmas."

Las Palmas! We glanced at one another. We were not
at Tenerife at all. Von Haart's navigation had gone a bit
wrong in the storm apparently. But no one cared to mention it. We went ashore. And it was noticeable that each

of us made a special effort to say something nice to von Haart.

He had a cold, and with the cold, a sore ear. Stubbornly, he stopped at several taverns, but finally he had to let us take him to a doctor. His ear was inflamed and the doctor gave him two medicines, a bottle of ear drops, and a bottle of nose drops. Von Haart emerged carrying the little flagons and looking puzzled.

One bottle was green and one was clear, and he was confused as to which was which. We got him back to the *Tuntsa* and put him to bed, where after considerable deliberation, the ear drops, a vile-tasting brew, went into his nose, and the nose drops went into his ear, where they stung like a hundred wasps. Von Haart cursed the whole pharmaceutical industry.

We reversed the bottles, repeated the operation, and in the morning his cold was better. But ever after, von Haart and all of us were apt to confuse the drops, and a cold on board would find the victim weighing the two bottles appraisingly and trying to recall which went where—and usually making a mistake.

*

We planned to stay three days in La Luz. Von Haart was determined to shorten the mast, and we were also in dire need of supplies. Von Haart predicted that we would need food for at least six weeks, possibly seven, for our Atlantic crossing. We went about with sober faces. We had long since sold all our tradeable goods.

There were none left. And we had almost no money at all.

Nevertheless, under von Haart's direction, we attacked the job of shortening the mast and adjusting the rigging and canvas to match. We cut off about six and a half feet. Von Haart made sketches of the rigging for Arvi and Karl. He marked the new shapes of the sails for the rest of us to cut and sew. We would now have a mainsail, fore staysail, and flying jib.

On the second day of our labors, a man and a woman came to our boat. The man was tall and well built, with a pleasing, open face.

"I'm from Denmark," he said. "I saw your Finnish flag and since we are neighbors, I wanted to say hello."

His wife was a handsome blonde in a white dress. While he spoke, she gave a model's smile and looked us over, staring (I thought) at each male rather too long. Kati, May, and Anna, who had been stitching away in their dungarees, stiffened noticeably. Anna tucked back her hair, May surreptitiously rubbed her stained hands on her trousers, but little Kati simply got out her glasses and put them on. I thought the blonde seemed to go a bit limp. She looked as if she suddenly felt overdressed.

"Won't you come below," May invited sweetly. "It's windy on deck. It will blow your hair."

We went below.

The Dane, whose name was Olle Borg, sat on a bunk in the galley, and crossed his legs as if he intended to embark on a lengthy conversation. His wife sat beside him, but she fidgeted. Either the girls had made her too radically uncomfortable, or the whole visit was not to her liking.

"We want to get out of the Islands," said her husband abruptly.

"So?" said von Haart. We looked at our visitor. His statement seemed irrelevant. Surely a Dane on the Canary Islands could leave whenever he wished?

"I wonder if you would smuggle us out on your boat."

"Smuggle?" I repeated. Von Haart raised an eyebrow. He looked suddenly interested.

"Why should we smuggle you?" Karl asked finally. "People come and go as they please here, don't they?"

"Well . . ." Our visitor cleared his throat. "I happen to be—uh—what you might call a political exile. After the war, I had to leave Denmark. I went to Spain. They shunted me here, and I don't like it. But I am here for the rest of my life unless I can get out."

We were all silent. It was not hard to guess the problem. The man had either collaborated with the German occupation, or he had been accused of collaborating. All of us on the *Tuntsa* had fought in the war, and there was a residue of keenest bitterness. But too often those accused of collaboration were not actual collaborators— a fact we all knew. After the war, people were denounced who had done nothing to cooperate with the enemy. In many cases, simply to have remained alive during the occupation had looked to zealots afterwards like collaboration. Many denunciations had been baseless. Others resulted from personal spite. In the fury of the liberated peoples, many so-called collaborators suffered unjustly.

"I am an architect," said our visitor. "I haven't a chance here. But if I could get to America. . . ."

Karl spoke then. "I think we understand. But we couldn't help even if we wanted to. Our food supply is so low that we can't feed our own crew for more than a few days, let alone two extra people."

The man answered quickly. "My father is in Denmark, and he is ready to wire me funds as soon as I find a way to get out of here. I can get you all the food you need."

It was a temptation. Von Haart pulled on his pipe and looked at the strangers. The rest of us glanced at one another. Inwardly I shuddered at the dangers involved in smuggling a man out of this country. All too vividly I recalled the mentality of the guard who had sat on our deck with his machine gun.

The woman had been looking around the shabby little cabin. Now she spoke for the first time. "Maybe just Olle should go with you. After he arrives, he could send for me and I could take a regular ship. Wouldn't that be better? There would be one less person for you to feed."

Her husband said warningly. "Inga, we have been over and over that. We go together, or I don't go at all."

"You have to go," she replied. "You can't make a living here." Her mouth was sullen. One could tell this was the continuation of an old and bitter argument.

"Will you take us?" Olle asked Karl.

"We will think about it," Karl replied guardedly.

The Dane rose with reluctance. His wife was halfway to the hatch while he still lingered. "Please think about it seriously," he begged. "I'll come back tomorrow. In the meantime I'll wire my father for money."

After he left, we broke into a babble of discussion.

Arvi and Karl were both opposed to the proposal. Arvi said it was too risky. Karl wondered to what degree the man had been a collaborator. Lars said, "I don't like the woman," and Kati, May, and Anna nodded.

But von Haart looked at us reproachfully. "He can give us something we need, and we can do him a service. As for his having been a collaborator, I'm positive he wasn't."

"Why?" asked Karl.

"He hasn't the face."

Lars groaned. "You'll land us all in jail simply because you like some fellow's face!"

Von Haart shrugged. "All right. Let's spend the day making the rounds. Maybe we can find some other way to stock up on food. But I doubt it. We never do well in this kind of place."

"Why?" Karl asked again.

"The *Tuntsa* just doesn't appeal to the people."

It seemed to me this was probably true. Swedish, English, French, Americans—all had shown almost unbelievable generosity to us. Their sympathy seemed to be instinctive. But in Lisbon we had nearly starved. And here the atmosphere seemed somehow the same.

Karl, Arvi, and I went off to call on neighboring boats. Lars and von Haart went into town. As far as the boats were concerned, we found that there were far too few—only small fishing trawlers or motor boats. Furthermore, getting into conversation was almost impossible. The people of Las Palmas seemed to be without curiosity. Von Haart and Lars came back from town with the same report.

That left Olle, and the possibility of supplying ourselves by agreeing to smuggle him out of the country.

"I don't wonder that he wants to leave," remarked
Karl.

Lars, full of sherry but otherwise profoundly discouraged by his trip ashore, had completely reversed his
views.

"There's no problem," he said airily. "Let's take them
on board for a drink, up anchor, and go."

Von Haart shook his head. "That's not the nature of
this sort of place. Olle is sure to be watched. Some official will have seen him visit us, and we are probably
being watched too."

"We would never get out of the harbor with them,"
said Karl positively.

Anna raised her eyebrows. "Them? I feel sure that the
woman won't come." Kati and May looked suddenly
more cheerful.

"He said both of them," Arvi remarked tersely.

"She has other ideas," replied Anna.

"The thing to do," said von Haart, "is to weigh anchor
and leave the harbor as if we were heading out to sea,
then slip back and pick him up on some beach where
there aren't any houses."

"I suppose pick him up in a rowboat," I said.

"You mean our dinghy?" Arvi asked, surprised.

"Good lord, no!" said von Haart. "We would never get
three people plus baggage in that peanut, even if his
wife sat on Olle's lap. He will have to rent a rowboat."

"Night would be the best time for pick-up, wouldn't
it?" Lars asked von Haart.

"Yes. Even if someone suspected what was happening, it would be hard to follow us in the dark. Once at sea, they would never catch the *Tuntsa* with her running lights out."

"We talk as if we had decided to do it," I said.

"There's no choice," finished Arvi simply. "There is no other hope of getting food. Smuggling out the Borgs is the only way we will ever get to America."

❖

When we got up the next morning, Olle was already waiting for us on the pier. He was alone.

We invited him down for coffee. He watched us use the blowtorch to heat the water. "We haven't been able to fix our stove," Karl explained.

"Living on the *Tunts*a is pretty crude," I said, rather hoping I could discourage him.

He answered soberly. "I wouldn't mind, if I were sailing on her away from the Canaries."

He drank the bitter coffee without expression. "I expect to get money from my father today. If you will tell me what supplies you need, I'll get them for you."

"Can you also tell us how to get you away without being caught?" I asked.

His voice was humble. "I think so." He offered us cigarettes and lit one of his own. "I am being watched, as you probably guessed. But today, I'll drop out of sight and stay at home as if I were sick. When you are ready

to leave, we can slip out my back door and come down to
the harbor."

Von Haart shook his head. "Not the harbor. They
would stop you for sure. I can *feel* the eyes around here.
Don't you know some beach on the back of the island?"

"Of course. Of course!" Olle nodded vigorously. He
was most obviously and desperately anxious to please.
"We have some friends who live fifty miles north of
here, about ten miles from the coast. I know the area
well. I can rent a car. When we get to the beach, we'll
just abandon it. Then you can come in and pick us up."

"Our dinghy can't carry three," I said.

"Rent a rowboat too," von Haart told Olle.

"Of course!" Olle cried. "That's just the thing! We'll
leave it adrift, and people will think we had an accident."

An odd sort of warning ticked in my mind at that moment, but I ignored it. I liked the man. I wanted it to
be possible for us to take him almost as much as he
wanted it to be possible for him to go. Furthermore,
without the supplies he would furnish, we could not
continue at all. And so we all cooperated with him in
ignoring the facts—a joint bit of wishful thinking which
was to prove nearly fatal. For it should certainly have
been apparent that a man who was being observed so
closely that he had to slip out his own back door after
dark, could not manage to rent so compromising an
object as a rowboat without attracting attention.

Yet not one of us mentioned it.

"It's settled then?" asked Olle hopefully.

We looked at one another, and we nodded.

Olle jumped up and shook hands all around, even giving Tuntsa a pat on the head. "You won't regret it!" he promised.

An hour later, we had decided on time, place, signals. Olle drew a freehand map and marked his beach. We planned to be there four days later at midnight. One of us would row ashore in the dinghy, and Olle and Inga would follow us back to the *Tuntsa* in their rented row-boat.

Olle got supplies for the *Tuntsa* by having a friend buy them, pay cash, and deliver them to us. We were overjoyed. There was a quantity of "gofio" (a delicious ground meal of roasted whole wheat and maize); there were loaves of bread, boxes of crackers, root vegetables, and fresh fruit. "Three hampers of bananas!" exclaimed May. For the *Tuntsa*, these were riches beyond measure.

*

Our re-rigging and re-cutting of the sails were finished. On the last morning in La Luz we bought a log rotator and a spare, "in case another shark makes cutting overtures," May said; and we filled our water tanks, always the final job before leaving port. We were ready.

We weighed anchor at noon and headed south, sailing about three miles off the coastline.

The night brought fog. With increasing anxiety, we watched it thicken to a soupy gravy, so opaque we felt we could almost mold it in our hands. Finally, von Haart said that we were opposite the appointed place. I could not imagine how he thought he knew, but had my usual blind (and nearly always justified) confidence in him.

"Who will take the dinghy?" he asked.

No one was eager for the privilege of venturing into that murk. We drew cards, and I won with a black Ace of Clubs.

I got into the dinghy alone and started to row in the direction von Haart said would take me to the rendez-vous. After about half an hour, I heard waves breaking against rocks. We had decided on a flashlight signal, and I paused to direct the beam shoreward. I signalled one long and three shorts and swung the light widely from right to left. There was no response.

It is probably not quite midnight, I thought. I will row a little closer and try again. By now I could make out a beach. It was piled with rocks and there was white foam breaking. A wind was coming up. It might help by blow-ing out the fog, but it would be rougher getting out from shore. Once again I tried signalling. Again, no response.

Now, what to do? I rowed on, attempting to find a less formidable area where I could take in the dinghy. There seemed to be no let-up to the rocky barrier. Rowing was becoming difficult. I was soaked and shivering from spray.

Ahead I saw a group of rocks extending out from the coast for perhaps fifty yards. At least it would be calmer on the other side.

As I approached, I decided to signal once again. Fif-teen minutes had elapsed since I had given the first sig-nal. This time there was an answer! It came from the other side of the prominence. Von Haart had guided us aright.

I rounded it and found a protected bay. I could see two figures dimly in the foggy background.

I pulled the dinghy up on the pebbly beach. Olle ran down to meet me. Somewhat to my surprise, his wife waited behind him. At her feet were two immense suitcases.

"Where's your rowboat?" I asked sharply.

He shook his head. "I'm terribly sorry. I just didn't dare. I was being watched, and they would have seen me. We can get along in your boat. I will take you back to the ship now, and then come for Inga. I'll row."

I stared at him bleakly. His good will was pathetic. He knew our dinghy could hold only two, but he had thought he could manage by making a double trip. What he did not know was that on anything but the calmest sea the dinghy would swamp. In any sort of surf she could at best carry one. And there was a wind coming up.

"The wind's rising," I said numbly at last. "I guess it is better to try all three now, than to risk coming back after the waves get up."

Olle of course had no idea what I was talking about, but he moved forward at once. When I made him leave one of the suitcases, however, his wife started to sob.

"I don't want to go," she whimpered.

"Come on," urged Olle gently. "Please, Inga!"

She got in the boat.

I had some line in the bottom and lashed the remaining suitcase across the bow. Then together Olle and I pushed the boat into the water.

I steadied it while Olle tried to get in back with his wife. The dinghy rocked violently, and it was all I could do to keep it from overturning as he tried to seat himself. Then he used the oars as a brace on each side as I tried to climb in. With my added weight, the dinghy was barely afloat. It wallowed and shipped water with each roll.

Once I began to row, she steadied a little, but my forehead broke out with perspiration at the thought of what would happen when we reached open water. My God, I thought, how did I get into this?

Olle was talking with humble sincerity about his gratitude.

We passed the protection of the rocks and were in the open. The wind was rising steadily now and blowing the fog into shreds of vapor. The sea was increasingly choppy. I had rowed perhaps thirty yards out from the beach when the boat filled so full that it overturned, throwing us into the water. Inga screamed.

"Stay by the dinghy and hang on!" I shouted. Olle helped her to the craft and she clung there, sobbing. I looked around for the oars. I saw one being carried out to sea. The other had disappeared.

A woman's gayly flowered dress floated by me. A shoe. The suitcase had broken open.

Slowly we turned the dinghy upright. While I held it, Olle lifted his wife into it. She sat moaning.

I swam on one side of the boat, Olle on the other. Slowly we passed the tip of the rocky projection and reentered the little bay. We reached the beach and Olle carried Inga in. She seemed slightly calmer. But I looked at her face in the darkness and thought I saw an expression of purest rage. If it was anger, at least it was keeping her quiet.

Olle spoke. "Shall we try again? Obviously, only one of us can go with you at a time. I'll stay behind. You come back and get me."

His wife sat up quickly. "No! You go first. You are the important one."

"Now, Inga," began Olle.

"I won't go first. I won't. Come back for me." There was no trace of tears in her voice now.

I broke in. "Of course, Olle. Be reasonable. She has to have time to calm down. I'll row back for her."

"I'll row," said Olle.

"All right," I said in exasperation. "Anything you like. But now let's you and I get started for the ship or we will both be here for life."

Then I remembered that we had no oars. I got up to search the shore for something we could paddle with. Olle joined me. After several minutes of looking, we found a board. But only one.

I eyed it skeptically. "Well, let's try." We pushed off. Once on the open sea, however, one paddle did not give us enough power to drive the boat through the ocean swells. Again we returned to shore.

Ingo was sitting on the beach, motionless. She said nothing.

"We have to find another board somewhere to use as an oar. One isn't enough," I explained to her. Rather to my amazement she got up and helped us look.

We checked the beach in the opposite direction from where we had found the board. There was a little driftwood, and a few sticks, but nothing long or flat or strong enough to propel a boat through water.

"How far can you swim?" I asked Olle at last.

"I'm a good swimmer," he said. "I don't get tired easily either."

I had indeed noticed that he swam well, and there was certainly nothing wrong with his courage.

"Here's what I have in mind." I explained that I would try to paddle with the board while Olle swam holding on behind the dinghy. "When you get tired, we'll stop and rest."

He simply nodded and went aside to speak a few words to his wife. He kissed her. Then he took off his clothes, and we entered the water.

I rowed and Olle swam for nearly an hour. I could not find the *Tuntsa*. We had agreed that the motor would be running to give me a clew in the fog. But I could hear nothing.

I was almost exhausted. I wondered if I could go on, and I looked back at Olle. His legs were moving heavily, as if he were very, very tired. I stopped paddling. "Wait a minute. I have to try to hear the boat."

"All right," he replied. His voice was almost a whisper.

With my shoulders humped and my head on my knees, I concentrated with all my might on listening. At last I thought I heard a motor. My imagination's playing tricks, I thought. But the sound grew louder, and I looked up to see a dark mass far to my right. It was coming toward us. I learned later than von Haart had been circling methodically over the entire area.

I shouted, "Over here! Over here!" Olle took up the cry. A flashlight shone through the fog and finally centered on the dinghy.

"They see us!" Olle cried.

I made a last effort with the board and brought us alongside the *Tuntsa*. Arvi threw one end of the rope ladder down and reached over to us.

I fell onto the deck. Olle followed, and stood clinging to the rail. The *Tuntsa's* crew clustered around us. In my exhaustion the voices I knew so well were merely a babble. "Where were you?" "You've been gone two hours!" "We were afraid you had drowned." "Where's the woman?" The last question was Anna's.

I heard Olle start to explain, and then I fell suddenly and deeply asleep, still sprawled on the deck.

When I awakened, I was below on a bunk in the galley. Olle, in a shirt of Karl's and shorts of mine was lying on the bunk opposite. His eyes were closed and his face was as white as chalk in the light of the swaying oil lamp. May was sitting beside me.

"Karl took the spare oars and went back for Olle's wife," she said. "Olle wanted to, but he could hardly move."

Our voices woke Olle, and we went on deck to wait, occasionally sending the rays of the *Tuntsa's* two flashlights out over the water. Finally, forty-five minutes later, we saw the shadow of the dinghy alongside. No one was in the boat with Karl.

"Where is she?" Olle cried.

"I don't know," Karl said wearily. "There was nobody anywhere on the beach. I rowed back and forth for nearly ten minutes then went ashore and walked."

"Was the car gone?" Olle asked.

"I didn't see any car."

I said nothing. I had expected that Inga would be

gone and that Karl would come back again. The reason I had been so anxious to get Olle off the beach was that I had been positive from his wife's manner that nothing on earth would have persuaded her to try the dinghy again. But Olle would have argued nevertheless, and it seemed to me that we might have stood there indefinitely—until the waves came up, and we lost the *Tuntsa* forever. Olle could not have convinced Inga. It seemed to me that her determination was obvious, though he could not have seen it of course.

In retrospect, however, he apparently agreed with with me, for when Arvi offered to row ashore and search the beach in his turn, Olle shook his head. "She won't be there," he said shortly. "Inga has a Swedish passport and can use it to come any time I send for her. And she knows I will send for her," he added in a lower tone.

None of us cared to pry. It had been apparent from the beginning that Olle's wife much preferred to come later, in a way more comfortable for her. It had been equally apparent that Olle did not want to be separated from her, even for the space of time it would take him to reach the West Indies on the *Tuntsa*. Undoubtedly, he had his reasons. Undoubtedly, too, he had now been defeated. He had managed to get Inga and her suitcases as far as the beach, and I thought probably even that had been a minor miracle. But to have expected her to go on after her fall into the cold water off that desolate shore was impossible. As soon as we were out of sight, she must have thrown her remaining suitcase in the car and driven as fast as she could back to town.

Olle picked up a coil of line and fingered it awkwardly.

"You people will have to show me how to help you," he said. "What do we do to head out to sea?"

"We just put the wheel around—so," replied von Haart. Karl adjusted the sails. No one said anything further.

And thus we began our long, westward voyage across the Atlantic. It was thirty-six hundred miles to Puerto Rico, the nearest landfall. We planned to by-pass the Virgin Islands and other islands of the Lesser Antilles.

The *Tuntsa* would be its own self-sufficient world now for a stretch of six or seven weeks. Our course was quite apart from regular shipping lanes, and we might not see a ship in all that time. We were eight familiar friends and one new personality isolated on our thirty-foot deck. Tuntsa and Ahmed were our only other company. But neither difficulty nor loneliness seemed significant as we began the longest part of our voyage. We were more and more bound together by our determination to reach our goal. It was a determination which grew in intensity with every advance we had made. And now—well, surely we were almost there!

CHRISTMAS AT SEA

our new passenger

boredom

games of chance

the whale shark

a ship!

the Sargasso Sea

It was Wednesday, December 17th when we left the Canary Islands. We would be spending Christmas and New Year's Day on the Atlantic.

The green land disappeared below the horizon and the ocean surrounded us. In our nostrils the sharp tang of brine replaced the warm moist smell of vegetation, the horizons opened again, and once more we seemed to be looking across the rim of the world. A school of dolphin had again found us, and there were fifteen or twenty of the great shimmering creatures playing near the surface. They seemed to delight in going ahead of the boat. Their leaps had almost military unison—ten or twelve would seem to be jumping at once. We felt that we were being escorted by friends. We loved dolphin as much as we hated sharks. There seemed at the moment to be none of those sinister pursuers behind us, or if there were, they were staying in the deeps. They would be around later, of course. We had nowhere to put our garbage but over the side, the sea was our disposal, and the sharp fins would soon be back on the *Tuntsa's* trail. But for now we rejoiced in the open water and the gay plunging of our dolphin escort, whose smiling, pointed snouts seemed almost to beckon us onward over the silver water.

Our plan was to make our next stop the Dominican Republic, where Karl, who had lived there before the war in his rice-farming days had friends with whom he was in correspondence, and who would be able to advise us about how to be admitted to the United States. No doubt there were technicalities, but they would soon be over, I thought. Then we would sail the *Tuntsa* to the Florida coast, disembark, and by next June be sending for Eero to join us. I envisaged nothing more complicated or difficult, and nothing now for the *Tuntsa* but a successful passage and fair weather. How wrong I was —on every count!

*

Olle, our new crew member, gave us much amusement during the first portion of the journey from the Canaries. Like ourselves when we left Helsinki, he was all thumbs. He couldn't coil a line or handle the sheets, and he was helpless at the halyards as a two-year-old. To add to his difficulties, he had not yet got his sea legs, and was queasy even in calm weather. My own impression was that he was also in a state of inner tension which was nearly tearing him apart. What the circumstances were between Olle and Inga, I did not know and was never to discover, but we could tell that he labored under strain and disappointment, and we thought our joking about his seamanship helped him. There were certainly plenty of jests at his expense. If poor Olle was tangled in the rigging, Karl and Arvi would chaff him mercilessly, "Much harder than building a house, eh?" and make a production of unravelling the mess. Under their good-humored teasing, and the necessity for concentration on his role as novice, Olle gradually put his troubles behind him, until he was usually thinking of nothing more serious than how to trim the mainsail when von Haart changed course.

He was a likeable man. We respected him both for his silence about his own troubles and for his wholehearted entry into life on board the *Tuntsa*.

We were all by now a little bored with our regular pastimes—cards for Kati and Karl, May and me; sketching for Anna; motor-tinkering for Arvi; philosophical arguments for von Haart and Lars. Olle did not fit into any of these diversions. Our card game was designed for four, Anna sketched alone, and Olle knew nothing about motors. As for von Haart and Lars, they had arrived now at a peak in their non-stop argument, which had begun when we left Helsinki and would go on as long as the *Tuntsa* continued to sail. Lars was a pessimist, von Haart a perpetual optimist. Lars plumped for the sciences; von Haart lived by simple faith in the beneficence

of the universe and man's ultimate destiny. Lars was a
strict determinist, convinced that the course of each life
was pre-ordained, set from birth by rigid mechanics of
heredity and environment. In proof of his convictions,
Lars would cite his books. Freud and Darwin were his
authorities, and he considered them infallible. But von
Haart was an iconoclast who perpetually demolished
arguments and left systems in splinters, simply by pointing with infuriating confidence to daily experience.

"If everything is pre-determined, Lars, then why are
you here, eh? What has made you set out to try to find
what you long for? If there were really predestination,
you would know it. Your blood cells would carry it. Your
instincts would sense it. You wouldn't worry. You
wouldn't even move. You'd be a vegetable. But you're a
man, and the fact that you are on the *Tuntsa* proves it.
Opposition to tyranny is instinctive. Not to oppose tyranny is treason to one's fellow man and one's own pos-
terity. That's what you're demonstrating. That's why
you're on the *Tuntsa*—not because your nurse gave you
a fixation on your bottle and so you had to go to sea, or
because you subconsciously want to return to the waters
of the womb. Nonsense!"

Poor Lars felt his ink-and-paper heroes, Freud and
Darwin, growing pale before his living hero, von Haart.
He would argue stubbornly, but it was plain that he was
giving way. Lars was changing before the onslaught of
von Haart's simplicity. Von Haart was making him leave
his world of books and forcing him to consider reality.
But it was painful, and Lars fought like a hooked fish.
Olle was not used to the struggle as we were. The pes-

simism of Schopenhauer, I remember, was Lars' theme
one sunny day and Olle retreated from the after deck
with a look of amazement on his matter-of-fact face.
"Does he go on like that all the time?"

"Von Haart is educating him," Karl explained.

Olle smiled. "I think he is over-educated already."

"That's what I mean," said Karl. "Von Haart is undo-
ing the damage."

Olle, however, shook his head. Finally he devised a
new pastime—one which all could enjoy together.

For a whole day he whittled steadily and carefully at
two little pieces of wood, constantly testing them between thumb and forefinger for balance. Finally, after
hours of dedicated labor, he proudly tossed them onto
the deck and called, "Come and look! Let me show you
my dice!"

After a while, however, rolling dice for no specific
gains seemed futile and we began to play for cigarettes.
Then Olle suggested, "Arvi, I'll roll you for ten minutes
of wheel duty. Just think, you might win your way out
of a whole watch."

"You're gambling!" Kati protested, shocked.

Olle laughed. "It's science. Ask Lars. Gambling gives
and gambling takes according to definite principles."

"That's quite true," agreed Lars soberly. He fetched
the encyclopedia and read aloud to Kati about the his-
tory of gambling. It began, he said, way back with the
Babylonians.

Kati was not impressed. Babylon, she said, was noto-
riously unharmonious and came to a bad end.

But there was little she could do; Olle's dice were new,

and they became the fashion on the *Tuntsa*. We diced for cigarettes, watch duty, and deck-cleaning. There was no job for which we did not gamble. Lars once handled the sails for seven straight hours, while Olle lolled at leisure before his envious eyes. Then later Olle had to scrub the deck alone every morning for four days to repay his own losses. One day von Haart won three packs of cigarettes. The next, he stood double duty at the rudder. We would exult when we won, complain bitterly when we lost, but win or lose, it was still a break in our old monotony. The gambling fever caught all but Kati.

*

During this first week at sea, we forebearingly ate watered-down soups, made extra thin "gold miner's sand-wiches" (a fried cake of gofio), and ate fresh fruit to stretch our food staples. Sometimes we fished, and were successful. We could not identify the different kinds of sea creatures we pulled in on pieces of salt pork and bits of tinfoil over our hooks, but there were some monsters which would surely have fascinated a scientific expedition. Lars would search his encyclopedia in vain, and bitterly bemoan our lack of reference works. Von Haart simply had us cut a small piece of flesh from each catch and put in a bit of silver—a coin or a little silver locket which belonged to May. If the silver turned cream-colored in ten or fifteen minutes, we must throw the fish to the sharks, for its flesh, said von Haart, was poisonous to man. If the silver remained clear, however, we ate

our catch for dinner. Whether this test was mere super-
stition as Lars claimed, or whether it had some accuracy,
I don't know; but the fact is that we were never ill from
any fish von Haart let us keep. Perhaps all denizen of
the deep would have been equally salutary; the silver
only clouded for one catch in twenty; but none of us
cared to chance a doubtful case.

There was another thing to which von Haart was also
unalterably opposed. He would not let us fish for dolphin. This, indeed, we did not want to do in any case.
We would have felt like cannibals if we had eaten one.

On the silent sea, one is constantly influenced by
glimpses of the life beneath the water. A beautiful fish,
a glowing mass of plankton, a luminous eye near the
surface at night (usually belonging to a small octopus)
gave one a sense of beauty, or mystery, or uncanny fear.
Each sight had its specific effect. I remember one day
when we passed a group of manta rays. The flat gray
triangular bodies were nearly twenty feet wide. They
flipped wickedly along the surface, trailing long powerful whiplike tails which were said to be able to rasp
the flesh right off a man. I shuddered and looked away.
They seemed the very embodiment of the pitilessness
of the lonely waters now surrounding us.

On December 22nd, our sixth day in the Atlantic, we
had a disaster on board the *Tuntsa*. Just before the evening meal, I heard excited voices in the cabin. Anna
raced up the galley ladder to the deck. "It's awful! Just
awful!"

Arvi looked at her in alarm. "Is someone hurt?"

"The food!" exclaimed Anna. "Come look!"

We hurried below.

The galley table was covered with fruit, potatoes, carrots, opened boxes—all of it furry with an odorous green mold.

"It's got almost everything," said May, looking ready to cry. Kati stood by limply, a picture of dejection.

Our first reaction was that it simply could not be true. We hurried to the hod where our potatoes, carrots, onions, and some of the fruit were stored. There our disbelief turned to horror as we found the first maggots. Some portions of our cherished supplies were literally alive with them. Whether they had come on board with Olle's stores or whether the eggs had got into our bins in some other port and were now hatching because of the tropical warmth we could not tell, but it was plain that nearly all our food was infested. The odor, faint at first, became nauseating as we gingerly moved away the top layers. I had never experienced anything like it except during the war, and the memories were not the kind one wants to return. I glanced at Karl. His tan was yellow-white. I was sure I looked the same.

Von Haart shook his head. "I've eaten moldy food on shipboard," he said, "and even scraped maggots out of bread, but this I wouldn't touch. The worst of it is probably not what we see but the invisible stuff that must be in it along with the worms to make it smell like that. I would rather take chances with shark than with putting it inside of us."

We stared somberly at one another. Our unopened cans, sealed boxes, and a little food kept on the galley table or otherwise in the open air had escaped. Our scant remaining stock of smoked meat hanging on deck, and two hampers of bananas lashed near the mast also were safe. Some of the food in the bins near the top was still edible. But that was all.

"If we threw it away, I don't think we would have a week's supply left," protested Kati desperately.

"Have you ever seen anyone die of food poisoning?" asked von Haart. "It's the sailor's most lethal enemy. If certain organisms get into his gut when he is miles from shore he is finished. And for agony, the Borgias had nothing to match it."

We were silent.

"Why didn't you find this before?" Arvi asked at last and looked accusingly at Anna.

"We did notice a strange odor the last two days but it wasn't until this morning that we saw anything," May answered defensively.

"We were going to refill the cupboard from the hold this afternoon," Anna said, "and we started about an hour ago. That's when we found out."

"Throw everything that is infested overboard," ordered von Haart. "We have to scrub the bins absolutely clean or it will spread to whatever is left, and to anything we may put there from this time on."

While the girls took turns alternately scrubbing and going on deck for air, for no one could remain at that work long, the rest of us carried up pound after pound of our precious food and threw it overboard. We went about the task in silence, but it took a special stoicism for Olle to see the loss of nearly all the supplies he had contributed. The sharks had a bacchanalian orgy. There suddenly seemed to be fins cutting our wake in all directions. They feasted and fought over the vile stuff, and there was blood on the water. We saw two of them frenziedly attack a third and eat him—I swear—while he still lived. They seemed to have gone mad. God knows what went on underneath the surface.

The meager food supply remaining to ourselves was put in the dryest spots we could find—lashed atop boxes in the galley, or on the higher shelves in the cupboards.

No one could contemplate eating dinner. We each smoked a cigarette in the open air at the bow. None of us went to the stern. The sharks were still at it. Lars, whose watch it was, stood alone at the helm, his back turned to the obscene feasting.

"With the best of luck, we still have three more weeks before we see land," von Haart said.

We had only seven or eight days' supply of cereal, canned sardines, meat and bananas, at most. Were we destined to starve—all alone on the vast Atlantic? No one would know our plight. Our radio had no transmitter. We had not seen another boat since the first day out of the Canaries. Von Haart had told us earlier that we might not see any ships at all until we reached the West Indies.

"Is there no way of changing course so we might meet a boat which could give us food?" I asked.

"The best thing might be to put back to Las Palmas."

Olle gave an exclamation. His face went white. "I would rather starve!"

"All right," returned von Haart. "On to the Indies

then. The fact is that, although we are only a week out, it might take twice that long to go back. The wind would be against us." He made his way to the after hatch and went below.

When he came back he was using his cane. I often noticed that in moments of discouragement von Haart's legs seemed to suffer. But his face was cheerful and he was carrying several charts.

"As I remember," he said, "the steamship route from Europe to South America crosses our course about mid-ocean." We gathered around as he sketched our route westerly and showed the approximate area where steamships might be found.

"Our problem is that almost no one uses this route. And the Atlantic is a mighty big puddle. We would be lucky to sight one ship during the part of the day we were planning to be in that particular area. Then whether we would happen to be close enough to signal is also a question. What we have to do is make for this spot and then alter course to parallel the shipping lane until we meet a steamer. Does any one have a better idea?"

We shook our heads.

"When should we reach this point?" I asked.

"Not for another ten days—with good winds. So we start rationing immediately. You women can stand it," von Haart said with a smile.

It was good to jest. Anna reached for an oil can and threatened to heave it at his head. Von Haart raised his arms in mock terror.

"Your figures are perfect! I only hope we'll sight a ship quickly so that not an ounce of your divine proportions will be lost!"

He went to relieve Lars at the helm, and the rest of us ostentatiously busied ourselves about the deck. But the silence was profound.

When I went to take over at the end of von Haart's watch, he sighed deeply as he gave me the helm. Karl and Arvi were sitting by the rail and watching the empty horizons.

"We could fish," I said.

"Not with *them*," replied Arvi with a jerk of his head. Without even looking carefully, I could count six or eight of the ugly triangular fins.

"We will try anyhow," said von Haart. "Things may get serious. I am not much for formal devotions, but here is one time I am going to turn to prayer. And I'll tell you this—it may be hard for a while, but we will manage somehow."

No one replied. Lars would normally have launched into a lecture upon the necessity for atheism for all intelligent people, but he simply went below. It was as if even he felt that we were in danger of a curse from the heavens. I looked beyond our boat, beyond the seas, to the westernmost horizon. The sun was setting into purple and gold brilliance. Something of von Haart's own feeling for the sea and its ways seemed to enclose me. As I steered, I prayed and felt inexplicable inner peace. The *Tuntsa* did not seem a foreign, insignificant dot upon the waters. Surely she and every soul on her were integral parts of the universe. We were part of an overall

plan, and like von Haart I believed that somehow our
need would be met and we would not perish.

Hunger and anxiety cruelly tax endurance. As I look
back, however, it seems to me that our endurance had
already been drained, and that the bleakness of the mid-
Atlantic, our fear, and our hunger only made evident
what had been happening in each one long before. Physically we must have been already very low. Poor food,
the confinement on board, the change of climates and a
thousand other factors had taken their toll. In spirit we
had undergone great strain—the wrenching departure
from home, leaving our children, the seemingly endless
journey with its incessant privations, the many times we
seemed unable to continue and lived from day to day in
terror of being marooned in some strange and repellent
land, the storms at sea which had endangered our lives—
at each crisis the energy to overcome it had somehow
been found, but the cost had been cumulative and now
pressed down upon each one aboard.

The *Tuntsa* crept at tortoise pace between an endless
sea and a cloudless sky. The breeze was moderate and
monotonous. We fished each day, but there seemed to
be no quarry of any sort around us. We attributed the
fact to unseen shark, but I do not know whether this
was true or not. On all the expanse of ocean there seemed
to be nothing alive but ourselves. Sometimes, indeed, at
a distance of a mile or two, we saw the rounded fins and
backs and water spouts which announced the passing
of whales, and some seemed as gigantic as ocean liners.
We would not have welcomed their company in any
case, but when we remembered our smaller, playful vis-

itor off the African coast, it seemed eerie that now not one of the monsters approached. Was the *Tuntsa* in some weird quarantine? Did an aura of doom surround us, and could the sea creatures sense it? Absurd imaginings, which would be dismissed on land, have strange tenacity at sea. Upon this endless desolate plain of shimmering water, anything seemed possible.

We reacted in our different ways. Lars abandoned his beloved encyclopedia and took to scanning the horizons earnestly. The real world became real to him with a vengeance. With our severe rationing, tempers became short and petty quarrels flared. Olle had an unusually sunny nature and remarkable resilience (were we like that, I wondered, back in the long-ago days when we left from Helsinki?); Karl still maintained perfect courtesy, which simply became more mannered under stress; and he, Olle, and von Haart stayed clear of the disagreements constantly setting the group on edge, but the rest of us were prey to losses of temper which later we would recall with amazement and shame. Anything could cause them, it seemed—a few minutes delay in coming on watch, a moment of sloppiness handling the sails. Annoyances which had never bothered us before suddenly assumed mountainous proportions. Even May and Kati, whose friendship had seemed unshakable, got into arguments in the galley. The strain on them was increased because both were worried about Anna. So indeed were we all.

For Anna, our robust almost boisterous friend, who could work beside Arvi in a storm or unblushingly return the quips of dockside loiterers, seemed to be retreating inside herself. The sensitive sketching she had loved no longer attracted her. Nor, apparently, did anything else. Her companions were almost exclusively Tuntsa and Ahmed. She would sit alone, staring silently at the sea and patting Tuntsa absently. At our meals, Ahmed in his tin container would be at her elbow, and she would feed him crumbs with silent attentiveness as if compensating for her own hunger. On deck, she would hold the little turtle in her hand. He had apparently learned to like the warmth and would stay as motionless as she. Arvi tried to distract her, but when he, or May or Kati, or indeed any of us approached her, the result was usually either tears or an outburst of reproach.

"We will never get there!" she cried once to Arvi. "The whole idea was crazy. We're going to die out here. I know it!"

"It doesn't help to talk like that," said Arvi.

"You're all fakes," she returned bitterly. "All of you feel the same. You just aren't honest enough to admit it."

Arvi said, "Be quiet, Anna!"

"Oh, I'll be quiet. But leave me alone."

Arvi left her alone, and Karl came to sit in silence beside her. The brother and sister, so different in character, nevertheless had an inner understanding, which did not need to be spoken.

Indeed it was Karl who helped us all. Karl was the one to whom we took our disagreements, who made peace, and reestablished mutual tolerance. But with nine people crowded on a thirty foot boat, existing on short rations, and wearing on one another's nerves after an association of months, the task was exasperating. Sometimes I thought that Karl, outwardly so controlled, was actually closer to breaking than any of us. With him the toll was, I thought, being taken physically. Under his deep sunburn, his skin appeared to be almost bloodless on some mornings, and his tan gave an effect of having been painted on. At other times, usually later in the day, a flush would come up on his cheeks. And it seemed to me that exertion at the sails made him shorter of breath than he used to be.

We were all smoking a great deal because of the emptiness of our stomachs. It was obvious that we would soon run out of cigarettes—a little thing, seemingly, but our crises were made of little things, and I feared that the powers of even Karl's diplomacy might someday reach an end. Surreptitiously, I began to save every discarded cigarette butt, and collected the tobacco in a flour can I kept under my bunk. On the day before Christmas we had one pack left. Everyone smoked the remaining ration with slow watchfulness, spacing out a cigarette almost a whole day, a puff or two an hour, until not a quarter inch remained. I decided it was time to get into my secret cache.

All were sitting in the galley after one of our frugal meals. I went to my bunk and quietly filled my pipe with tobacco. No one paid any attention. I returned, and the aroma from my smoke circled the galley. Lars sniffed suspiciously. Arvi turned in my direction. I sat calmly.

"Teppo, where did you . . ." Arvi began heatedly.

Lars' gaze followed the wisps of smoke from my pipe. I looked up in apparent unconcern.

"What's the matter?" I asked in feigned surprise.

"Didn't we agree to share our tobacco!" cried Lars. He was furious.

"Look, gentlemen," I said. "A gift to us from the Christmas Magi. They left it under my bunk."

I had been concealing the flour can full of tobacco on my lap. Now I put it on the table and opened it. There was a tense silence.

"How did you get it!" exclaimed Arvi.

"Not unfairly, I swear. A week ago I didn't have it. Now I do. Who can solve the riddle?"

The truth must have burst on all of them at once. We started to laugh. Arvi rose, came round the table, and joyfully pounded me on the back. Lars picked up a book and flung it at my head. We roared with laughter. Now I cannot imagine why, but then it seemed the most hilarious joke on earth.

We each filled a pipe a quarter full and had one smoke. Von Haart showed us how to stretch my salvage with other ingredients—dried used coffee grounds and tea leaves. Astonishingly, the mixture was not unpleasant, and a real quencher of hunger. We were all still occasionally sputtering with laughter, with shouts of "God bless Teppo!" and "Merry Christmas, Teppo!" I could not have been more pleased if I had caught the biggest tuna in the Atlantic.

The next day we had our Christmas dinner. Before the meal, everyone—except May and Kati, who did not smoke—had an entire pipeful, including Anna, who sat quietly enjoying Arvi's pipe. Kati laughed, and Anna gave her first wan smile in days. Then we opened two cans of sardines and made coffee. That was our Christmas dinner.

We sang carols and reminisced about former Christmases. In other years, some had been traveling, several had been visiting relatives or friends, a couple of us had been at the front. Von Haart commented that he had spent nearly all his last ten or fifteen Christmases on shipboard.

"I remember one particular year when I was a third officer on a luxury yacht," he told us. "We were in the Pacific approaching a beautiful island. Most of us were waiting for the time we would get off duty and celebrate the holiday with real spirits. But we never celebrated. We hit a reef and dived into lifeboats as the water began flooding the engine room. The yacht washed off the reef and sank. We reached shore, but I felt unhappy for weeks at the thought of all that good liquor going down to the fish."

The day after Christmas, von Haart told an amusing tale during our dawn coffee break.

In his early years, he had spent some time in the Orient. It was the beginning of his addiction, in the days when he had just begun to drift about the world on his endless pursuit of change and adventure. "I was a bartender in Shanghai, and you would think if anyone should be allowed to drink, it would be a bartender," he said. "But after I got fired twice for sampling the merchandise, I looked around for different work. I wanted a job which would let me lead my own life.

"I finally found one. I joined the police force. Those

were happy days," he recalled wistfully. "Since I never had the heart to arrest any one, I let everyone settle their charges by taking me out for a drink. I met a lot of interesting people that way. But then—" von Haart shook his head ruefully—"the Chief of Police came around after I had been on my beat two months and asked why I had never made any arrests. That was the end, of course. If one is a policeman one has to arrest people, not drink with them. But it was fun while it lasted."

"Where did you go after that?" asked Kati with interest.

Von Haart seldom talked about himself. If he was doing it now to distract us, he was succeeding, for we were listening attentively.

"Oh, wandered here and there," he said. "After a while, I signed on a ship to go to the United States. Another sailor and I worked our way across the Pacific, through the Panama Canal and up to New York. We were offered regular jobs on board but I wanted to see the city. So my friend and I jumped ship and rented a room in Brooklyn. We saw the sights for a week and then went on. We stowed away on a boat for Cherbourg." He described it all as casually as if he were discussing a motor trip from Helsinki to Kotka.

"What is New York like?" May asked eagerly.

"The most glorious city on earth," von Haart replied, smiling at her. "You'll love it. Wait till you see the shops! When you first come upon the city from the water, you can't believe it. Buildings twenty, thirty, a hundred stories tall point like fingers into the sky. God, what confidence! It's magnificent!"

"One atom bomb," said Lars. "Only one. The whole thing would be just a big cemetery."

"There won't be any bomb," said von Haart. "There will never be another war. This is the age of peace we're entering. War isn't possible any more."

"On the contrary," returned Lars acidly, "war will explode any minute. Five years from now, Russia and the United States will be at war. Humanity will be wiped out. You'll see!"

It was an old argument between them. "*You'll* see," retorted von Haart tranquilly.

"One thing," interrupted Karl, "if Lars' prediction is true, no one will see."

"Quite right," agreed von Haart. "That's what is so good about it."

"Good!" said Lars. He subsided into exasperated silence.

"It's like heaven and hell," said von Haart. "If there isn't any, we won't know about it anyhow."

Lars snorted and went on deck.

*

Kati and May were light sleepers normally, and guarded the container which held the blow torch alcohol, but we were all sleeping more than usual because of weakness, and our slumbers were deep. Comparing dreams, we found that most of us were dreaming of food. Von Haart, presumably, dreamed of drink. In any case, the craving finally became more than he could endure, and no one woke up on the night he rose from his bunk. He drank straight alcohol until he fell into a stupor. We found him stretched out on deck when we changed watches at dawn.

Efforts to rouse him brought a single wakeful moment of raucous good cheer, followed by childlike mutterings as he dropped off to sleep. Finally we carried him below, where it was simpler to let him slumber on. But without von Haart, the empty ocean seemed to increase the pressure of our solitude. Clouds were trailing long white shreds, and we feared an impending storm. We were all so weak I wondered if we could survive one.

Olle insisted that we try fishing again. "There's been a change of weather," he said. "And maybe we have come to an end of the fishless area."

I doubted it, for we still saw no fish anywhere. In seas where there were fish, we usually glimpsed them jumping or swimming near the surface. Little squid would scoot along, their legs clustered together to give them a sort of jet propulsion. At night they surfaced and their eyes gleamed on the water. But here there was nothing. Even the sharks seemed to have deserted us. Perhaps they knew that we were now quite hungry enough to try eating one of them.

Olle fashioned a spear from a long iron bar, which he hammered into shape against the base of the motor. The rest of us dipped into our precious salt pork and baited all available hooks, letting the lines drag farther and farther out behind the *Tuntsa,* for there was certainly no life close at hand. Olle was entirely unsuccessful with his spear, for he never even saw a fish. But Karl, Arvi, and I brought in six small bright perch-like quarry. There was only enough meat, however, to give each person "a bite and a sniff," as Kati put it.

Afterwards, as if to make up for our momentary peace, the biggest shark I ever saw began to follow us. He was a great mottled creature with an oddly flat head. He swam behind us, beside us, and under us, and when we looked at him hovering close below, we found him peering up speculatively out of evil little black eyes. He was with us all that day and was still there when we got up the following morning.

Von Haart was up at sunrise, apparently in perfect physical repair and in excellent humor. He was not in the least apologetic. "I needed a little drink," he said simply. "It's been too long."

"Little drink!" repeated Lars. "My God, von Haart, you'll kill yourself."

Karl informed him that he had missed a fish dinner.

"I don't like fish anyhow," said von Haart, "particularly that one." He nodded at our new attendant, who was so close to our starboard quarter that one might have supposed he was fastened to the boat. "That's a whale shark, a nasty customer."

Could he capsize us, do you think?" asked May.

"He could, but I don't think he is that clever about filling his stomach."

To relieve May, however, I went below and got my pistol, loaded it carefully, and shot studiously at the creature, steadying my arm on the rail. It happened that he was swimming at some distance when I came back on deck, but I felt sure of being able to hit him. He seemed fully as large as the boat. He dove, but resurfaced, and I saw no effect of my fire whatever.

"I wouldn't annoy him," advised von Haart, who had watched in silence. "You can't kill him. You might frighten him off, but I think it's better if he doesn't get excited."

In view of his size and his apparent imperviousness to bullets I thought so too, and returned my pistol to its place in my under-bunk locker. If I had fired again at a moment when he was directly under us, I might have been lucky enough to put a bullet into whatever area of that ugly flat head contained his brain, but his death throes could have damaged or even upset the *Tuntsa*. and it seemed foolhardy to meddle with him.

I think in any case our prevailing feeling by then was less one of outright fear than of helplessness. In the three days since Christmas, the edge had worn off our anxiety as it had off our hunger. Perhaps we were getting too weak. In any case, I know that I felt we were simply in the hands of fate. Arguments among ourselves had subsided. We did our work in silence.

We had a storm. It was as bad as any we had met, yet we must have experienced it with dulled faculties, for in retrospect I scarcely remember it. I recall that the wind changed capriciously as the storm came on, and one could predict only its violence, never its direction. We manned the wheel in pairs for twenty minutes at a time. The gale tore off the tops of waves and filled the air with spray which stung like flying needles. Our faces and hands burned, then became raw, and finally swollen. We were grateful for our shorter mast; the *Tuntsa* had to rise almost perpendicularly from each trough. We fought desperately to keep her riding the waves. Finally the wind came from dead ahead so that we had to fall off course, and when the storm was over, we found that we had lost almost five hundred miles. It would take an additional three days even to regain our old position.

On December 30th, all food was gone. At the same time my tobacco supply was finished.

The sea had quieted. Again there was that peculiar absence of life. The whale shark had disappeared. We seldom left the deck. Often one or another would imagine he saw something on the horizon. As we approached, however, it would turn into a bit of driftwood.

Then on the night of the 31st, I heard Lars, whose watch it was, call out excitedly.

"Lights!" he shouted.

I sprang from my bunk and raced on deck, followed by Arvi, Olle, and Karl. Lars gestured wildly. "It's out there. I tell you, I saw a light!"

We could see nothing. "It's imagination again," Karl said to me. "Better relieve Lars and let him sleep."

I hesitated. By the time Karl finished speaking I thought I, too, actually saw a light far away. Did I imagine it? We were all very suggestible. Many times in the last few days one of us had convinced another that a floating log was an approaching liner.

Von Haart had seized his binoculars as he ran on deck. He gazed through them for a long time without speaking.

"I think it really may be a ship," he said. "The light is getting brighter, so it must be moving. It must be coming toward us."

We shouted. We slapped one another on the back. The girls ran up on deck.

"Is it . . . ?" cried May, not daring to finish.

"We think it's a ship," I said.

"I don't see it," murmured Anna fretfully. "Where is it?"

May put her arm around Anna's shoulders and pointed. "There."

"I don't see it either, Anna," Kati said consolingly. "But von Haart sees it through the binoculars."

We lighted our two running lanterns and Arvi climbed the rigging to fasten them as high as possible. The kerosene lamp was hastily brought up from below and pointed over the rail so that its beam would be reflected on the water. Karl and I each took one of the flashlights. I practiced the S.O.S. As the *dot dot dot, dash dash dash, dot dot dot* played across the waves, the beam seemed to reach a pitifully short distance. I wondered desperately if the ship—if it was indeed a ship—would ever see it.

"Save your batteries," said von Haart. "They will see our lanterns first. Don't signal until they are about three miles away."

Minutes seemed like hours. We began to see the light clearly. Then the single spot of white grew to a triangular cluster. Von Haart nodded, and I began to signal S.O.S. in Morse code, over and over, until my fingers and arm ached. Karl began with his light. By now I could easily make out the silhouette and some of the detail of smokestack and lifeboats. But it was too far away to see figures. And I thought the ship seemed to be swinging away from us.

My throat muscles tightened and I couldn't speak. Olle cried, "It can't be turning! It has to see us!"

Anna sobbed. "Hush," said May.

"Why don't they answer?" I heard von Haart mutter.

But the ship was not swinging away. The changed shape of her lights had merely meant that she was coming about. Now she bore down on us. A light flashed from her bow. *She was answering.*

"Merciful God," murmured von Haart.

Very slowly the ship came within one hundred yards of us. We could see her rail crowded with figures. She was a cargo boat—Greek—on her side we saw the name of her port—Athens.

"We have no food!" called Lars in French. Karl took up the cry in Spanish, and von Haart in English. "Will you help us?" he shouted.

"Can you get closer?" someone on her bridge bellowed back in broken English on a bull horn.

We had dropped our jibs. Now Arvi started the motor as I lowered the mainsail. Von Haart maneuvered the *Tuntsa* to within fifteen feet. We did not dare get too close for fear waves would smash us against her hull.

At last the *Tuntsa* wallowed in the big ship's lee, next to two wicker fenders the freighter lowered to keep us apart. The *Tuntsa* was like one of the steamer's lifeboats in size. By then the captain and von Haart were shouting a regular colloquy in broken English. Von Haart explained that our supplies had spoiled, and that we had eaten what little we had left two days ago.

"Glad to help . . ." the captain called back. "I think you're crazy to be out here in that . . . that . . . thing!" He pointed to the *Tuntsa.*

"Where the hell are you going?" another voice cried.

"America," Arvi shouted. The crowd looked down on us incredulously.

"We have come from Finland," called von Haart.

"Finland!" There was another rumble of startled voices.

Then someone on board shouted a command in Greek, and there was comparative silence as actual operations began. They made several attempts to drop lines but missed our deck by several yards on every cast. "We're not used to throwing lines to toy boats," a sailor called. Laughter followed.

We laughed politely also, then hastened to follow the captain's orders to cleat the hawser which finally landed on our deck near the stern. We started the motor and headed away until the hawser was taut. This would steady the *Tuntsa* and keep her a constant distance from the larger ship.

It was nearly eleven o'clock when our S.O.S. had been answered. Now it was one in the morning. Maneuvering into position and securing the lines had taken more than an hour. Then we waited nearly another hour while the Greek crew readied our packages.

While the food parcels were making their slow trip down the line, von Haart and the captain exchanged nautical information. "What is our position?" von Haart asked.

The captain gave the exact latitude and longitude and von Haart called back in triumph.

"The *Tuntsa* and my inborn genius calculated our position to be within fifteen miles of yours. She is perfectly on course." Von Haart joined the laughter, but he

was at least half serious. To him the *Tuntsa* was a remarkable ship. All his own miracles of seamanship he
attributed in large part to the excellence of his beloved
boat. Seeing her bobbing like an insignificant cork at the
feet of the big freighter brought forth his boast.

It was two-thirty before the final package reached our
deck and the Greek crew pulled back their lines. Fervent
thanks were voiced by all of us, in every language we
knew.

The captain called down in his broken English. "This
will give you energy for the rest of your crazy trip. I
hope you make it." He sounded dubious, and I thought
a good part of the men around him were in agreement.
But many more cried, "Good luck!" "God bless you!" and
"Happy New Year!"

As the freighter steamed away, we looked hungrily at
the bread, butter, canned beef hash, bologna, apples,
and other food on our deck. Someone among our unknown benefactors had even sent down a dozen cartons
of cigarettes. Olle led a cheer and we continued to shout
as long as we thought our departing samaritans could
hear. Then May cut slices of bread, passed butter, and
we ate hungrily.

"Slowly!" warned von Haart. "Your stomachs will
cramp."

Little Tuntsa, however, was not worried about his
stomach. He gobbled voraciously and barked for more.

But we ourselves found to our amazement that we
were satisfied with very little, and that we immediately
felt excessively sleepy.

We decided to postpone our real celebration dinner

until the following evening. The strain of two days without food and of the last four hours of physical effort had all but exhausted us. We longed now to sleep away the tension, the fear, the desperation, and the inner torture we had known so intimately the past ten days.

We tossed Olle's dice to see who would take first turn at the wheel. It turned out to be Arvi. We arranged to relieve the helmsman every hour until morning, and then crept below to sleep.

Von Haart and I were the last to leave deck.

"Well," I said, "tonight nine people got their heart's desire. It's not often one sees that."

"No," he said soberly. We were adjusting the mainsheet so the night helmsmen could handle the sail.

"If you had your heart's desire, von Haart—for life I mean—what would it be?"

"To own a tavern," he replied promptly.

We laughed. I could imagine von Haart's tavern, filled with personalities, each one different and fascinating in some special way, as von Haart's cronies always were—von Haart himself the center, as if on some perpetual land-going *Tuntsa*.

*

New Years Day on board was an exuberant feast. We ate on deck and everyone gorged. The girls fixed a delicious stew. We had fresh rye bread, fresh fruit, and cookies. We made it a New Year's celebration, and toasted the coming year with canned fruit juice, pretending it was the most potent Patagonian swizzle. At midnight, we went wild. We cheered, toasted, and blessed the Greek ship—the new year—the *Tuntsa*—von Haart—our crew—and our imminent arrival in America. The girls had never been hugged so enthusiastically. We were all glowing with happiness. Only Anna was a little quieter than the rest, and Karl a little weary. By five minutes past twelve, we were all hoarse—and exhausted. With a few last croaks of "Happy New Year!" we went to our bunks and slept soundly until eight o'clock, with hour long watches until morning as on the night before. We were too physically exhausted and too nervously keyed-up to trust ourselves yet with regular four-hour spans.

But on that night we had a repeat on our earlier disaster with von Haart—he got to the blowtorch alcohol once more. Morning found him in a state of happiest inebriation, barely able to stand. May shook her fist at our befuddled but joyful navigator. But it was difficult in our present mood to maintain anger.

"I kiss your hand, Miss May," said von Haart, teetering into a mock solemn bow. "I forgive your lack of understanding. But I bless your sound sleep!"

May smiled. Indeed it was hard not to laugh. Von Haart was an accomplished clown and could be most marvelously funny when he wished. Olle and Lars finally carried him below to sleep it off.

Meanwhile, however, sharks again cut our log line, and until a new watch discovered the severed end and installed our spare rotator, we were without a record of the *Tuntsa's* progress.

As if in devilish cooperation, the weather on that evening chose to span the sky with dense clouds. When von Haart got up the next morning, he found that he was not only uncertain of our position but because of the weather, could not take star or sun shots. We had no idea where we were upon the vast Atlantic, nor had he. A brisk wind was pushing us onward, but until the clouds broke, we could not know whether we were headed toward Puerto Rico, Bermuda, or the Lesser Antilles. Our compass told us we were on a course north northwest. That was all the knowledge we had.

During the night the brisk wind died, and a strange stillness surrounded us. Von Haart looked about him scowling. "I don't like this. It doesn't feel right."

At daybreak Karl, whose watch it was, looked upon an unearthly and amazing spectacle. As the damp night blackness, which had lain upon hands and face like layers of wet felt, slowly gave way, and the eerie light of the new day surrounded the *Tuntsa,* he saw that the silent seas around us seemed oddly mottled. The wind, which had been dying all night, barely filled the mainsail. For some time before the darkness lifted, he had been wondering why the *Tuntsa* responded so sluggishly to her helm. Now he saw the reason. We were not receiving the benefit of even the faint wind which still remained, for the *Tuntsa* was pushing through a mass of seaweed. As the light increased, he realized that the spotting of the water was caused by other clumps of weed which increased in thickness and number every moment.

Karl went to the hatch and shouted to von Haart, who

alerted by the unwonted stillness, and perhaps a linger-
ing uneasiness from the night before, was already sitting
up on the edge of his bunk. He came on deck, and Karl,
Arvi, Olle, and I followed. As soon as he looked around
in that eerie light, von Haart stood still as though thun-
derstruck.

"God in heaven," he murmured at last. "The Sargasso
Sea."

There was now an almost complete layer of brown
weed upon the water and not a breath of wind. Our canvas hung like rags—we were a tattered ship upon a tattered ocean. The seaweed gave an effect of an enormous
coverlet, torn and patched by water. The weed was a
rubbery substance with ragged brown tentacles sprin-
kled with little air bladders like millions of blisters. In
and out of the lacy tatters ran rivulets, like the veins of
countless autumn leaves. It was strange to see that although there was no wind, the *Tuntsa* moved steadily
into the mass. Around and under us must be currents,
which had brought the weed here, trapped, and held it.
Our drift was slight. Slow though it was, however, the
great water jungle now extended all around us.

"We must have got into it quite a way," said von Haart.
He peered through his binoculars. "This infernal haze!
I can't see more than three-quarters of a mile. The edge
can't be far, but which direction? Let's come about and
try to find the way we came in. Olle and Teppo, get the
dinghy and pull our bow around. Arvi, see if you can
start the motor."

In the dinghy we were almost level with the weed. I

saw that the whole evil jungle was swarming with life—
not fish, but the sort of creatures one sees under rocks
and on mudflats at low tide. Spider-like crabs legged
their ugly way along the rubbery leaves. Little octupi
of a singularly repellent bluish tinge skittered around
and under. The whole obscene, floating mass heaved
with the movement of water below, like a great mass of
brown jelly; and with the dinghy weighed down by the
two of us, we were all but immersed in the nauseous
stuff. The fetid air, reeking of wet decay, was suffocat-
ing. Arvi's motor started and we felt a moment of hope,
but the propeller was at once fouled by weed. Olle and
I, sweating and thrusting to get the oars into water, had
brought the *Tuntsa*'s bow around, and now we tried to
clear the propeller by using the oars and a pole von Haart
passed down from the deck.

But our spare oars, which were all we had left after
picking up Olle, were quite helpless to push aside the
coarse blanket of weed. Our poking was useless. The oars
were too short; the pole was too thin. We would have
to dive physically into the brown mass. Olle stripped
and went first. He cleared the propeller blades and they
turned. He came back aboard shuddering and cursing.

"It's alive," he said. "The whole damned thing is alive
with things crawling."

The motor ran awhile, then choked and died.

I dove in my turn and felt my arms and legs, back
and neck being softly explored by creeping creatures. I
swore and fought the weed.

Arvi would run the motor five minutes, turn it off, and

then we would dive again to clean the propeller. This gave the motor a chance to cool before Arvi started it again.

It was a miserable, exhausting torment. All through the day we repeated the short motor runs and long propeller cleanings—each man taking his turn at diving. We brought up the dinghy and used the rope ladder to lower ourselves into the water, for the dinghy had begun to fill with little scuttling creatures. Soon even the *Tuntsa*'s deck skittered with crabs. Tuntsa chased them and barked. The air was motionless, the heat and stench unbearable. And with all our labor we had probably moved less than half a mile.

The sluggishly heaving vegetation was a floating graveyard, its density supporting relics of the sea, ragged portions of old life jackets, chunks of ship's planking, pieces of oars—mute memorials to God knows what forgotten storms, washed here by the currents and caught forever.

At nightfall, there was still no end to the ghastly jungle, nor any wind to clear the haze or speed our progress.

Exhausted, we let the *Tuntsa* wallow where she was and went to bed.

The following day we started again. At noon, we took time off to eat a sandwich.

"Who would ever see us way out here?" May asked. But she knew the answer as well as we. Ships avoided the Sargasso Sea like the plague.

"Do you honestly think we can reach open water?" I asked von Haart.

"I think so—if our fuel holds out," he said. "There used to be tales that the Sargasso Sea could trap and hold a boat, but it's been proved untrue. . . ."

"By whom?" asked Lars with angry skepticism. "Was there a scientific expedition, I'd like to know?"

"I don't have the least idea," replied von Haart tranquilly. "But it's a fact. The Sargasso can't hold a boat. I never heard of it happening, and it won't hold the *Tuntsa*. You'll see."

We were silent. All of us, even Olle now, were accustomed to von Haart's "you'll sees."

"All we have to do," said von Haart, "is keep moving. If we go in the same general direction and have no breakdown in the motor or propeller, we have to get out eventually."

No one replied. It seemed to us that the weed was constantly thicker. We could not tell if we were really making progress or not, for the devilish haze was all around us. The heat and mugginess, the constant odor, the diving into that crawling mass, were endless torture.

After lunch, von Haart was first on deck. Below we listened to his cane pound slowly across . . . stop . . . then tip-tap quickly back. I heard his excited voice at the hatch. "Come up! The weed is moving." I didn't understand until he exclaimed, "We are in a stronger current!"

But when I came on deck, I felt keen disappointment. As far as I could see the same gulfweed still enclosed us, and seemed motionless except for its steady, jelly-like heaving. Then I looked more closely and saw that there was a slight directional floating of the smaller clumps. Seconds later our mainsail showed a ripple. Indeed, it was true—the water was sluggishly flowing south. There must be open sea ahead. The air, too, was faintly in motion.

"We're coming to the edge," von Haart cried. He moved to the wheel.

Standing at either side of the bow, Arvi and Olle pushed away the heavy growths with poles. It was slow work. Olle, more impetuous, finally got back into the dinghy and hacked once more at the weed from water level. Karl and I tenderly nursed the sails into cupping the tiny breeze.

But at nightfall of this second day in the Sargasso Sea we still could not discern the ocean. We had covered only about a mile with the help of the faint wind and by riding the weak current.

Once more we left the *Tuntsa* where she was, dropped sail, and fell dispirited and exhausted into bed.

By morning, however, the current was swifter, the haze was gone, and we saw a solid bluish mass in the near distance. Von Haart scanned the horizon with his binoculars.

"It's open water, two miles away!"

We knew then that we must have been at least four miles into the jungle.

It took us almost all the third day to fight through the remaining mass. The growth persisted thickly right up to the rolling ocean. But the last mile was almost enjoyable. A breeze touched our foreheads and fanned our backs. Our sails filled. We entered the open sea in late afternoon, and our spirits matched the swift movement of the newly freed boat. Tuntsa barked and raced about the deck, beguiling us to throw sticks and play with him, as if he understood the release from our prison. Ahmed sunned himself in his favorite spot atop a coil of line near our oilcans. In spite of our heavy use of the motor, we still had two quarts of oil and half a dozen cans of gas left.

"Plenty to reach the West Indies," von Haart declared. "It will be smooth sailing from now on. Fate wouldn't dare order more bad luck for us."

But we were to have a few uneasy hours our first and second nights out of the Sargasso Sea. The skies clouded over after sunset, and we began to see lightning all along the southwestern horizon. The tremendous flashes spread until they climbed half way up the sky, making it look like a white wall. We were heading southwest and certainly were not eager to sail into the mysterious electrical phenomena visible in the distance.

Von Haart shook his head. "Something unpleasant is getting ready over there," he said. "I just hope it moves the other way."

We fell off course and watched the distant horizon. There was no sound, but in the eerie stillness the jagged sheets of lightning continued to whiten the sky throughout the night, were occasionally seen near the dark horizon the next day, and repeated their silent flashes as soon as it was dusk. We finally became used to them and since the brilliant display seemed to come no closer, we simply enjoyed its grandeur and sailed serenely on. More than three-fourths of the ocean voyage was now behind us. We had been on the Atlantic a month. Within another week we might catch sight of seabirds again and finally see land once more. It was an exhilarating thought.

On our sixth day out the Sargasso, however, von Haart complained that the rudder would not answer. Arvi and Olle tested the wheel and cable controls. They discovered that the welding to the iron rudder post had broken.

"We haven't enough heat to re-weld it," Arvi said. "We have to unship the rudder, drill through the neck of the drive gear and rudder post and get a steel pin through."

It took three hours to drill through the welding on the gear neck and another two to drill the rudder and find a pin which could be filed to fit. Every man took turns drilling, for each became exhausted after a few minutes. It was grueling work.

But finally the rudder was working again to von Haart's satisfaction, and with no further setbacks we resumed our journey, with hope higher than ever. Only Anna continued her strange silences, and sat on deck alone for hours, looking at the water or stroking Ahmed's indifferent shell. It was seldom now that she played actively with Tuntsa.

"I feel that I will never get there," she would say to Arvi when he tried to talk to her.

"Of course we will!" he would answer heartily. "Don't be foolish, Anna!"

Indeed it was obvious that the greater part of our long journey was now over, and we were, in full truth, "getting there."

"Anna's in one of her moods," Arvi said to us reassuringly. "She always had them."

"Not like this," Karl told me later. "I'm worried."

Kati and May began persistently to bear Anna company, taking a book or sewing on deck and sitting near her to chat. But Anna answered absently. Her old exuberance had quite disappeared.

We were six weeks out of La Luz when we saw our first birds. They were winging toward a distant cloud on the horizon far ahead. Then we saw a ship, and a sailboat heading the same direction. At last, a faint jagged line gradually appeared below the cloud.

"Land ahead!" Arvi shouted from forward on the cabin roof. I was at the mainsheet, and called to Karl at the helm. They heard us below and von Haart stumped up carrying his charts and sextant.

"We are coming to Sombrero," he said. This was the easternmost island of the British Leewards in the Indies. "We should see her lighthouse in about two hours."

We sailed on. The gray line thickened, turned green, and disclosed beautiful fertile hills. We waved to the lighthouse keeper's children as we passed. We did not plan to stop, but to by-pass the Leeward Islands, sailing from Sombrero through the Anegada Passage, then on by Anegada, Virgin Gorda, and Tortola. We hoped to continue past the other Virgin Islands, make a brief stop in Puerto Rico, and then sail on to the Dominican Republic, where Karl had friends.

Von Haart did not want to put in at Sombrero or any of the Leeward Islands. "The whole area is full of coral," he said. "It's the small boat's death trap." He planned to go around, although it would require two full extra days to reach Puerto Rico.

"We will bear northwest when we leave Sombrero. That should let us clear reefs."

Tuntsa smelled land. He seemed to sense we were not

to stop, and whined complainingly. Von Haart patted
him and threw a stick to the foredeck. Tuntsa ignored it.
Instead, he started barking.

As the island faded astern, Tuntsa continued his tem-
peramental outbursts. He occasionally ran to Anna and
buried his head in her lap.

"What's wrong with Tuntsa?" she asked.

"Nothing," Arvi said. "He wanted to go ashore at Sombrero, that's all. You know he always barks when we get
near land."

By mid-afternoon we were well into the Anegada Passage and bearing northwest. Tuntsa continued his wild
barking, alternating with spells of sitting moodily in
Anna's lap. We tried to get him to play but he responded
half-heartedly. We offered him food. He showed no interest. After nightfall, he intermittently woke up, as if
from a nightmare, and yapped fitfully or whined. Finally
Anna took him in her lap again until we were ready to
go below.

"I hope he isn't getting sick," May commented with
a look of concern.

"He's all right," said Arvi. "Dogs can be tempera-
mental as well as people."

We went below and Arvi snapped his fingers to order
Tuntsa "to bed." Still whining in protest, the little dog
went reluctantly to his blanket.

Lars had the watch until two. Arvi was to take over
until six.

The rest of us fell into peaceful sleep.

WHITE HORSE REEF

wrecked

a night in the surf

von Haart takes a drink

rescue!

the Tuntsa *is pillaged*

As the thunderous impact threw me from my bunk to the cabin floor, my first thought was that we must have been struck by a squall and been demasted. Then came the sickening grind of timbers and I knew we must have run upon a reef.

The cabin was in total darkness. The kerosene lamp which usually hung on the hook outside the lavatory, must have fallen and gone out when we struck. I could not see the others. Nor could I hear them, for the noise of water overhead was a continuous roar.

I felt my way to the hatch ladder. I fell as the boat gave another tremendous lurch, and fought back to the ladder where I crawled up almost on my back, so careened were we. The ship seemed to pitch almost from end to end. When I forced open the hatch, I was nearly blinded by spray. Dimly I could see three figures clinging to the lifeline at the foredeck rail, and I thought them to be von Haart, Karl, and Olle. I was stunned to see them outlined against line upon unending line of white combers—the most feared sight upon the ocean, the dread sign of underwater shoals. I turned to look behind me. The sea was heavy. Almost upon us was a wall of water cresting to either side as far as I could see. As I glimpsed, I gasped. Then it struck.

My instinctive gasp probably saved me from being swept into the sea. I clutched the cabin roof, lost my grip, clutched again, felt my lungs bursting for air but still had the strength to grip a third time without losing consciousness. Tremendous force raised the ship under my feet and flung her forward once more with horrifying impact.

The water receded—released me—I could breathe. The last enormous thrust seemed to have steadied us somehow. We had been driven over the porous edge of the reef and were impaled on the solid coral beyond. Now, although the *Tuntsa* reeled sickeningly from side to side with every wave, she did not pitch so violently. I could hear the grind of timbers, and in the trough between each swell, could see on either hand the cruel stag horns of the reef's inner edge. The bow must have struck almost dead center and been thrown forward until the hull literally channelled into coral. Vividly I could picture the gouging of our timbers with every lurch upon the hundreds of smaller horns beneath us.

I crossed the tilted deck to von Haart and Karl. Olle

stood with them, and Arvi, who had been at the helm, staggered forward to join us.

He shouted to von Haart, "I was watching the compass. We were on course!"

"It's White Horse Reef!" shouted von Haart. "Drop canvas!"

Olle and I struggled with the wildly flapping jib while Arvi and Karl brought down the mainsail. White Horse Reef! I could not believe it. I had seen it on the chart. We should have been miles to the north.

Lars emerged from the after hatch and ran across the canted deck, clutching the cabin roof to steady himself in the sweep of waves across us.

"Water!" he shouted. "It's rushing in below. The women are terrified."

I left Karl wadding the sails into a soaking mass at the foot of the mast and hurried below. Anna had relit the lamp. One side was shattered, but it gave an unsteady light which dispelled the blackness in patches. I could see the sheen of water already over the walkway, and rising so fast that I could note its ascent, the surfaces gleaming moistly in the flickering light. May was struggling with the emergency pump. Kati had the discharge hose in her hands and was apparently about to try to carry it on deck. I seized it from her, and Lars took over the pumping.

I put the hose over the side and joined the others around the mast. For a moment we huddled together, faces shocked and unbelieving. Von Haart had wakened minutes before we struck. He had been restless earlier, aware that the sea was rising, and had gone briefly on deck. All seemed in order and he went back below, where the accustomed whine of the rigging, the cry of the wind, and the monotonous rush of water on the other side of the hull beside his bunk lulled him back to sleep, until suddenly his trained ear caught another sound which he sensed was not right. Once more he got up, and was heard by Karl and Olle. They followed him on deck, and the three had just made their way to the bow to peer into the darkness ahead, when the *Tuntsa* struck.

Von Haart looked up at the mast which slewed violently from side to side with each wave. "We have to cut it down," he shouted.

Shivering and soaked to the skin, we took turns chopping at the spar's thick base. It was miserable, murderous work in the biting spray and plunging walls of water. Dawn came before the mast finally fell and the *Tuntsa* eased her wild swaying.

Our next concern was that the sea would work us off into deep water and sink us. Von Haart ordered the anchors thrown out to either side of the bow. When I went below to get the second anchor, I found that the water now reached my thighs. Anna and May were taking turns relieving Lars at the portable pump. Kati was ill.

"It's no use, Teppo," she said as I bent over her. "The sea is coming in everywhere. We had better go on deck with you." She was sitting on her bunk holding a drenched and terrified Tuntsa on her lap. Ahmed scrabbled in his little can beside her.

"You can't stand it up there, Kati," I protested. "Better stay below as long as you can."

But Kati shook her head. Lars was at the pump now, and Anna collected an armload of blankets. "If we break up, Teppo, we would drown down here. The pumping doesn't help anyhow. We would all rather be on deck."

May sloshed from the midships cabin toward me, holding a large can under her arm. "I filled it with drinking water," she said quietly. She also held three jackets. The girls quickly put them on.

I helped Anna and May spread blankets around their shoulders and fastened the top button on our two raincoats for a more waterproof covering. "When we get to the deck, we'll put Kati in the center and spread a part of each raincoat around her. Then you will all be partly protected."

As the queer procession started for the ladder, with Anna now holding Tuntsa, while Kati carried Ahmed, I stressed the danger of being swept overboard. "Go slowly and hang on to something solid."

I went first and Lars brought up the rear. I saw that he had wrapped an old jacket around a few of his beloved books and some of our photographs and ship's papers. We made our way across the deck, and the girls huddled on the cabin roof, the highest part of the ship. Lars and I tied lengths of line around their waists, and secured the other ends to the stub of the mast, where Lars also fastened his bundle.

The sea rose steadily higher along the low side of the increasingly tilted deck. Tuntsa panted in Anna's arms and rolled his eyes, too frightened even to whine. In his can, Ahmed drew in his head and legs and turned himself into a pebble. I wished that I could do the same. In the cabin, the water was creeping half way up the hatchway ladders.

Then von Haart noticed air soughing out the portholes

on the roof. He shouted to clamp them tight and fasten down the hatch covers in hope of sealing in the remaining air to keep us afloat.

It was still not completely light. We no longer tried to call to one another above the noise of breakers, but sat in silence, hunched together for warmth, with our faces lowered to escape the driving force of the waves. The larger ones almost dragged us overboard.

If this was indeed White Horse Reef, I knew it was a coral barrier southeast of Anegada and perhaps ten miles northeast of Virgin Gorda. This curving fringe of shoals between the two Virgin Islands had been the graveyard of countless ships. Years ago, unsuspecting helmsmen had been lured onto the coral by plundering natives. They would flash false beacons; and pilots, who thought they saw a lighthouse, would head into disaster.

How could we have erred so greatly? We should have by-passed the reefs by nearly ten miles. Had Arvi mistaken our course? Was there an error in the compass? Had the wind blown us westerly instead of northwest? Or had von Haart plotted our route incorrectly? He had admitted earlier that he had no detailed maps of the White Horse area. We were never to know the real reason, but our map of ocean currents was more than two years old, and it seems probable that the fault lay in the false economy of not buying a new one. In those waters, the course and velocity of currents often varied from year to year.

We shivered, clung to the ship, and strained to see through the gray dawn. With heavy clouds overhead, visibility was poor. By some miracle my wristwatch was still running, and I noted that it was just past eight when the clouds finally broke and sun filtered through.

The first things we saw were hulks of other wrecks. One was no more than a hundred yards away, its rusty bow driven into the first long line of coral. This was the reef we had struck before we had been lifted onto the larger reef beyond, where we were now impaled and slightly protected from the seas. Had we remained on the outer edge, the *Tuntsa* would have broken up by now. No craft could long survive the full force of the breakers. Two other wrecks were out there, rolled onto their sides, with great holes in the exposed hulls. They had obviously weathered a long time. Numbly I wondered if fifty years from now, some other unfortunate crew of a freshly shipwrecked vessel would be viewing the shell of the *Tuntsa*.

Suddenly Olle pointed and cried out. "There's land!"

In the dim new light a rounded hill appeared to rise out of the sea to the northwest five to ten miles away. I also made out a lower but closer rise to the southwest. Row after row of thunderous racing combers appeared between our boat and the rounded farther hill, but only a short span of foam-capped breakers was between us and the lower land. The wind was flinging the spray in a southerly direction.

"Shouldn't one of us try to go round the end of the reefs to the south in our dinghy and get to shore? I'd be glad to try," Karl shouted to von Haart.

"That's probably Virgin Gorda," cried von Haart. Although we huddled close together, the roar of surf was still such that we had to shout. "It's British," called von

Haart. "Someone who speaks English should go—not you, Karl."

"I'll go," offered Olle.

Von Haart, who had half risen, sank back. "Then I'll stay with the ship."

Only Olle and von Haart had any fluency in English, and none of us cared to have von Haart be the one to leave. If the *Tuntsa* began to fall to pieces, we would need all his seamanship to survive until Olle fetched help—if indeed he got ashore, and found someone he could bring to us.

Olle detached the line from his waist and fought through the waves to the stern, where the dinghy was still intact. We watched the little craft bob up and down between the rows of raging surf. Each time it disappeared into a trough, we wondered if it had been swamped. Then it would rise into view and we would breathe again. Finally, Olle was on the open sea and drawing farther and farther away.

Inside the *Tuntsa*, the water had now risen almost to the hatch openings.

"Are we starting to sink?" Arvi shouted.

Von Haart shook his head. "The coral is crumbling under us, that's all. We dropped our iron keel. I heard it go. Losing that weight should help."

Arvi shouted, "Suppose she goes onto her side?"

"Then we stick to the mast."

It seemed a forlorn hope. Nevertheless, after a shouted consultation we began to move precariously about the tilted, wave-lashed deck to cut the remaining stays still holding the fallen spar. When it was free, we fastened empty oilcans on either side to make a narrow raft and secured it by a line to the rail so it would not drift away. But it seemed a pitifully inadequate object on which to depend in that vicious surf. It would float, but it would be tossed like a matchstick. I thought we would probably have our brains dashed out on the first coral it struck.

"It won't work," Arvi said curtly.

"It may have to," replied Lars.

Arvi gave him an angry glance and turned away. Arvi, who had instinctive skill in his hands and understood at once how a thing would or would not "work," had a quite normal scorn for Lars. Yet if the *Tuntsa* rolled over or broke up, von Haart's raft would indeed have to be used. It would at least put some protection between our bodies and the sharp horns of the reefs.

Gradually the morning air turned warmer. The sun of an early tropical day slanted over us, and birds began to circle and call. We were a little dryer and the girls put aside their blankets. The surf rocked us less violently and we no longer had to shout.

But now we recognized a new peril.

In our preoccupation with the raft, no one had noticed that our stern settled steadily deeper into the water with the advancing tide. The *Tuntsa* had begun to sink.

Von Haart pointed. "Somehow we have to manage to lighten her," he said.

What could we do? Certainly we could not hope to hoist out the motor and cast it overboard? It weighed a quarter ton.

Karl said, "What about the anchor chain?"

Our deep-sea anchor chain weighed a good five hundred pounds and was stored in the after hold. If we could get that out! We ran across the deck, and Arvi took off the hatch. Then we stared in dismay. There were now only ten inches of air left between the water at the top rung of the ladder and the cabin roof. Even that small space was visibly diminishing.

Arvi stripped to his shorts and plunged head first down the ladder. We watched bubbles rise as he exhaled beneath the dark water. He surfaced and clung panting to the ladder's top.

"The cover is tight on the bin. I can't get it off. I have to find something to pry with."

He dove again and found a tool kit wedged between an upper bunk and the bulkhead. He came back to the ladder with a crowbar and hammer.

"Let me dive now," said Karl.

But Arvi had already plunged back under the water. He managed to loosen the cover, for I could hear the resonant sounds of his struggle with masses of chain.

Again he came up, and clung to the ladder. "I can't find the blasted end," he gasped.

"Let me. . . ." I began.

But he was gone once more, leaving us peering into the dark water and the shrinking air space above it. Eight inches now. All sorts of objects were afloat—caps, shirts, bits of paper.

"My books," said Lars in a voice of despair.

Arvi surfaced once more. "I've got an end loose." His face showed his exhaustion.

I shed my clothes and dove head first, clutching rung after rung of the ladder deeper into the chill water. Our cabin where for months we had slept, lived, and dreamed, was now this black inlet from the sea in which my lungs seemed about to burst.

I found the loose end of chain and thrashed about with it. Karl was in the water with me now. The chain lay in a devilish tangle but slowly, slowly, we got it out, and Arvi standing on the ladder passed it link by link to Lars and von Haart above until they were able to slide it into the sea. As the heavy weight came out of the hatch and plunged into the breakers, the stern gradually rose until it was almost a foot higher than it had been when we began our labors.

"Merciful God," said von Haart, and wiped his forehead.

The water-logged *Tuntsa* was floating.

The sun was past its zenith now in the rapidly clearing sky—a tropical, lovely liar of a sky, all peace and radiant beauty.

While we had struggled with the chain, articles from the cabin had also come out the hatch. Pots and pans, clothing, scraps of cloth and bits of flotsam from "Kati's treasures," wooden poles and shelves, and countless other items sloshed about the deck. To Tuntsa it apparently looked like an interesting new game. Barking, he plunged off the cabin roof and launched himself half-running and half-swimming to seize whatever he could. He would have been washed overboard if Arvi had not made a harness out of rope. In the calmer water between the lines of reefs, we now saw several of the familiar triangular fins. Tuntsa did not seem to mind being tied, and bounced around merrily at the end of his impromptu leash. Remembering the whining and peculiar disquiet which the little dog had shown before the storm, I hoped his joyousness now might be a good omen.

Constantly, we watched the shore. Von Haart, however, appeared to be transferring his attention back to the boat.

"She's sunk as far as she is going to sink," he murmured, almost to himself. I was next to him and glanced at his face. He returned my look soberly. "You know," he said, "it may take Olle till tomorrow to find people and get them here. Meanwhile, if the sea comes up at dusk again, the *Tuntsa* will be in for another pounding —maybe break up."

I nodded. If the sea rose that night, it would probably be the end of us. May, her face lifted to catch the sun, was leaning against the stub of mast. Kati lay covered by a raincoat, her head in May's lap. Her eyes were closed and blue hollows below her lashes made her face look like an exhausted child's. Anna was hunched over Ahmed, whose little can she held in her lap.

"The tide is rising," said von Haart. "If we could lift the *Tuntsa* off the reefs and get into quieter water, we would have a better chance."

"Then let's all stand on the reef and push," May said simply. She and Anna got to their feet. May held out her hands to Kati, who rose and stood looking bewildered. She had been asleep.

"We're going to stand on the reef and push the *Tuntsa* off," May told her matter-of-factly.

"What about them?" asked Kati, pointing to the fins.

"Nonsense," said May briskly. "It's too shallow. We won't be bothered."

Kati shivered.

We all fastened ropes about our waists and lowered ourselves into the water until we stood on the coral. Then we lined up along the hull, while Arvi and I wedged a length of lumber between the bow and a pinnacle of coral.

A great wave headed toward us.

"Now!" shouted von Haart.

Arvi and I pried at the bow. We heard the crunch of breaking coral as the giant breaker passed over us and hurled itself upon the boat. We gasped for air, but there was little time. Another breaker was upon us. Von Haart shouted again and all pushed once more. I could feel more coral breaking up and slipping past.

The boat moved free. We helped the girls scramble back aboard. Arvi and I threw our plank on deck, then clambered after it. Lars and Karl were hurriedly cutting loose the anchors. We began the slow job of propelling the *Tuntsa* toward the next line of surf. Crossing it, we had to fend on either side with poles and pieces of wood, but we managed to guide the prow through a narrow opening. Crashing waves broke over us, and the *Tuntsa* reeled with each one. But in the moment's respite between combers, her water-logged hull would level grudgingly.

At last, wearily and numbly, we poled into deeper water. It was now late afternoon. Exhausted from our labor, we sank down again on the cabin roof. At least we would not break up or overturn if we had to remain through another night. The sun was sinking over the island.

When we had gone overboard to push the *Tuntsa* off the reef, Anna had tied Ahmed's can to the stub of mast. Now she discovered that the can was empty.

"He was a salt-water turtle," said May quickly. "He will swim ashore and start a family in the new world—a whole batch of Virgin Island Ahmeds."

"Of course," said Kati.

"Any animal knows the direction of land," added Lars. "He's ashore all right."

Anna did not reply. In silence she untied the can and threw it overboard.

Then we saw two small boats rounding the point.

"It's Olle!" cried Karl. Arvi stood up and waved his shirt like a flag. But, instead of heading in our direction, the boats began to swing out toward the end of the long line of breaking surf.

We shouted, but the sound would not carry above the roar of waves. Although we could see clearly the tall sails in the pinkish light of the setting sun, the demasted *Tuntsa* was so low in the water that she was not visible.

"It will be dark any minute," said Anna in despair. Kati began quietly to cry.

The boats came about again. They sailed up and down until dark. They seemed unable to find even the place where we had first struck. Finally we saw their lights as they went back around the point.

Night fell. The wind came up, and the surf turned into murderous ranges of white-crested mountains. The strain of keeping our balance on the swaying cabin made us tremble as if stricken with palsy.

I had my arm around May.

"What an end to the dream," she murmured in my ear.

"It's not ended," I said.

But by eleven o'clock, when my wrist watch finally stopped, we were starting to discuss the possibility of trying to swim to land. Every comber submerged the *Tuntsa,* and each time we would gasp for breath and wonder how much longer she would stay afloat. We might have panicked and actually tried to swim, if von Haart had not argued violently against it.

"Stay with the ship," he kept repeating. "That's elementary. Stick to anything that floats."

"You call this floating?" Lars asked with an attempt at humor.

"God, if I had a drink!" von Haart cried suddenly. "If only I had a drink!"

I tried to see his face in the dark. The sky was overcast now, and there was no moon. Von Haart's ingenuity had brought us through the day, and his iron will was keeping us on the ship. What if he came to his own breaking point?

"Good God!" I heard him exclaim. "Of course!"

He got shakily to his feet. "I'm going to get a swizzle, Teppo." He spoke as matter-of-factly as if he were leaving for a moment to stop at the nearest bar.

I stared up at him. It had always puzzled me that unlike most heavy drinkers, von Haart never suffered delirium and seldom showed even such minor traces as unsteadiness in his hands. If von Haart was hallucinating, it must be from strain and shock, and this I could not believe either. It was not his nature.

"Excuse me," he said, and I heard laughter in his voice.

He lowered himself into the water, and I could see him working his way aft. I suddenly suspected what he intended to do. The compass was mounted in front of the wheel. But it was about twelve inches under water, and even with his ingenuity he would find it impossible, I thought, to get it off. His only tool would be his pocket knife.

I saw him bending over, working diligently. The line from his waist dangled over the edge of the cabin roof. Lars took hold of it. "What's he up to?" he muttered.

Suddenly he, too, realized von Haart's objective. "Don't!" he shouted. "Von Haart. . . ." He started to scramble after him.

"It will poison you!" Karl shouted.

Arvi said to me in bewilderment, "What's the matter?"

"Von Haart is after the alcohol in the compass," I told him. "He can't get it though."

Even as I spoke, von Haart lifted a bowl shaped object from beneath the water. A wave swept over him, then sprayed over us. In the interval before the onrush of the next wall of water, I saw him getting the plug out of the filler hole. We watched him outlined against the white combers—his head thrown back, swiftly drinking.

The giant breaker struck him like an avalanche. It knocked him off his feet. "Damn!" he shouted as it passed. "And damn every shark that drinks my swizzle!"

Then laughing uproariously he made his way back to us. The wave had taken his treasure. All he held was the empty bowl.

But he felt wonderful. He laughed and acted the clown, prodded and infuriated us until in sheer anger we regained some of our spirit. He forced us to make the blankets and two raincoats into a pair of improvised shelters. Kati was in the lee of one, with Karl, Lars, and Arvi making a crude circle. Over their heads, von Haart stretched the first raincoat. Across their backs to windward he spread a blanket which broke the spray. The center, toward which all faced, was comparatively dry. Then he and I, with Anna and May, made a shelter of our own. With our heads on our knees, we were even able to seize a few moments of precious sleep.

It was a fearful night. Every few moments a deluge of water swept over us. At times the *Tuntsa* would roll heavily, and one shelter would lunge into the other. Minutes seemed like hours—the night like a week.

Finally there was a scarlet sunrise. Our eyes were then burning so painfully from spray that we could not look upon the shimmering spectacle. The watercan May had filled and which had been placed in the center of our circle, was nearly empty. We sipped sparingly. We had had no food for thirty-six hours and were fearfully weak. We dared not run out of water.

It was mid-morning before we saw the boats again. Arvi fastened his white shirt to a pole, and held it high.

The boats came within a mile of us—a half mile—a quarter. Slowly they sailed round and round among the reefs. One came so close we could see the helmsman point to what was probably some of our clothing, afloat on the water.

"They will think we have drowned!" cried May in despair.

For the first time I felt absolute hopelessness. The leading sailboat turned back toward the island. Judging from the sun, it was only about two in the afternoon. They must be giving up the search. I have never felt greater panic in my life.

By now we were too hoarse to call, and too weak to move. May was sobbing herself as she comforted the weeping Kati. Anna sat like a woman carved in stone, her dark face brooding, her spirit seeming utterly withdrawn. When Arvi spoke to her she did not answer. Lars had buried his head in his hands. Even von Haart had nothing to say. He sat quietly, feigning to occupy himself with rubbing his lame leg. Finally he stood up, stretched his arms deliberately, sat down. The sight restored me somewhat. It was necessary to move, to stretch. Von Haart as usual was quite right. We were so weak that without movement any one of us might fall into a stupor which might result in slipping off. No one was in condition to endure the water now, and we were so exhausted that our united efforts could scarcely have drawn a fallen member of the group back on board, even by the line around his waist.

I stood up to stretch too, and urged May to brace herself upon the rolling surface and get up beside me. Slowly and wearily she stood.

"Teppo!" she cried. "Look!"

The other sail had come about and was heading in our direction.

Arvi got up and began to wave his pole again. The boat veered and came directly toward us.

"They see us!" Arvi cried.

They drew closer. We could make out their faces. There were three colored men, and in the bow, Olle. Our eyes met. Olle suddenly wiped his face with his sleeve, turning away for a moment.

The rolling surf made it too dangerous for them to come near enough for us to climb directly aboard. They tossed us a tow cable which we fastened to our bow cleat. Then we each got into the water and pulled ourselves to them hand over hand. The women went first. Then Lars, Karl. Arvi with Tuntsa under his arm. Myself. Von Haart, traditional to the last, insisted on bringing up the rear. Was not he our captain?

Once on deck, we looked numbly at each other, too full of emotion to speak. In silence Olle shook hands all around and led us to the sunny side of the boat. We fell onto the deck, letting the sun dry our clothes.

At last, with the hulk of the *Tuntsa* tied astern and wallowing in our wake, we began the journey to the island. The water-laden *Tuntsa* was a heavy weight. The wind was behind us, and our rescuers started their motor to reinforce the pull of their sails. The black men of the crew seemed kindness itself. They made us strong tea, and gave us biscuits, urging us to eat slowly, for fear of cramps. The sun was slowly drying us, but best of all was the warmth of feeling that we were with other human beings. Smiles shone white in the crew's black faces.

Olle got a rag and began to dry Tuntsa's wet coat, while the little dog wriggled delightedly. As the tea and biscuits strengthened us, we began to feel alive again. May and Kati tidied each other's hair and laughingly teased one another about their appearance.

We pressed Olle with questions. "What took you so long?" Lars asked.

"Believe me, I sure tried!" Olle said earnestly. "It took three hours just to row to the island. I landed where no one lived, and it was almost another hour before I found anyone. Once I got to the village, we started the search immediately with two boats. But we couldn't find you. Finally it was too dark to look further and we had to go back and wait for morning."

"We saw you go," said Arvi laconically.

There was a silence as we gazed back at the rough sea. The whitecaps breaking over the distant reefs looked now like gentle dribbles of milk upon the deep blue of the ocean.

Olle continued. "Both boats came out again this morning. It never occurred to me that you could push off the reef and get into open water. They all said that even if you lived through yesterday you would have broken up in the night. The other crew turned back. My English isn't good, but I got it across to these men that I wanted to search until we found a body or some proof that going on was hopeless. We started to circle inside the reefs about three this afternoon. But I was almost ready to give up."

"Thank God you didn't," said von Haart feelingly.

We sailed through a spectacularly beautiful lagoon,

bordered by palms, flame trees, and fantastic flowers. Projecting into the water were several shabby wooden piers. The one for which we were headed was crowded with jostling figures—stringbean men as black as ebony, sausage-shaped women, round black children with shining smiles which seemed as wide as the Atlantic. All reached out to shake our hands, call congratulations. They were excited, and laughing with happiness.

Surrounded by the crowd, we were hurried off. There was such a babble that for a moment we had no idea where they were taking us. Then we found ourselves before the village church, a one-room frame building with a simple wooden cross on its peaked roof. They stood aside for us to enter, and then poured in after us.

Since the service was in English, I understood very little. But each of us added his or her "Amen" to the native minister's oft-repeated, "Praise the Lord." There was rich, enthusiastic singing. The voices had a special resonance, a velvety deep beauty. I had never before heard colored people sing. It seemed to me the most moving sound I had ever known. Even now I cannot hear negro singing without special emotion.

✱

Afterwards, we were told that the women of the village had prepared a meal for us. It was at "Sister Bessie's." We were escorted to a small house in front of which was a great mango tree. Platters of several kinds of fish, yams, beans, beets, slices of flat unleavened bread, and huge baskets of cassavas, mangoes, bananas, and papayas covered two large wooden tables—each beautifully exotic with petals of canaria, bougainvillea, hibiscus, and other tropical flowers.

"Someone has the soul of an artist," von Haart said.

The women, picturesque in long loose flowered dresses and straw hats decorated with bright colors, waited on us. Sister Bessie was tall, statuesque, smiling, and coal black. We thought she was wonderful.

When we had eaten, they told us that we would be taken to the capital city of the British Virgin Islands in the morning. We were in an outlying district of Virgin Gorda, but already—we were told—"the governor has a report of your shipwreck."

Something in the way it was said, and in the manner of the people, made us think that administration here was strict—or that they had something on their consciences. In spite of our exhaustion, von Haart wanted to go see to the remains of the *Tuntsa,* but we were told that she was being looked after and was lashed safely to a pier in the lagoon.

The natives were consulting among themselves about where we could best spend the night. After a long, excited conference, they finally told us we were to have two houses to ourselves. We protested, but it was useless.

The women and their husbands—Arvi and Anna, Kati and Karl, May and I—were to sleep in "Uncle Ed and Aunt Sarah's house." The other men—Olle, Lars, and von Haart—could have the "house where Sister Mary and Fisherman Joe live." Nearly all seemed to call each other by titles of "uncle," "aunt," "sister," "brother." At first, we thought the connotation was perhaps part of their religion. Then we discovered that most of the people in the village were actually related to one another, and the names usually expressed actual consanguinity.

The meal had put us all into a state of torpor. We trudged the few steps to the houses. "Uncle Ed's" house held two lump-mattressed double beds, sagging in the middle, and two cots pushed together, but they seemed the softest luxury as we threw ourselves down. Without undressing, and with scarcely a "good night," we closed our eyes—and remembered nothing until we were roused at dawn.

As we gathered at the pier for our departure, von Haart asked again to see the *Tuntsa*. Finally, at our united insistence, we were taken to where she was tied to a pier some distance from the other sailboats.

We gazed in silence. With her stub of mast, her sea-stained deck, she was a derelict indeed.

Then I noticed that the mast which we had brought in with her was not there. At the same time I saw, with a stab of incredulity, that she had been pillaged. Oil cans—compass—wheel—everything was gone. The deck had been stripped.

Some of the men with us began now to touch our arms, urge us to hurry. The governor must not be kept waiting. Others simply stood silent. It seemed to me they avoided looking at us.

Von Haart turned on them. "You looted her!"

No one answered. They shifted their feet and looked at one another uneasily.

"Came in like that," a man muttered at last.

"Where's the boom?" cried von Haart. "It's a big job—getting that off. Who unshipped the rudder? What have you done with it all!"

We gazed at them in sickened silence. It seemed impossible that while one group of these people had been taking us to church, feeding us, and giving us their own beds for the night, another could have been systematically robbing wayfarers as helpless as we.

A man shrugged, and said to von Haart, "The waves were bad. They took it all away." His hands gestured vaguely.

"Waves?" von Haart shouted. "Waves don't dismantle a wheel and neatly strip fathoms of line. You know it."

The man shook his head. "You will have to talk to the governor in Road Town."

It was no use to protest. If our good rescuers of yesterday and our kindly hosts were not themselves in on the looting, it was plain they must be afraid of those who were. It was impossible to tell thieves from friends. Undoubtedly, some were good and some were bad—and like the human race, they were all brothers and sisters. The entire crowd had gone silent. The black faces were resolutely masked.

We sailed out of the lagoon. The crew was sullen and quiet. We looked back at the pier, again crowded with figures, some of them waving.

I smashed my fist against the railing, scarcely feeling the pain of the impact, not noticing until later that I had scraped off a patch of skin. The *Tuntsa* was a derelict, and all her gear stolen. We had no money at all, no way to buy or work our passage. How could we go on now?

the **JOURNEY ENDS**

the governor's island

we provide entertainment

an inquiry

rebuilding the Tuntsa

who would send us out to drown?

the crew of the Tuntsa *separates*

on the texture of dreams

The native crew tossed mooring lines onto Road Town's small pier, and a dark, Spanish-looking young man, who had apparently been awaiting our arrival, stepped forward to greet von Haart who was the first ashore.

"Welcome to Road Town," the young man said cordially.

"Thank you," replied von Haart, leaning on his cane. I saw his shrewd gaze appraise the young man, and his eyes narrow slightly, whether in puzzlement or disapproval or merely discomfort I could not tell. The young man's white shirt and spotless white tropical trousers made me feel how wretchedly dirty and shabby we were —and this feeling would particularly affect von Haart, who always took pains to dress as immaculately as possible when ashore, as befitted his rank as our skipper. Now, however, we all still wore the clothes in which we had been wrecked, and there had been no chance for baths or shaves since then. May in sudden self-consciousness, fingered a rip in her sleeve, and instinctively I moved to take her arm. Anna stared at the ground. She seemed to be in a state of mingled shyness and fury.

"I am Governor Chilton's assistant," the young man said. "I am to take you to his quarters."

We followed our escort up steep, winding streets. It was a sun-drenched, unpaved town populated by, I guessed, several hundred persons. But the shabby little houses, scarcely more than huts, were surrounded by such a profusion of flowers—scarlet, orange, yellow, azure—and everywhere was such a wealth of green, that there was no air of poverty. I thought that native life must be easy on these islands. There were fruits on the trees and fish in the sea, and assuredly little labor could be needed. The people watching as we passed had plump, if somewhat sullen faces. No one approached us. As we had noted earlier, the natives seemed to lead lives closed to all but their own race except under the most unusual circumstances. Our guide was the only white man we saw.

"Suppose we had to stay here," May murmured. "It would be more hopeless than Safi."

At the top of a hill we came to a large white house of painted brick with a broad veranda. The governor's "quarters" apparently served as both offices and residence, for as we passed through the double front doors shining with brass, I saw on either side musty, official-looking empty parlors, which might have been transplanted, dust and all, directly from nineteenth-century London. Our guide led us upstairs to what was obviously the residential portion of the mansion. Furniture here was heavy, dark, substantial. I felt as if we had stepped into a bygone era, into one of Conrad's novels of Victorian colonialism.

The governor had obviously been waiting for us and rose as we entered. He was extremely thin, a stooped man of apparently forty-five or fifty, but who looked older than he was. With his narrow nose and harsh line of a mouth, his bent shoulders and long thin legs, he had the air of a lean tropical bird. He, too, was smartly dressed in tropical white. He took a step or two to meet us as our guide led us in.

"We are glad you're safe," he said with an abrupt nod of his narrow head, and I was immediately sure that in the routine of his life we must represent an annoying interruption. This was a man who did not care for complications.

In contrast was his wife, a pretty, red-headed, vivacious little woman, who came quickly forward with exclamations of concern for May, Kati, and Anna in their torn and sea-stained clothes.

She hurried them off to a guest room, and we men were taken by a colored man-servant to another, where at last we were able to shave and shower. When we put our clothes back on, we still looked like scarecrows, but being clean did wonders for our self-respect. We returned to the governor's living room feeling like men

again. The governor stood stiffly and offered us a drink.
Von Haart's eyes brightened, and Lars moved cautiously
next to him. It was a foregone conclusion that the governor would not understand von Haart's ways with a
bottle.

It had taken us more than an hour to shave and
shower. The women were gone much longer, and when
they came back they were utterly transformed. Powder
and lipstick brightened their faces. They had washed
and set their hair. And, marvel of marvels, each had on
a fresh summer dress! Kati's was a little long for her,
Anna's a little short, and May's was in between. It was
clear that our hostess had given them clothes from her
own wardrobe. We rose with exclamations of pleasure
and appreciation. Nothing which could have been done
would have seemed to us half as wonderful as this unexpected kindness. We overwhelmed Mrs. Chilton with
thanks.

We sat down again and called on all our resources to
be as interesting and pleasant guests as possible under
the circumstances. A butler brought in a delicious white
rum distilled on the islands, but von Haart had only
three drinks, and consumed them with what was for him
heroic slowness. He recounted our adventures with all
his inimitable exaggeration and charm, seconded by
Olle in his broken English. Together they soon had Governor Chilton roaring with laughter. But the governor's
laughter had a peculiar quality. He would sit expressionless, drumming his hands on his knees. Then when his
wife and assistant would begin to smile, he would sud-

denly shout with merriment—a haw-haw-haw which was almost a bellow.

"I ought to keep you around as my court jester," he cried to von Haart. Von Hart stiffened perceptibly. Karl gave our odd host a stare.

Opportunely, Mrs. Chilton invited us into the dining room for a magnificent lunch. After feeding, the governor seemed somewhat more relaxed and less inclined to spasms of mirth at our expense, so von Haart took the opportunity to mention the looting of the *Tuntsa*.

The governor looked at him a long moment without speaking. His hands again began to drum on his knees.

"You are mistaken," he said coldly at last. "The breakers here sweep a ship clean. I am sure that is what happened."

"I am afraid not in this case," replied von Haart firmly. "Breakers could not leave screw holes where the wheel was, or freshly cut ends of wire where the shrouds were sheared off."

"No one steals on my islands," said the governor. "Your boat will be towed in here later today or early tomorrow. I am sure you will find that nothing is missing."

"And if we find we are not mistaken? If everything is still missing?" von Haart said.

The governor shrugged. He nodded at his assistant. "Then Juan here will have to take care of it." he replied petulantly.

I glanced at his wife. She seemed to be absorbed in looking out a window. Whatever her private impulses

of kindness and generosity, she was clearly either helpless to interfere with her husband's attitudes, or had
decided long since that she did not wish to.

The governor's assistant bowed slightly. "I will see to
it, sir," he said.

Soon afterwards, he ushered us out.

The governor's assistant, whom I shall call Juan Gon-
salez, and who was to play such a part in our destinies,
would remain for us ever after an ambiguous figure. An
agreeable, quiet, and charming young man, he may have
been the real power in an administration whose actual
head did not want to be bothered; or he may have been
merely a factotum who carried out orders. Personally,
he may have thought of himself as our friend—as from
his manner he always outwardly seemed to be—or he
may have been secretly a villain of the deepest die—we
could never tell.

However it was, our stay on Governor Chilton's island
would be for us one of the most terrible of ordeals. We
would in the end feel the most baffling helplessness, the
most inexplicable injustice. Words would be quite inadequate to express it.

"How can they have a bureaucracy with just two people?" May would say later.

"It's English," answered Lars, as if that explained
everything.

"It's the world!" Anna cried passionately. "The whole
world is like this. It is useless for people to try to get
away."

In Road Town, there was an old man who was mad.
He dwelt in a one-room shanty. He was an ancient dere-

lict, who once upon a time had come here from—of all places—Boston. Running out in the dusty lane ahead of us, he would dance along, nodding and slobbering, and holding up his fingers to show how old he was. We would find that he, the governor, Juan, and three or four men connected with an agricultural experimental station, were the only white people on the island.

*

The *Tuntsa*'s castaways were quartered in an old inn built years ago for tourists who had never come. It was an unpainted, rundown building with an outdoor privy. Juan led us there, and told us that as indigent castaways, we were to receive an allowance* with which to buy food and other necessities at "the store," which was owned by Juan.

The subjects of the governor's kingdom lived simply. Fishermen brought in their catch of bonito, red snapper, kingfish, and Spanish mackerel each dawn and sold them on the pier. Once a week a cow was butchered there and its meat used the same day, since the island had no refrigeration. The only other activities were the agricultural station and a few casual one family distilleries, where the natives refined their magnificent white rum. To von Haart, of course, this made up for everything.

"It may be the kingdom of the devil," he would say, smacking his lips, "but as usual angels have sneaked into it."

* Our group allowance was approximately three dollars a day.

Kati, who shared von Haart's faith in the ultimate good, but was quite without his special interpretations, would gaze in disapproving amazement.

The *Tuntsa* was towed in the day after our own arrival. About two in the afternoon we saw a sailboat with a small spot astern, and we hurried to the pier. A half hour later the black spot appeared to be a rowboat. By three o'clock, we knew the "rowboat" was our de-masted *Tuntsa*. She looked disreputable, tired, and battered, as she wallowed helplessly behind. Moored at the pier, she listed heavily to starboard, and I could see the sinister small craters along her exposed hull.

The deck was bare. Our boom, rudder, line, oil, and gas cans and other gear were all still missing. We jumped on board, and Arvi peered down the hatchway to the galley. A look of dismay, then of anger crossed his lean face. I followed him. Water still rose midway up the ladder, but there was a complete absence of anything whatever floating on the surface. The upper bunks were bare. The galley and navigation tables were gone. Von Haart's fury at this completion of the looting of his beloved boat knew no bounds.

"By God!" he shouted in English as he clambered back to the pier. "I'll see to it that this governor's name is known all over Europe! The man has no honor. I know people in England, plenty of them. I'll write letters. The bloody fellow won't have a shred of reputation!"

I thought Juan's smile more than merely agreeable. He was amused. His bow was polite enough, however.

"We will send a boat to Virgin Gorda today," he said.

"You had better!" cried von Haart, flourishing his cane. "By heaven, young fellow, you had better!"

Juan went off, ostensibly to inform the governor.

Oddly enough, to us who knew von Haart, the outcry was not comic. Von Haart, who had so readily appropriated money intended for his cousin (a family matter), who was self-exiled from his class and an outcast from society, was quite serious about honor. To him honor was a matter of character. In his own strange but very definite way, he scrupulously observed it. What he despised in the governor was his lack of character, and the nature of the atmosphere enclosing this island, like a projection of the governor himself.

We were in an agony of uncertainty as to whether we would ever see our gear. At best, we expected lengthy delays in finding the thieves. We were amazed, therefore, when we came down to the *Tuntsa* the following morning to find on deck coils of line and wire, our gas and oil cans, our boom, and in the water by the boat, our mast, still with the lashings with which we had tried to make it into a raft. There were boxes of our clothes, washed and folded—boxes of bedding and blankets— our tools, one of our flashlights, our radio, and the compass assembly. There were even a few books—the bundle Lars had lashed to the mast with maps and some of our snapshots and undeveloped film.

Lars fingered the film and papers with delight. "Look," he said, "here's the original blueprint of the *Tuntsa*. It's been soaked, but you can still read it."

Books and papers, however, were the least of our interests. On the pier stood Juan directing the natives who were replacing our wheel and reshipping the rudder.

"Who took them?" Olle cried.

"Undesirable elements among the population," replied

Juan ambiguously. "They have been punished. I may tell you, incidentally, that they are exceedingly sorry." Juan spoke with emphasis. "This might have embarrassed the administration."

Something about the way he said it made me look at him, and I caught Karl doing the same. I think it occurred to us both that embarrassing the administration might be the one major crime on the island.

The following day, the governor held a formal inquiry into our case. It seemed that a full report of every wreck was expected in London, and our restitution therefore had come just in time. The "inquiry" was held in a musty little office downstairs in the official portion of the mansion. Von Haart and Olle recounted to the governor all over again the story of our wreck, while a portly colored clerk took a transcript of the testimony.

Had false lights or any other device lured us onto the reefs?

No, indeed. We had seen no lights whatever.

The government then was legally absolved of all responsibility. Were we missing any of our possessions?

Our two cameras, most of our books, our ship's log, lanterns, and some of our clothing were gone, but we believed that these things might have been washed overboard during the storm.

We were then, in full possession of our belongings?

Well, we thought so. We certainly could not contend the contrary.

Then there, too, the government was free of all responsibility.

That ended the inquiry. The governor had been distant, anxious, peevish, and finally—I thought—bored. In spite of the fact that we brought no accusations, I thought that we had made no progress whatever in gaining his approval.

"It seems to me," said May thoughtfully as we left, "that perhaps we 'embarrass the administration' just by being here."

"Do we embarrass it enough for the governor to help us get away, do you suppose?" Olle asked.

"Help us? How?" inquired Arvi.

"Well, he certainly knows we want to reach America. Would he telephone San Juan to find out about entry visas for instance?"

"Or he might know some sea captain who comes by here and would take us to the Dominican Republic," suggested Kati.

"I suppose he might," Karl said doubtfully. "Somehow it doesn't seem likely, though."

Von Haart shook his head. "Visas—sea captains—I don't think he has it in him. You have to have friends to be able to do things like that. Furthermore, he wouldn't put himself out."

"His wife seemed nice," observed Kati.

"Juan told me he met her in the States and married her six months ago," May said. "I bet she's sorry."

"She might urge him to help, though," Kati said.

"I don't think so," replied May. "I believe she has already decided not to interfere with him in any way."

Olle laughed. "No woman exists who has decided not to interfere."

"On this island," said May, "anything can happen."

That seemed to be the one thing on which we agreed. Since the astonishing return of our possessions, we had no idea of what might develop next. We felt that it might quite literally be anything.

"But we can't stay here forever!" cried Anna.

"I think," said von Haart slowly, "that while we don't embarrass the administration sufficiently at this point to have the governor take any action, nevertheless our presence may annoy him enough to get us help of some sort—if it doesn't require too much effort. Let's try Juan. If he would find us block and tackle and some old lumber, we might patch up the *Tuntsa*."

We glanced at one another. After our look at the *Tuntsa's* hull, repair seemed impossible. How could she ever be made watertight?

"She has been a good ship," said von Haart. "And it is only three hundred miles to the Dominican Republic."

We discussed it some more. None of us liked it. But I think in our hearts we all had known it would come to this.

So finally we approached Juan in his general store and told him we were thinking of repairing our boat and setting sail. It seemed to me that he appeared pleased when he heard we planned to leave, and I felt encouraged. Something agreeable to report to the governor, I thought. But when we mentioned our need of help, and specifically of block and tackle, he looked suddenly dubious.

"Listen, Juan," said Olle. "You have a truck. If you would let us use it and will find block and tackle for us, we can haul the boat up on the beach and make her seaworthy. Then we'll be on our way."

Juan said enigmatically that he was sure there was no block and tackle on the island, but he would see about it.

"If there is no block and tackle on the island, how can he see about it?" asked Arvi in disgust when we were again out on the dusty road.

"He's our only friend," said Kati, "and I am sure he will do his best."

"What makes you think so?" asked Anna bitterly.

❋

Our "inn" was not an encouraging environment. A one story building, it had four small bedrooms around a single central space containing a pot bellied little one burner coal stove. Its uncommunicative attendant arrived each noon and prepared the large bowl of fish and potato soup on which we then lived until the same time the following day.

"It's a jail," said Anna.

"Oh, come," protested Kati. "It's quite pretty here, really."

Usually we sat on the veranda, on benches that leaned against the wall. All around were crimson flowering trees, and in the background the vivid purple and green of the hills.

"The whole island is a jail," said Anna—"the whole damned world, for that matter."

Anna's moods troubled us now as much as her silences earlier, but in sober truth the governor's island did infect us all with somewhat the same feeling as she seemed to suffer with such intensity. The inquiry, the inn, our treatment—everything seemed to combine to give us the sensations of prisoners.

"Well," said Kati reasonably, "suppose we were in the governor's place? How would it look to us? Nine strangers suddenly appear out of nowhere, and they have no money and no place to go. It would be terribly hard to know what to do with them."

"The governor," replied Anna, "is simply like every other modern governor. The supreme wrong, as he sees it, is if anyone moves around without his consent. It's an attack on authority—that's what it is. If he were a really modern governor, he would just have us shot and tidy up the whole affair. But England is behind the times and there would be a fuss at home. So he'll have to find some other way to dispose of us."

"Anna!" exclaimed Karl, sincerely shocked.

"Look at the mountain, Anna," said May. "Wouldn't it make a lovely picture?"

But Anna got up in silence. She went to walk on the beach. There she would wander alone with Tuntsa and gaze out over the endless water.

Von Haart leaned back against the wall and contemplated the mountain. "First thing tomorrow," he said at last, "we'll start repairing the boat to get out of here."

There was no sign of Juan in his store the next morning. The few natives about just shook their heads when we asked where he had gone.

"They're absolutely illiterate, you know," said Lars. "You can't expect them to know anything."

"Don't kid yourself," replied Olle. "They watch everything that goes on. Probably they know exactly where he is, and why. They just aren't telling."

"Why would they do that?" asked Karl.

Olle simply shrugged.

Finally we went to the beach and began to hunt for driftwood to make a crude corduroy way on which to pull the *Tuntsa* up on shore without sinking in the sand. We were just beginning to use coral rock to weight the first pieces in the water, when we heard Juan's truck stop by the pier. He had block and tackle for us, and nothing could have been pleasanter than his manner, or more cooperative and agreeable. He would help us, he said, in any way he could. He would be glad to use his truck for power if we needed it. Just let him know.

"It will take all of today to make a passage up the sand and get her ready," said von Haart. "Could you come tomorrow morning?"

Juan said pleasantly that he would be on the beach at seven o'clock.

In wonder we gazed after him as he drove away.

We labored on the *Tuntsa* and with the driftwood all that day. Von Haart said that she could sail again, and in spite of ourselves we were beginning to believe him. I was amused to see how Lars, seconding von Haart, combined his own faculty for dreams with an imitation of von Haart's knack for leadership.

"We'll make it!" he would exclaim to one of us as he brought wood to be put in place. "See if we don't!"

Or again, to another, "Von Haart's checking the hull. It's not nearly as bad as we thought. She wasn't designed for that iron keel in the beginning anyhow, you know."

Lars must in fact have been in process of change for a long time, but I had never until now realized how little resemblance was left between the new Lars and the defeated man who had sailed with us from Helsinki, surrounding himself with books for refuge.

We slept restlessly that night. Hope coming after despair is a poor sedative. By six o'clock, all of us, with May, Anna, and Kati, and with Tuntsa chasing seagulls, were waiting by our homemade marine railway. Juan, all smiles, arrived at seven.

Immediately we began the task of attaching lines securely to the stern of the *Tuntsa*. We rigged a block at the base of a mango tree and fastened the end of the rope securely to the rear of Juan's truck. Juan slowly inched the truck forward. The line grew taut but the boat barely budged. The first pieces of wood slipped forward under the pressure. Arvi dove to anchor them more securely with extra rock. We tried again. The truck wheels spun in place.

"Put rocks in the truck to get more traction," Arvi said.

This done, we tried once more. The *Tuntsa* lunged forward some three feet. Her stern was six inches higher in the water. But we could not move her at all on our next attempt.

"We have to let her drain," said von Haart.

We watched water stream from the holes along the hull exposed by the first lift. A faster stream came out a gash near the prow. It took some time for the water to stop gushing and leave the boat as light as she could get at that level.

Juan turned on the ignition and again inched forward. The *Tuntsa* slid painfully ahead another foot and a half. This raised her two more inches. We waited until the newly exposed holes also ceased gushing, then laboriously moved her once more.

Inch by inch we advanced. It was a slow and agonizing process.

At last the *Tuntsa* was off the sandy ocean bottom, and onto the wood runway. It was mid-afternoon before we were halfway up the beach, and when the quick tropical darkness descended we had just reached our goal. Juan, patient to the end, trained a flashlight onto the line as we unhooked the block and tackle.

Despite our exhaustion, we trudged through the village with excitement and hope. The crazy man ran out in the moonlight and held up his fingers to show how old he was. The natives ignored him, as they ignored us. But now these things had lost their power. We were no longer prisoners. We were leaving!

Juan was on the scene again the following day. He looked at the *Tuntsa's* hull and shook his head.

"She'll never sail."

"She will," von Haart told him.

We were all silent, watching Juan's face. We had to have help and materials. Would he get them for us? Arvi listed what we needed—"old lumber, rags, nails, some tar, used metal sheeting," he pleaded. I could see how he longed to get his skillful hands on the hull. "Please," he begged. "It needn't be anything good."

"I'll ask the governor," Juan said at last.

While he was gone, we turned back to our riddled boat. Olle and Arvi started to trim the splintered wood around the edges of the holes to prepare for putting in plugs. Von Haart seated himself on a log and took a long swig from his rum bottle. Since our arrival in Road Town, he had found a group of fishermen to whom he was giving lessons in navigation, using his sextant, chronometer, and compass for demonstration, while they in return kept him supplied with rum. The men were intelligent and seemed to learn with an enthusiasm which somewhat broke down their usual aloofness. Later, we would wonder if we did not have cause to bitterly regret von Haart's "classes," but at the time we saw no harm in them. We disliked the governor and were sorry for his subjects.

Juan came back that afternoon. He had a small load of tools, used lumber, tar, sheet metal, some nails, and old rags. We thanked him as if he had brought us nine tickets on an ocean liner. He left without comment.

We cut pegs and pounded them into place, stuffing the rags tightly around them as they went in. We searched the beach for scraps to supplement Juan's lumber and we cut driftwood for the smaller holes. It was slow, hard, discouraging work. The holes seemed innumerable. We stopped at noon, walked the mile to our barracks for the daily ration of soup and then returned. The sun blazed over us. We were bathed in sweat. By four o'clock, even with all of us laboring together, the girls cutting rags and holding plugs, we had filled only a few dozen holes. And there were places which were literally peppered with gashes, many less than an inch apart.

"We will just have to tar heavily and nail sheets of metal over some of these places. The holes are too small to plug," Arvi said, wiping perspiration from forehead, cheeks, and chin. "We have to do it over some of the long cracks, too. There are just too many. We would weaken the hull even more if we try to wedge pieces of wood into all of them."

Nevertheless, we finished that day in high spirits. It was good to be working hard, good to have a goal again. In this place where it seemed so few really worked and no one had a goal, our progress was a sort of triumph. We felt as if our labor and our rising hope were proving the island's powerlessness over us.

Juan came down every day. To us it seemed that the work was going magnificently, but he said little. Finally he remarked that after we decided to "give up," he might be able to sell our motor for us on commission.

"Give up!" exclaimed Olle. "We aren't giving up! We're going to sail her, can't you see?"

Juan gave one of his enigmatic smiles and went away.

"I hate him," said Anna violently. "I just *hate* him!"

"He's a good chap," protested Karl. "Look at all the help he's been."

"Don't give him too much credit," said von Haart.

"Why not?" asked Olle. "He has been awfully good, really."

We never could agree about Juan. In any case, we were too busy and too tired for argument. Soon the island and its mysteries would be left behind.

Olle and Arvi constructed a new wood keel and reinforced the bow. It took eight days to ready the starboard side for a coat of pitch, then two more to build supports to keep the *Tuntsa* upright on her rebuilt keel. When the outer hull was completed, we gave it three coats of pitch and began inside. The precious lumber Juan had brought was used for new ribbing and planking for the galley sides, where the biggest holes had been. Reinforcing timbers were nailed along the lower hull. Then three more coats of pitch covered everything.

While Lars, Olle, Karl and I worked on the inner hull, Arvi went over the motor. He repaired the radio and restored the hand pump to working order. These were miracles of craftsmanship. But even for Arvi our auxiliary pump was beyond fixing.

By the end of the third week, both the outer and inner hull were finished. Von Haart was exultant. "I never thought she could be that solid again. She's a wonderful ship!"

But when we filled the *Tuntsa* with water along the keel line and left it overnight, the next morning brought bitter disappointment. The sand underneath was horribly wet, and damp showed all along the keel and lower bow.

"A half inch of pitch over the whole hull and it still leaks," Olle said in despair. It was a heavy blow.

Von Haart said, "Well, she's too light anyhow. Let's pour two or three inches of cement in the bottom. That should not only stop the leaks, but give us some of the ballast we lost with the old keel."

Juan supplied us with cement, but it seemed to us that his manner was more and more equivocal. "She won't float, you know."

"She will," said von Haart. "You'll see."

Nothing was heard from the governor. We had neither visits nor comments through Juan, nor any contact whatever. He was invisible. It made us uneasy.

At last came the morning when we laboriously pushed the *Tuntsa* back down our homemade runway into the water. After three or four days at the pier, there seemed to be only a normal amount of moisture in the bilges. We were full of excitement then, and sure of success.

There remained only the mast to be reset, and the sails to be cut down and sewn. We took out the stump of the mast, cut the base of the remaining spar square, and secured it into the socket. Our new mast had a height of less than sixteen feet, but it was sturdy and we wedged it well.

The possible sailing of the *Tuntsa* was becoming the talk of Road Town. The native fishermen learning navigation from von Haart predicted quite openly that we were certain to drown. Their own sailing was usually limited to areas around the islands, and our projected journey in the crippled ship seemed to them sheer suicide.

There was a voluble little group around von Haart one morning when I came down to the beach. The fishermen brought him cigarettes and the delicious island rum each day, and having thus paid their tuition, settled down to enjoy his class. He sat in their midst like some tropical god receiving the offerings of his devotees—or some honored elder prophet in the midst of a band of disciples. What a professor he would have made, I thought. Indeed, it seemed to me there was nothing von Haart could not have done—if he had wanted to. The black faces around him were rapt with attention. Von Haart's own gargoyle features were alight with good fellowship and enjoyment.

"Hey," he said laughingly to me in Finnish, "this is going a little far! I think they believe I have some sort of magic which is going to lead them automatically to tons of fish."

"Don't overdo it," I said.

"I'm trying not to. It helps that they think we're all crazy and doomed to die. *Moriturus eos salutat.* It lends glamor, but at the same time it keeps them from taking my goings-on too seriously."

"Look," I said, "if they understood what it is really about. . . ."

Von Haart's audience had a certain allure that morning. I sat down beside him. In my broken English, and with a great deal of assistance from von Haart, I tried to express some part of what our dream meant to those of us who were determined to get to America so that our sons and our sons' sons would grow up in freedom and opportunity not possible in our own darkening land. But I did not seem to get through to them. Perhaps it was my English. Or perhaps freedom and opportunity did not seem particularly relevant in Road Town. Anyhow, they began to fidget.

"Don't sail in that boat," was all the answer I got. "Better to stay here—and be alive."

It was a point with which I did not agree, but which my limited English did not qualify me to dispute. I got up and left them to von Haart. In any case, I could not tell how much of their reluctance to see us go came from concern for us, and how much arose from reluctance to lose our navigator, whose generous demonstrations with his sextant so fascinated them. I do believe, however, they were most sincerely convinced we would drown.

Some rumor of this spreading conviction may have reached the governor, for one morning Juan arrived on the pier and made an announcement.

"You are officially denied permission to sail from here in that boat," he told us abruptly.

We gazed at him in consternation.

Olle said angrily, "I thought your governor was so anxious to have us go that he coudn't wait to see the last of us. How can he refuse permission?"

"I said 'officially,'" Juan repeated. He winked.

"What the Hell do you mean?" Olle shouted. Juan made no reply. Olle returned to pounding furiously at the hull.

After Juan left, we looked at one another in amazement. "Juan certainly can't have been helping us without the governor's knowing it," said Karl.

Arvi scratched his head. "The governor must have wanted the boat repaired, or we would never have got supplies."

"But now he tells us we can't go!" wailed Anna.

"'Officially,'" said von Haart. "It's *'officially,'* remember. I think that it has suddenly occurred to our precious governor that we may be wrecked again. Talk has probably reached him, you see. He may be afraid that in case of our deaths, he might be held responsible."

"If we drowned, would the governor be embarrassed?"

asked May. "It's almost pleasant to think we might be that important."

"Do you think he could legally keep us from going?" Lars asked von Haart in alarm.

Von Haart spread his hands. "How do I know? He may be content to let us sail, while at the same time refusing to make it official. Juan certainly implies as much —so it seems to me, anyhow. But I don't know what to expect."

"In this place, who does?" asked Arvi.

We went on with our last bits of work on the boat. But we had a sense of continual helplessness. What would happen to us next?

We were not long in finding out.

❁

Meanwhile, however, we discussed our plans as if they were certainties. We would land in the Dominican Republic, find work, and settle down until we could supply and refit the *Tuntsa* to carry us on to the coast of Florida. Since the *Tuntsa* had been made to float again, we had quite abandoned the notion that after Ciudad Trujillo we might have to make the last part of our journey to America on a commercial boat of some sort. We were hazy about the actual mechanics of entering the United States by sailboat, but we were convinced it would somehow work out. It was all quite irrational, but as I look back on that time, it seems to me that we talked ourselves into a state of certainty precisely because of the constant, nagging, invisible, and perilous uncertainty we felt surrounding us. Simply to keep sane, we had to think of our plans positively. But I believe we all sensed the quicksand on which they were built, and merely hid our anxiety from one another in our various ways—Anna with her silent walks by the sea, Olle with jokes, Karl with politeness, Lars with learned lectures on the vegetation of the Virgin Islands—with which he bored us so successfully that if we had had any tendencies to despair they would have become quite submerged in the sheer exhaustion of listening to him.

Then Juan appeared upon our scene once more in his official capacity.

It was then our sixth week in Road Town. We were planning to sail within days. Arvi was about to install the motor. We were all below—the girls in the galley, Lars and I in von Haart's quarters, and Olle was helping Karl put back the old curtains across the mid-cabin bunks. They were torn and water-stained, but they would still give a measure of privacy.

Juan came down the after hatch, by-passing the motor in the walkway. He glanced at it—then at us. He hesitated, took a breath, and looked into the air over our heads.

"The governor is confiscating your motor, your compass, your radio, your sextant, and other navigation equipment in payment for supplies, lodging, and food furnished you since your arrival." He spoke as if he were reading a proclamation. All that was lacking was a ceremonial roll of paper in his hand.

Stunned, we could only stare at him. I noticed that he would not meet our eyes.

"Juan . . ." began von Haart.

"I am to take it all back with me in the truck. Now," Juan said emphatically.

"But how are we expected to leave without a motor or navigation equipment?" demanded Olle. He was crimson with rage.

"The governor has officially forbidden you to leave in this boat," Juan replied stiffly. "You can't claim that anyone here is responsible for what happens if you don't obey his orders."

"No, we can't claim that," von Haart said soberly. "The governor is quite correct, Juan. But what do you say? You yourself?"

"I say—" Juan drew a long breath.

Von Haart looked at him.

"I have nothing to say!" Juan exclaimed. "If you take this boat out, you will all drown. I am just glad the equipment won't go to the bottom with you."

He went to the ladder and beckoned to three natives, who had been waiting on deck. Tuntsa snarled as they came down the ladder, and would have bitten them when they approached. Anna had to hold him.

Helplessly we watched while they dismantled the motor and carried it ashore. Then the compass, sextant, barometer, chronometer, and radio were put in Juan's truck. They drove away.

"I think it's Juan's own idea!" Arvi said bitterly. "The fishermen on this island would mortgage their souls to buy von Haart's equipment. Since the navigation lessons, everyone knows about it."

"Juan will sell it in his store," cried Olle.

"That can't be," Karl protested. "Juan has been our

friend. He wouldn't deliberately send us out to drown."

"I believe it's the governor," said Lars. "That governor thinks one thing one day, and something else the next. First he saw to it that we got help to repair the *Tuntsa*, so we could relieve him by getting off his island. Then he was frightened that he would be blamed if we drowned, and 'officially' forbade us to go, and for a while that seemed to him a good solution. But as the time for our leaving got nearer, he panicked and decided we really must not go. So he hit on confiscating our equipment."

"It can't have been like that, Lars," said von Haart. "The governor knows we put in six weeks' work on the *Tuntsa*. He knows we will sail—equipment or no equipment."

"Then what *did* happen?" exclaimed May. "It was a horrible thing to do. How could they!"

"I don't think we will ever know," I said.

"Von Haart!" Olle cried. "You said the governor knows we will sail—equipment or not. Is it possible? All I want in the world is to get out of here!"

There was a chorus of assent.

"It's only three hundred and fifty miles," said von Haart slowly. "The currents are in our favor. We'll navigate by the stars, and pray to God."

✿

The following day—Friday, March 26—one of von Haart's fishermen pupils towed us out of the harbor before dawn. It was supposed to be, of course, a "secret" departure, but everyone knew we were going, and Juan himself appeared, camera in hand, to see us off. Nothing could have been more affable than his manner. His friendship had never seemed more genuine. He came on board smiling and said that he would ride with us until we caught the wind. We were all a little at a loss for conversation, however—the governor did not seem an appropriate subject—neither did our confiscated equipment. Finally May and Kati went below and made some coffee, and we chatted on the after deck about neutral topics: our children, our hopes of reaching America, the climate of Ciudad Trujillo, and other non-controversial matters.

"You must write to me," said Juan, winding his camera. "And I'll write you—send some of the pictures if they turn out."

"Thank you," I said. "We will be glad to write you, Juan—if we arrive safely."

He made no comment, but stood to get a shot of the boat towing us.

The morning wind began to rise at last. The fisherman threw back our tow line and took Juan aboard to return to shore. The last memory I have of the governor's island is Juan's white figure, standing well aft and poised to take a final view of the *Tuntsa* as we got under way. She was pathetically short masted now, and her patched and cut down sails were a wretched contrast to the tall white canvas she had once carried so proudly.

"It was nice of Juan to come to say goodbye," said Kati.

"Nonsense," snapped Anna. "Those pictures are to show that we left the island alive. They're for evidence in case the governor has to hold one of those 'inquiries' of his. On the subject of our dead bodies."

"Don't, Anna!" exclaimed May.

"I'm sure it isn't that," said Karl firmly. "Juan has done a great deal for us, and he came to see us off as an act of final courtesy. I shall write him our thanks from the Dominican Republic."

"Oh, for God's sake!" said Anna. She got up and wandered below.

The hills of the island were fading into the rosy morning horizon. Beneath us the wavering coral was a constantly shifting rainbow shimmer through the translucent water. It was one of the most beautiful sights I had ever seen, and it seemed a radiant symbol of our new freedom. Juan, the governor's island—that was past. Whatever the danger, we were our own masters once more.

"I think I'll write Juan too," I told Karl. All bitterness seemed behind us.

We set our course westward. I brought von Haart a cup of coffee at the helm and asked him how the *Tuntsa* was behaving.

He looked up smiling. "There isn't a boat of her size in the world that could do what she has done, Teppo."

"I mean how is she going now?"

"Well," he acknowledged reluctantly, "it's not good, if you must know. Even with this breeze, we are terribly slow. We will probably be lucky to average a hundred miles today."

Silently, I did some elementary arithmetic—three hundred and fifty miles—that made four days—six at most. It could not, I thought, possibly take longer. I hoped the sea would be calm, with fair winds in our favor.

It was noon on the fifth day when Puerto Rico, our first landfall, became a certainty. That evening we could see the far-away lights of buildings on shore. By sunrise, we were within five miles of the northeastern tip, and that afternoon it had almost faded from sight beyond our wake. We expected to sight the Dominican Republic by nightfall.

But we had no charts now—only a page from a child's geography book, which Juan had once given us.

Von Haart studied it and swore. "How in Hell do I know what's under us?" he asked bitterly. I saw him glance at what seemed to be cross-currents near our bow. They appeared to intersect the main ocean current we were following.

Von Haart shrugged. "Well, I can make an obvious general guess. We are entering the Mona Passage. It's a nasty piece of water."

The Mona Passage lay between Puerto Rico and the Dominican Republic. I knew it had a reputation for high, changeable winds. Furthermore, the whole area was full of coral. In these seas it was the commonest of growths, and over the eons had formed hardened, jagged, subterranean peaks which protruded off the ocean floor like mountains and tore the bottoms out of ships.

It seemed to me the wind had a suddenly colder edge against my cheek.

Von Haart turned to May, Anna, and Kati. "Better

make a pot of coffee. You may not be able to later, and we might need it. I don't like the feel of the air. Take Tuntsa below with you."

But Tuntsa turned up his nose and ran to Arvi's side.

"Still thinks he's a member of the deck-crew, I see," Karl said with a faint smile.

Reluctantly, the little dog let himself be dragged below, Anna's hand in his collar. He was sniffing suspiciously. He was a weather-wise animal by now. He too could smell the change.

Suddenly the wind dropped. The water showed scarcely a ripple.

For about thirty minutes the calm continued. Glancing at our motionless sails and then back at the sea, von Haart gripped the wheel expectantly.

Karl and I took positions at the jib sheets. Arvi and Lars stood by the main. We knew enough now to share von Haart's apprehension.

Suddenly the boom swung violently across. It crashed back. The *Tuntsa* lurched. The jibs were luffing wildly, and Karl and I ducked the boom again just in time. Arvi and Lars crouched out of its reach.

The *Tuntsa* rolled from side to side. Karl and I clung to the sheets and fought to fill the flapping canvas to steady us and give us way. But there was little we could do. Von Haart shouted to Lars and me to see what was happening below.

Gripping the life line and cabin sides, Lars and I crossed the deck. As I went down the ladder holding the rails to keep from pitching forward, I suddenly heard a sinister crack-crunch beneath the walkaway. It was the cement we had put in over the keel. It was working loose.

In the galley, the coffee-pot, drained of its contents, lay fallen on its side, wedged between a table leg and a bunk. Kati, white as paper from the motion, was being ill. Anna sat on her bunk clutching the side in an effort to keep from being thrown to the floor.

As she saw me, she screamed wildly, "I can't take any more of this. Do you hear? I can't! I won't! I can't! It's no use! I'm tired of living. Do you hear me? It's no use!"

"Anna, Anna," I said in alarm. Lars and I stood beside her, holding to the galley table to keep our feet.

"What's the matter with her?" Lars whispered. "Look at her face."

Anna's features were wooden. Her eyes were staring.

"Listen, Anna!" I said. "It's only a lot of wind. There's nothing we haven't had a dozen times before."

She did not answer. Finally she looked up at me. "No one gets away, Teppo," she answered almost calmly. "It is only fools who try." Suddenly she clutched the bunk again. She threw her head back and cried, "I won't go on! I won't! No one can make me!"

At her feet, Tuntsa whined and nuzzled her hand. She paid no attention.

I heard May call, "Teppo."

She was sitting beyond the curtain on our bunk amidships. "Let Anna alone," she said softly.

"Has she acted like this before in a storm?"

"It isn't the storm. It's . . . well, it's everything. I understand but I can't explain." May spread her arms and drew a long breath. "Anna has simply decided that everything is hopeless. She has been deciding for a long time, I think. No one is going to change her mind. And,"

May spoke slowly, "I know what she feels. But it's dangerous, Teppo. No one should allow feelings like that. You have to keep them away."

"May, we are almost there," I said. "Surely . . ."

"You don't have to tell *me*, I *know!*" May smiled at her own vehemence. 'You see, I have my own unreasonable feelings too. Hope—I am almost crazy with it. Tomorrow we will be there, I say to myself. If not tomorrow—well, then, the day after. I know it—I mean to keep on knowing it. No one is going to change *my* mind either." She got up, holding on to the bulkhead. "I had better go to Kati. She's awfully sick. She feels just as I do, but bad weather is certainly hard on her stomach."

We returned to the galley. I pushed past Lars. He was clutching the table and lecturing Anna on the nature, location, and temporary difficulty of the Mona Passage. She was staring unseeing and unhearing at the wall.

I went to Olle at the pump. In the last three days we had been using it eight hours out of every twenty-four.

"Seems like it's coming in faster," he said briefly.

I took over from him, and he went on deck. Lars abandoned his lecture and spelled me. We assured each other that the only reason for so much water below was that we were shipping more from the rising sea.

After pumping, I relieved Arvi at the sails. The waves were mountainous. Von Haart gave the wheel to Karl.

"Going below," he shouted. "I'll get a nap. Watch out for reefs."

He yawned, stretched, and then disappeared, closing the hatch swiftly after him.

Karl was smiling. "That von Haart! Told me the Mona Passage is like a mistress—has a habit of losing her temper to keep a man down. The way to get the best of her is to outrun her. So he had me keep the *Tuntsa* before the wind, while he—if you please!—goes to sleep."

"That always means he expects worse later on," I said.

Already we needed two men at the wheel. I stayed with Karl until Olle came up to tell me it was my turn again to pump.

When I went below, von Haart had braced himself into his bunk and was sleeping as calmly as a child. He did not wake until dark. We cursed and sweated at the wheel, the sails, and the pump. But we let him sleep. It was well that we did.

That night was an inferno. The wind rose to gale force and would strike from different quarters within seconds. Waves rolled across our bow, our stern, our port and starboard sides. To supplement the permanent lifeline along the rail, we had to rig one across the deck.

The labor became so exhausting that we reduced watches to two hours each. Two men were on deck constantly, another below at the pump. Von Haart himself, however, scarcely left the wheel after nightfall. The waves seemed to scrape the sky. We would rise dizzily, only to plummet as if we were dropping into a bottomless pit. Even von Haart could do little to make the *Tuntsa* ride the crests. Our rudder was almost constantly out of water. We had no light except the weak beam of our one remaining flashlight. The lanterns had been lost in the wreck.

As the sky began to show the beginning of day, we saw no sign of land, only endless water. But by nine o'clock the winds were abating and the waves were smaller.

Von Haart stood at the bow watching the direction of the rising sun. "We were blown southwest by south," he said at last. "Let's tack back. We should see the coast in a few hours."

We began to tack. The water-logged *Tuntsa* answered her helm sluggishly.

Two hours passed. Noon.

We had a lunch of sardines, crackers, and coffee. Three more hours passed. Von Haart eyed the *Tuntsa's* list with apprehension. "If we don't sight land soon. . . ." He did not finish.

The cement, which had begun to work loose beneath the walkway the day before, had now collected to starboard, giving us a permanent list. In the *Tuntsa's* weakened condition, it was an ugly phenomenon. Von Haart kept going below to check the leaks. Each time he returned I expected him to say, "It will be all right. You'll see." But he was silent.

In mid-afternoon Arvi came up from the pump and reported that the hull planks seemed to be separating beneath the tar.

All, except Kati, who was still desperately sick, now spent their time at the pump, the wheel, or watching for land. Anna sat in silence gazing ahead. Tuntsa lay at her feet.

Finally, about five o'clock, Olle thought he saw a shadow on the horizon off our port bow. It was faint, but stretched out in such an irregular shape that it could not be another boat or a large fish. May slipped her hand into mine.

An hour later, we had no more doubt. The white gulls flew out to meet us, circling and crying. Kati crept up from below and stood beside Karl at the rail. By seven o'clock we could see ahead the outlines of buildings. A freighter was unloading at a dock.

Lights of other ships guided us to the harbor entrance. But without a motor and because of the sluggishness of the *Tuntsa* to her helm, we were helpless to make our own way in. We hailed a small boat to send customs men out to us, and we anchored offshore.

Around eight o'clock a motor boat approached. We signalled that we had no motor of our own, and one of the men turned a powerful beacon on our boat and tossed us a line. We were towed to a pier, and learned that we were at San Pedro de Macaris, nearly a hundred miles from the eastern boundaries of the Dominican Republic. We had been blown clear across the Mona Passage into the Caribbean and past the southern coast. Originally we had expected to reach the northeastern tip first.

The harbor commander stepped hesitantly aboard and regarded our listing deck with misgiving. "Where are you heading?" he asked in Spanish. Karl explained that we wanted to land in the Dominican Republic, and showed a letter from his friends in Ciudad Trujillo.

The commander shook his head. "We have no authority to let you stay here. You have to enter directly at Ciudad Trujillo for official clearance."

Karl protested, saying we were exhausted from the storm we had just been through, and from almost steady pumping. "We're in no physical condition to go on tonight," he pleaded.

San Pedro de Macaris' harbor chief again shook his

head. "You can only get your clearance in the capital."

"Oh, please," Karl entreated. "Couldn't you call the authorities in Ciudad Trujillo? Our wives are nearly ill from shock and exhaustion. Couldn't an exception be made to let us anchor here just tonight?"

The official looked doubtful. "At this hour, I don't think anyone can be reached." He hesitated, taking in our weary, strained faces. "Still, I'll try." Karl thanked him, and followed him ashore.

Fifteen minutes later, Karl returned. "We have permission to stay tonight only," he said tensely. "I had to promise to start for the capital at daybreak."

"Can the *Tuntsa* make it?" I asked von Haart.

"I wish she didn't have to," he said. He was like a doctor with an exhausted patient, of whom too much is being asked.

Pumping was now a constant necessity, so each was assigned a two hour stretch during the night. "I'll take the first deck watch," said von Haart. "I might talk some passerby out of a drink."

We managed a faint smile.

Von Haart was irrepressible. But I felt that he might be expressing more than his usual need. His beloved ship was dying under his feet.

At dawn, Lars came up from below in sudden alarm. "The water in the bilges isn't going down. I can see moisture all along the seams."

Arvi agreed soberly. The planks were indeed separating. Our patchwork on the governor's island was starting to come to pieces. We studied von Haart's face. He shrugged. "We don't dare offend the authorities here.

The *Tuntsa* can't take us on to Florida now—that's obvious. We had better start for Ciudad Trujillo no matter what."

The same motor boat which had towed us into San Pedro the evening before took us two miles out, and the *Tuntsa* limped on.

"If the *Tuntsa* were her old self, we would cover the fifty miles to Ciudad Trujillo by noon," said von Haart, "but as things are, I am afraid it will take a lot longer."

It was five that afternoon before we saw the city's harbor. We had to navigate a narrow entrance and go up the Ozama River. Even getting near the slender opening would be a hazardous feat without a motor. Rocky shoreline stretched away on either hand. A single breakwater jutted on the side we were approaching. Opposite were rocks, breaking waves, and a giant, deceivingly lazy whirlpool.

It took nearly two hours to get close to the mouth of the river. We made it just at nightfall. There were no lights on this part of the shore. We could only be guided by the crash of breakers.

The sound grew louder. "We are being pulled past the river," von Haart called suddenly. "It's the current from that damn whirlpool."

While Karl and I worked frantically to coax the wind into the sails, Arvi brought up the pole and began to probe for bottom.

"Get the flashlight and start S.O.S. signals," von Haart shouted.

The current was drawing us steadily closer to the rocks. Arvi was plunging in the pole, striking bottom now with each desperate thrust. Von Haart spun the wheel and shouted instructions to us at the sails.

Gradually we checked the *Tuntsa's* drift and slowly inched away. At one point the whirlpool was less than ten yards off our bow.

"We were meant to get in, Teppo," May said. "We will be all right now, I'm sure of it." As if in afterthought, she added the phrase von Haart had used so often, "You'll see."

Anna sat by the rail in silence. She stared at the coast as if already she hated it.

There was still no response to our signals.

Karl joined Anna at the bow and gazed toward shore. "They told me on the telephone they would be waiting for us," he said, puzzled.

"They couldn't have expected us to be so long," replied von Haart. "Probably they went home to bed."

He was right. It took an hour and a half of intermittent signalling before we finally got a response. When we were safely in the tow of a motor launch, one of the men called back that they had given us up.

"We decided to get some sleep. Just lucky we came back to make sure."

Our emotions were too mixed for anyone to think of a reply.

✸

The journey of the *Tuntsa* really ended that night. When I came on deck to relieve von Haart, I sat with him a while. He was in a peculiar mood. I remember thinking wryly that it might have been different if anyone had come by to give him a drink. It was an unjust stroke of ill luck certainly, but we needed him sober to get him by the entrance authorities in the morning.

"Well, I brought the *Tuntsa* in, didn't I?" he asked. "I'm a pretty good navigator. Maybe the best in Finland, eh?"

"The best in the world, von Haart," I said fervently.

Even in the starlight I could see his gargoyle features crease with pleasure. Praise always delighted him.

"So you are content, Teppo?"

"Why, yes," I said, "I'm content."

I hesitated. What ailed von Haart? "Don't think," I went on finally, "that any of us mind not getting to Florida. We remember the places we could have been stopped—Lisbon, Safi, the governor's island. All that is over. We've won."

"Have you indeed?" he murmured.

"Of course," I said heartily. "And you did it for us, von Haart. This is a modern industrial city. There'll be no problem here. We can get jobs, save our money, and buy our passage the rest of the way. And I know as sure as I'm sitting here that May's children and mine will grow up in America."

"Fine, Teppo," said von Haart. "But, you see I don't want to go to America."

"What *do* you want?" I asked curiously.

"I told you once," he replied laughing. "To own a tavern."

"I mean really?"

He shrugged and made no reply.

On arriving at Safi, May and Teppo chat with the port police officer, François Dupré.

Friends of Dupré on board the *Tuntsa*. From the left, Kati's "fish canner," Kati, unknown guest, Anna, another guest, and a little boy. Teppo is in the foreground.

New Year's feast on the Atlantic crossing, with food provided by a Greek freighter after the *Tuntsa's* crew had been three days without provisions. From left to right, von Haart, Kati, Teppo, Karl, Arvi, and Anna. Olle is behind Kati.

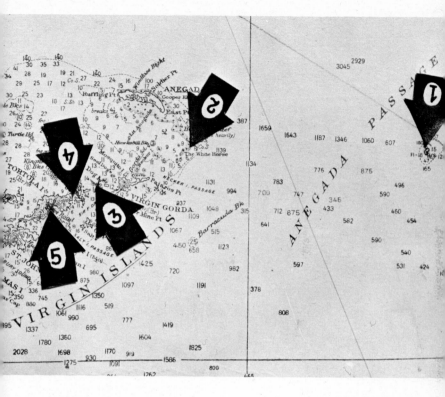

The *Tuntsa's* chart, showing the shipwreck. (1) Sombrero Island,
(2) White Horse Reef, (3) the point of rescue, (4) the native village,
(5) Road Town, the "capital city" of the governor's island.

May and Teppo on the governor's island.

Leaving the governor's island. Top, the fisherman's boat which towed us out of Road Town. Olle is holding to the stay. Bottom, left, von Haart on the after hatch. Bottom, right, the *Tuntsa* under sail as she left the Virgin Islands.

The *Tuntsa* arrives in the Dominican Republic.

The end of the voyage.

A final view of the *Tuntsa,* stripped of her cabin and watertanks, as she waits for her new role as a humble log carrier along the Dominican coast.

At last he said slowly. "There's a special feeling in a defeated country. I don't know if I can explain it, but I think you know what I mean. The people want to throw defiance into the face of things. They refuse to accept what the world is. They *won't*. So they have to prove that the impossible is possible. There's a fury inside of them."

"Oh, I don't know," I said uncomfortably. Finland seemed far away tonight.

"You had that feeling awhile, Teppo, whether you remember it or not. The difference between us is that I have it always. What was temporary in you is permanent in me. I won't take things as they are, you see."

"But Finland . . ." I began.

"I don't mean only Finland."

"Be reasonable," I said at last, looking at the lights on shore.

"Reason is something that doesn't go with it. Were you reasonable? You have just crossed the Atlantic in a thirty foot sailboat, remember? You could have stayed home, saved your money, and left in a few years by steamer."

"Maybe," I said. "We couldn't be sure. The Soviets could have taken over any day. Listen, von Haart, you have seen practically the whole world. You have done some wonderful things. Why not settle down?" I hesitated. "You could take a cure and. . . ."

He got up, stretched, yawned. "Well, I'm going to bed." But behind me, he paused. "Never mind, Teppo. I loved this trip. For me it was probably the last of the big ones. I'm getting old. It was worth doing— to bring the *Tuntsa* in."

I sat out the rest of my watch with a sense of loss I could not explain. For a moment it seemed to me that I bitterly regretted the end of the voyage. But as I sat idly staring at the lights on shore, my mind automatically began to make plans. Tomorrow I must see Karl's friends. May must find us a place to live. Then we must write Eero. There was a great deal to be done. . . .

The end of the voyage divided the crew of the *Tuntsa*. Once past the port authorities and the formalities of entrance, we went our separate ways. Karl found a position as supervisor on a banana plantation owned by the United Fruit Company. Arvi joined him. I also went to work there, as a soil analyst in the plantation laboratory. May and I began earnestly to save money—first for the day when we could send for Eero, then for the final passage to the United States.

Meanwhile Lars and von Haart were employed somewhat briefly by the owner of a fishing fleet. It could not last, of course, for von Haart inevitably did more drinking than fishing. Lars then contracted malaria and had no recourse but to go home to Finland. To Lars, who on the *Tuntsa* had ceased to be a dreamer in favor of combining dreams with reality, his return to his point of departure must have looked like the deepest sort of defeat. Having finally learned to understand action, he was condemned to inaction because he was sick. But he had sailed on the *Tuntsa* for eight months. He had watched repeatedly while what seemed our last possible step turned out to be only a transition, and every disaster crippling our ship only made it necessary to find one more way to push her on. The *Tuntsa* never stopped because she could not. In Finland Lars got well, left the country again, and reached Sweden. There he found work he enjoyed, and ultimately success which would, I am sure, never have been possible for the bookish, defeated man who had first come on board with his ragged volumes of Freud and Schopenhauer.

After Lars left, von Haart for a long while was simply around the waterfront. It took considerable time to make the full tour of the taverns with new companions and complete telling everyone about his best loved ship. Finally he stowed away on an outbound freighter, and from time to time there would come to us joyous, if occasionally incoherent postcards, stamped in far-away places and bearing colorful scenes which dropped through our mail slot like fragments shot off from the spirit of our old navigator. Invariably their arrival brought back the sense of loss I had felt the last night on board the *Tuntsa*. I would always feel it. Indeed, I have it yet.

Olle fared well in the Dominican Republic. He found work quickly, and as soon as his savings made it possible, he sent for his wife. Whatever may have been the puzzling painful bond between them, however, it failed to keep her with him, just as it had failed to make her leave the safety of land that night on the dark beach, and risk with him the trip through the surf to where the *Tuntsa* waited. Soon after her arrival in Ciudad Trujillo, we heard that she was leaving Olle and was to marry his employer. After the divorce, Olle was tormented and silent, as he had been on the *Tuntsa* after we left the Canaries. But the man who had transformed himself

from landlubber to sailor in a space of days, who had
come out of his own moods to invent games which con-
quered the tedium of the more than six months we had
spent in our cramped quarters, was not the sort to disin-
tegrate under pressures of any kind. "What the hell do
you mean!" he had shouted at Juan on the governor's
island, and gone on pounding at the *Tuntsa*. In Ciudad
Trujillo, Olle soon recovered. He found work in his
chosen profession, married again, and is now a successful architect in the Dominican Republic.

Kati and Karl, May and I saved our money until we
could send for our children. After they joined us, we felt
we had made another enormous advance. We were "families" again—no longer voyagers. We completed our
transformation into quite another species, and the call
of the sea, which once we had felt almost as dangerously
as von Haart himself, receded so that we could scarcely
hear it. All during the long voyage, our sense of close-
ness to our young son had never diminished. It was for
him, this child who carried my father's dream and my
father's blood, that we were on board the *Tuntsa*. It
seems possible that in some way beyond our understanding, Eero himself may have felt the extraordinary depth
of the bond, and perhaps even our danger, for while he
was staying with my mother in Finland he woke one
night crying in terror, and he would not be consoled.
He was a tranquil, healthy child normally, and the
occurrence was so unusual that my mother remembered
the date. Later we found it was the same night that we
were shipwrecked and lay helpless on White Horse Reef,
where our voyage so nearly came to an end and all on
the *Tuntsa* nearly perished.

When we had left Finland, Eero had been eighteen months old. By the time we were able to have him flown to us in the Dominican Republic he was a husky boy who would soon be four—no longer a baby but a son indeed. I could see May's face in his, and she said she could see mine. At some moments he resembled my father, at others he reminded us of May's, or my mother, or someone else in our two families. In him all our past seemed with us, and all our future before us. Our joy knew no bounds. We looked back in triumph, and ahead with expectation. May became pregnant with our second child, and Eero had a baby sister. We began to save again, with even greater earnestness, for the last and final step of transporting us all together to America.

But tragedy struck our little group. Anna never fully recovered from the despair which had marked the last part of our journey. She finally became mentally ill, and Arvi had to send her home where her citizenship would make possible better care than he could get for her in the Republic, and perhaps let her get well enough to join him after he reached the United States. But the diagnosis of Anna's illness was a cruel blow. Arvi for a time seemed to lose all purpose in life. He and Anna, Karl and Kati, May and I had been with the *Tuntsa* from the beginning to the end. Now both Karl's household and mine were centered about our children, while Arvi was suddenly alone. The tall, quiet, skillful man, who had been able to do such miracles with his hands, began to drift in and out of work. He became shabby, and he aged so quickly that the change in him was hard to believe. Finally Karl found an opening for him and insisted that he take it.

"It's not up to what he *can* do, but maybe for a while it is what he *should* do."

I agreed. Although it seemed a grim contract, nevertheless, it would, I thought, accomplish exactly what was needed—force Arvi to work diligently and persistently with his wonderful hands. He was assigned to a pile of corroded, hopelessly worn-out oil pumps, and paid only for those he put in commission. The pumps were wrecks, survivors from years of service. It was the engine room of the *Tuntsa* all over again. In a few days, Arvi brightened almost visibly. His prompt salvage of an incredible number of pumps astonished the management, and they hastened to make him shop supervisor. Arvi found hope again. He, too, began to save once more to enter America.

But fate was not through with us yet. Of those aboard the *Tuntsa*, the man to whom I felt closest was Karl. It was Karl who kept harmony among us. His innate courtesies were not mere manners, but the expression of a nature which longed for peace and order. Shrewdly discerning the troubles of others, he was a man of almost incredible generosity, and probably he had for years been taxing himself too severely. The voyage on the *Tuntsa* perhaps only completed what had been begun much earlier during the war and postwar period. In Ciudad Trujillo, when the long journey was over, when he and Kati had been joined by their two little daughters and Kati was pregnant with their third child, Karl began from time to time to look suddenly tired, as he had during the second part of the voyage. Then, just as all at last seemed to be going well, and Kati was in the hospital being delivered of a son, Karl had a heart attack and died. To us the loss seemed unbelievable, and for Kati, her grief and loneliness were at first almost more than she could bear.

But the quiet courage of the girl who had without complaint endured so many storms aboard the *Tuntsa* did not fail. She had been keeper of accounts for us on the voyage, and now she found work as a professional bookkeeper. Like von Haart, Kati had always had confidence in the ultimate goodness of the universe, and her faith did not desert her. She centered her life around her children. She kept busy—filled her days to the brim —held her job—tutored her daughters in English— played with the baby—interested herself in church work. The struggle of finding a new world for his family had cost Karl his life, but Kati and his children took up the future his sacrifices had won and entered it without bitterness. It was, I think, perhaps the greatest accomplishment of all.

The final step of getting to the United States was not easy, and it required patience and time. As soon as May and I had saved enough for our passage, I applied at the American consulate for visas, but was dismayed to find that the quota assigned to Finland was full. We would have to wait, we were told, "four or five years." After the Korean war, the quota was reduced. Meanwhile, I worked for United Fruit, for Texaco, and finally in a small way began to manufacture furniture, which sold quite well. Both May and I were on our guard, however, against letting such postponement grow permanent. As each month passed and then each year, we told ourselves firmly that when our baby daughter started school, it

would be in the United States. Meanwhile we talked
English at home for Eero's benefit and I worked diligently on my own accent—with, however, my American
friends tell me now, considerably less than complete
success.

A problem even greater than getting our visas was to
find a sponsor to guarantee that we would not become
public charges after our admission.

"Goodness, Teppo," May said wryly once, "it must
really be heaven in America. It's so difficult to get in!"

By working for several American companies, I had of
course come to know Americans, but it is hard to say to
a friend, "Look here, my visa is about due. Do you suppose you could get somebody in the States to sponsor us
for five years? In case we turn out to be paupers, you
know."

I had it on the tip of my tongue a hundred times, but
could never get it out.

"Teppo, you simply have to do it," May said one day
at last. "Or the visas will come, and still we won't be
able to leave."

Finally an acquaintance mentioned a man in Chicago.
This man had an insurance firm which had been extremely successful, but his activities outside his business
seemed even more astonishing. Our acquaintance told
several anecdotes, and then said simply, "All his life he
has been helping people. He is the kind of American you
know exists, but get to wondering where he is."

I decided to write this American and explain to him
as well as I could about our problems and our hope of
at last entering the United States.

The letter took a great deal of labor, but even after I had written and rewritten it, I still felt it left out most of the important facts. It did not mention my father's dream—I had found it impossible to put into words. It scarcely touched the *Tuntsa*—I was afraid that if I started on that I would never finish. As for von Haart, whose courage and ingenuity had got us almost to our goal, he was not even named—I could not think of any way to bring him up. I looked at the letter and felt that there was nothing in it of what we really were and why we had hope.

It was the best I could manage, however. I had spent almost an entire night writing, and there was nothing to do but send it off. I wrote the address: "Mr. W. Clement Stone, President, Combined Insurance Company of America, Chicago, Illinois"—and then regarded the envelope skeptically. What time would an American corporation president give an unknown Finnish refugee? When I dropped it into the mailbox, I already felt sure there would never be an answer. Next week I would start writing to governors of states.

But Mr. Stone's reply arrived before the week was up. I held his letter in my hand and could scarcely believe what I read. Not only would he sponsor our entry, but he offered me a job in his insurance company and suggested that he help find us an apartment in Chicago.

I rushed home to May. She read and reread the letter.

"Teppo, there really are such people!" Then she said slowly, "How von Haart would have loved him."

The rest of the time in the Dominican Republic passed with incredible speed—a whirling kaleidoscope of goodbyes and final arrangements. The reality of our new world was about to begin in earnest. The unforgettable journey was truly at its end.

*

It is a strange thing—a journey. I would not exchange even our mounting happiness in our Chicago home for the voyage which brought us here. The spirit of the *Tuntsa* became part of us and part of our children's heritage, for it is in our blood, and has gone into theirs. Finland won her independence in 1918 after centuries of struggle. But she was almost at once overshadowed by a people who had a false dream of freedom. After centuries of tyranny, they were possessed by such rage that their future inevitably delivered the wrong package. But our dream was—as I feel each day more and more—totally unlike that. It had another quality, a different texture—stubborn, not angry. It pleases me to think that even the *Tuntsa* passed from the scene still in character. After we landed in Ciudad Trujillo, the job of disposing of her fell to me and I dreaded it bitterly.

What I feared of course was that she would have to be junked, and sawed up before her time for used hardware and lumber. She was battle-scarred and had to be pumped almost incessantly but there was stubbornness in the way she rose to meet the ripples of the harbor, and defiance in the design of her hull which parted the waves to either side and had never let her be driven against any shore. There was good in the *Tuntsa* yet. I was sure of it.

I brought down a potential buyer, a man who had a mahogany shop in the city.

"In pretty bad shape isn't she?" he asked.

"It was a hard trip," I admitted. "But she's a sound boat. If you knew . . ."

"Oh," he said, "never mind that. I can see it. I'll take out the deck and cabin and sell the water tanks. She'll do."

"Do for what?" I asked.

"To pick up mahogany along the coast. How much do you want for her?"

Elated, I named a hopeless price and we went to bargaining. Finally we agreed on a sum. It was about a quarter of what we had paid when we first bought her in Kotka. Not bad, when one thinks that she had transported nine people across the Atlantic!

The *Tuntsa* was a sturdy boat, a working boat—that was her character, and anyone who knew boats and saw her, recognized it. Her middle life, her time of dreams, when tall-masted and shining she sailed for a new world, was only an interruption. In Finland her life had been to carry potatoes to the hungry ports of the Baltic. Now she was to carry logs in the Dominican Republic. There had been no danger of her being junked before her time —I should have known. That fate wasn't in her.

Of the four heads of families—Karl, Masa, Arvi, and I —who originally had the dream for which we outfitted the *Tuntsa,* not one finally failed. Karl is dead, and Anna still lives in a darkened world, but one cannot think for a moment that there was really failure. Kati came to the United States and is bringing up Karl's children in New York State, where her church group had a branch and sponsored her entry. Masa, who left the *Tuntsa* at Lisbon, returned to Finland to start again, and his family now is growing up in Buffalo. Arvi is working in Chicago, where he has just been joined by his son. I, who sold insurance in Helsinki, now sell it with much more confidence in Illinois, and May is constantly delighted by new acquaintances who meet our children and express amazement at finding they have no trace of Finnish accent.

We continued to hear from von Haart for only a short time. Before we left Ciudad Trujillo, the joyous postcards which had intermittently flashed into our lives, abruptly ceased. We heard that he died at home in Finland—some time, we think, in 1953. I believe that as he predicted when we docked on that last night, there was never for him another such ship, or another such adventure. There were trips still to come, and places to see, and drinks to have, and stories to exchange, but this was the climax of his journeys. "Nine of us in a thirty foot boat," he used to tell them in the Canaries—on the governor's island—in Ciudad Trujillo. "A thirty foot boat, mind you, with no modern equipment—and she took us half-way around the world."

He was a magnificent man, von Haart—one who could have been anything—if only he had wanted anything the earth could give him. I am glad that the *Tuntsa* seemed to him, as he said, "worth doing." He lived in a deeper dimension than we, and it is not surprising that he never found anything which could hold him for long. He would have made the last voyage of all with courage and dignity—indeed perhaps with expectation, and probably with an unquestioning joyousness a little disconcerting to the angels.

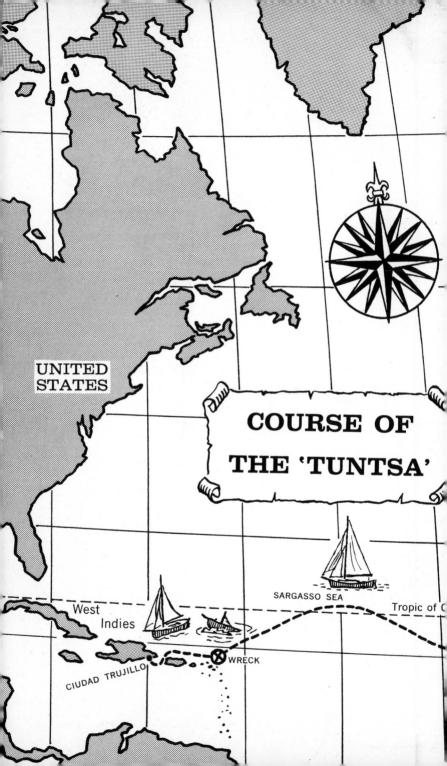

UNITED
STATES

**COURSE OF
THE 'TUNTSA'**

SARGASSO SEA

Tropic of C

West
Indies

⊗ WRECK

CIUDAD TRUJILLO